CUT YOUR LOSSES—
AND PLAY TO WIN!

Beat the odds by gambling smart! Learn:

- Which games you should play

- The simple secrets that will save you money over the long run—*and* help you win!

- Where to play, with a comprehensive directory of North American casinos, card houses, and tracks

- The key to winning at slot machines—five critical steps

- Why Blackjack is the only casino game in which a skillful player actually has a slight edge over the house—and a few simple principles that, once memorized, will make you an above-average player in a short time

It's all here in this essential manual designed to put beginning gamblers in the winner's circle.

THE ABSOLUTE BEGINNER'S GUIDE TO GAMBLING

ROBERT J. HUTCHINSON

POCKET BOOKS
New York London Toronto Sydney Tokyo Singapore

With the different forms of gambling described herein, there are varying elements of chance and skill. This book presents information that is designed to introduce beginning players, with little or no experience, to the basics of each of the games. It should be understood that none of the advice contained herein can guarantee winning. When betting is involved, never bet more than you can afford to lose. With any game, even a proficient player will lose at times. Therefore, when employing the playing information contained herein, a guarantee of winning is neither expressed nor implied by the author or publisher. The author and publisher disclaim any liability arising directly or indirectly from the use of this book.

An *Original* Publication of POCKET BOOKS

POCKET BOOKS, a division of Simon & Schuster Inc.
1230 Avenue of the Amerias, New York, NY 10020

Copyright © 1996 by Robert J. Hutchinson

ISBN: 0-671-52932-3

First Pocket Books printing August 1996

10 9 8 7 6 5 4 3 2 1

POCKET and colophon are registered trademarks of
Simon & Schuster Inc.

Cover design by Gerald T. Counihan/Altitude Design

Printed in the U.S.A.

To my mother,

MARY JANE HUTCHINSON,

*who taught her six children how
to live with faith and love*

Acknowledgments

With every book project, there are many people to thank. This book grew out of decades of playing cards with friends and family members, and to them I owe most of what I know about gambling. However, I should thank in a special way my father, A'lan Hutchinson, for teaching me how to play Cribbage, chess, Pinochle, and Poker before I could read. More immediately, I must thank my editor at Pocket Books, Emily Bestler, for believing in this book strongly enough to take it with her when she left another publisher, as well as my long-suffering agent, Lisa Bankoff, who is a gambler in her own right in taking me on as a client. I should also thank my friend and copywriting agent, John Finn, for his help in setting this project in motion, and my assistant, Lisa Hammer, for her painstaking typing and research.

I also want to thank my children, Robert John, James Timothy, and William Kelly for their patience as I locked myself away in the office writing. Finally, as always, I must thank my wife, Glenn Ellen, to whom I owe everything.

Acknowledgments

Contents

Contents

Luck is what happens when preparation meets opportunity.

—JACK VALENTI

I am sorry I have not learnt to play at cards. It is very useful in life: it generates kindness and consolidates society.

—SAMUEL JOHNSON, *quoted by James Boswell in* Journal of a Tour to the Hebrides with Samuel Johnson, *November 21, 1773*

The ABSOLUTE BEGINNER'S GUIDE TO GAMBLING

Introduction

The New Boom in Legalized Gambling . . . and How You Can Make the Most of It

In just ten years, from the mid-1980s to the mid-1990s, the entire gambling world changed . . . completely and totally. There have been so many new developments that a gambler from the 1950s, '60s, or '70s would hardly recognize the scene. Not only have the casinos been completely reinvented, transformed from the dingy rug joints of the Vegas strip to such lavish entertainment megacomplexes as Luxor, Excalibur, and the MGM Grand, but there are now entire games that did not even exist until a few years ago—such as Caribbean Stud, Let It Ride, and Pai Gow Poker. Even those gambling pastimes that existed in the past have been altered dramatically through the use of electronic gadgets. Slot machines now have ATM-like debit cards, which add and subtract monetary credits instead of coins, and video Poker and video Keno machines have drawn thousands of players who would never have gone near a Poker table or Keno parlor in the past. Furthermore, there are now gambling establishments everywhere—full-blown casinos on Indian reservations, lotteries in most U.S. states, flashy card casinos in California and Colorado, riverboat casinos that float up and down the Mississippi and on many lakes, video Poker games in the Midwest, even gambling sites "online" through the Internet. Over the past decade, gambling has become one of the most popular leisure activities around.

Someone who has never gambled before, therefore, is faced with a dizzying variety of choices. There are dozens of excellent books now on the market about gambling, some written by the greatest authorities and experts in history, but unfortunately many of them are now obsolete. Gambling books have always tended to stay in print forever because the fundamental principles of gambling, and most of the games, have remained the same over the years. That is no longer the case, however. It is almost impossible to find a book in a bookstore, for example, that even mentions the game of Carribean Stud—now one of the most popular table games in America; and with the advent of video Poker, the state lotteries, new megacasinos, and Indian reservation Bingo halls, the old books no longer serve the needs of novice, or even experienced, gamblers. That is why Robert J. Hutchinson's *The Absolute Beginner's Guide to Gambling* was written. It fills in the gaps that other books, even the very best ones, ignore. It provides the novice gambler with basic, step-by-step instruction on how to play the most popular gambling games and also includes up-to-date information on the latest trends in casinos, state lotteries, and reservation gambling.

What's more, this book includes a comprehensive directory of all the casinos, card houses, and horse and dog racing tracks in North America as well as the forms of gambling each establishment offers. This directory also includes a summary explanation of the laws regarding gambling in all fifty states.

Come explore the exciting new world of gaming at the turn of the millennium. First, we'll take a quick tour through the new gambling establishments and then move in for a closer look at each of the games you're likely to encounter. This book is not meant to be an exhaustive source of instruction for each of these games but it *will* supply you with a solid introductory knowledge of each game and where you can go to enjoy it.

The Gambling Revolution

Gambling, both legal and illegal, is now among the largest industries in the world.

In the United States alone, men and women wagered a record $330 *billion* in legal gambling operations in 1992—an increase of more than 1,800 percent since 1976.[1] State and municipal lotteries racked up sales of $24 billion that same year.[2] At this writing, the only American states without any form of legal gambling are Utah and Hawaii. And of course, legal gambling is only a small percentage of the total amount of gambling in a given country. If you factor in all of the floating crap games, Friday night Poker sessions, and illegally booked sporting bets, some analysts believe that gambling in the U.S. is easily a $1 *trillion* industry—that's one fifth of the entire U.S. economy!

The U.S. is not the only country witnessing a tremendous growth in gambling. All across the developed world, from Europe to Australia, gambling is on the rise and national and regional governments are cashing in. In the European Community, the estimated revenues from legal gambling are more than $50 billion, and gambling operations are springing up across Asia and the Pacific.

For example, in June 1994 it was announced that an Australian consortium won the bidding war for a twelve-year franchise on the new Sydney Harbour Casino, the first casino to be built in the state of New South Wales. Expected to open in 1997, the 100,000-square-foot casino will boast 170 gaming tables, 1,480 slot machines, a 350-room hotel, 140 private apartments, and parking for 2,500 cars. The consortium agreed to pay the state of New South Wales an upfront fee of $376 million or three equal payments of $441 million during the construction phase. New South Wales officials also estimated that the new casino would generate $100 million in annual revenues to the state.[3] Not to be outdone, the city of Melbourne announced in November 1994 that it would help to build a 5-star, 38-level, 1,000-room resort casino that would include at least 200 gaming tables, 2,500 slot and video machines, and the largest sports book in Australia.[4]

In Canada the legal gambling industry in 1993 showed gross revenues of $11 billion, double the amount of the entire Canadian federal budget.[5] A series of shining new casinos, many run by Las Vegas operators, have appeared or will soon appear in the chilly air of Canada's provinces. The Casino Windsor, Ontario's first, opened in May 1993; a $720 million megacomplex on Burrard Inlet in Vancouver is scheduled to be built; Quebec spent $92 million on the renovation of Montreal's Expo '67 facilities into a giant casino; Manitoba's Crystal Casino opened in 1989 in the Fort Garry Hotel in Winnipeg; and both Nova Scotia and Halifax have licensed privately run casinos as a way to raise tax revenues.

Changing Attitudes Toward Gambling

Experts point to a number of factors that are behind the incredible explosion of gambling outlets in the past two decades.

The most obvious factor, of course, is money. After years of deficit spending, many national and local governments are desperate to raise additional revenues and have found that gambling, from state lotteries to heavily taxed card houses, is a form of ''voluntary taxation'' that excites far less public antipathy than other forms of ''revenue enhancement.''

This government-run gambling began in the U.S. with state lotteries. After a nationwide ban than began in 1895, New Hampshire became the first state to legalize statewide lotteries, in 1964. Neighboring states soon followed suit. New York started its own lottery in 1967, New Jersey did the same in 1970, and the genie was out of the bottle. Today lotteries are legal in thirty-seven out of the fifty states. It is estimated that each week one third of all adults in the United States buy lottery tickets, the proceeds of which contribute an additional $8 to $10 billion to state governments.

As a result, some observers insist that state governments are now the biggest promoters of gambling in America and are the reason why gambling in general has exploded in past decades.[6] With the states pushing lotteries so hard, it is not surprising that soon other forms of gambling would reassert themselves—card rooms, reservation Bingo halls, riverboats, and full-fledged, Vegas-style casinos.

There is another reason why gambling took such a hold in the final quarter of the twentieth century—public attitudes toward gambling have shifted. For one thing, the association with organized crime—exemplified by such "sportsmen" as Bugsy Siegel, the Mafia gangster who founded the Flamingo Hotel in the late 1940s—has diminished over the decades. The major casinos are no longer fronts for the Mafia, having been taken over long ago by legitimate corporations. In addition, the focus of many of the casinos' marketing efforts has swung away from gambling as a chance at easy money to more of an emphasis on gambling as pure entertainment. The moral objection to gambling—that it preyed on the weak and offered something for nothing—has been diluted, somewhat, by the notion that casino gambling does not differ, in essence, from a Friday night Poker game. At least in theory, both are done purely for pleasure. As a result, gambling has gained a certain respectability that it did not have in the 1940s, '50s, and '60s.

New Locations to Gamble

Following the Lotto fever of the 1980s, in which states saw lots of positive effects and few negative ones from lotteries, state governments began to rethink their traditional opposition to any and all forms of legalized gambling. By the early 1990s, even the most casual observer could see that card rooms and slot machines were popping up in places they never were before— such as the sleepy hamlet of Black Hawk, Colorado. And in 1991 the people who lived along the banks of the Mississippi River saw the revival of one of the most picturesque and popular ways to gamble in American history: the riverboat. On April Fool's Day of that year, the tiny hamlet of Davenport, Iowa, set sail the *Diamond Lady,* the very first legal riverboat casino since gambling was banned nearly a hundred years ago. Buoyed by the romantic images of the old sternwheelers of the nineteenth century, patrons flocked to new riverboat gambling operations authorized in Iowa, Illinois, Mississippi, and Louisiana. These riverboat facilities have turned out to be quite popular and more are planned for Alabama, Texas, and Arkansas. In addition, President Riverboat Casinos, Inc., which owns and operates riverboat and dockside gambling operations in Iowa, Mississippi, and Missouri, announced its intention to operate a four-deck, 300-foot gambling boat on Lake Michigan. Some states now are not ready to part with the new riverboat revenue. When a judge issued an injunction in May 1994 halting the development of a riverboat concession in Indiana, the Indiana Supreme Court stepped in and ruled that riverboat gambling was a constitutional right under the laws of that state, overturning the lower court's injunction.

The riverboats, of course, got a lot of people to thinking. There is no reason why waterborne gambling ships have to be on a river, *or even on a boat.* In Mississippi executives built gambling "boats" along the river that have no engines and no crew and are, in fact, noth-

ing more than floating casinos. The idea behind riverboat gambling is that, because the gambling operation
is moving, there is no specific place that will draw ''un-
desirable'' elements to the community, such as prosti-
tution and crime. In some states waterborne gambling
is permitted, therefore, but not gambling on land. Now
that everyone has seen the success of the waterborne
operations, some entrepreneurs have even begun dis-
cussions to bring back the old gambling ships that operated off the coast of California in the 1940s.

In addition to the riverboats, however, there is now a
whole new generation of actual casinos that has arisen
in recent years. By the mid-1990s, it appeared that the
powerful monopoly of Las Vegas and Atlantic City on
the gambler's utopia, the casino, was finally coming to
an end.

In California, the once sleepy card rooms in towns
such as Inglewood and Garden Grove expanded into
gambling palaces that, although legally denied the right
to offer slot machines and Craps, look and act pretty
much like the big Vegas casinos. In the summer of
1994, the Hollywood Park Casino, its neon sign shin-
ing out toward Los Angeles International Airport,
opened its doors to customers eager to try their luck on
the 200 tables inside. It wasn't the only one. At least
40 percent of California's 1,700 card tables are located
in the L.A. area, and many more are planned. So-called
card casinos—to be distinguished from the ''full-
service'' casinos of Las Vegas—have been proposed in
cities such as Irwindale, Pomona, and even ultra-glitzy
Palm Springs. Much of the growth in the card casinos
comes from larger and larger groups of Asian immigrants, who enjoy playing such Asian gambling games

as Pai Gow and Super Pan Nine (see below). The Bicycle Club in Bell Gardens, for example, has a special Asian game section.

California is not alone in blazing the way for more casino-type operations outside of Las Vegas and Atlantic City. In the early 1990s, Governor Edwin Edwards, a notorious high-stakes gambler, helped ram a bill through the Louisiana legislature authorizing the development of a full-fledged casino in the heart of New Orleans. According to promoters, the casino that is to be built on Canal Street near the New Orleans convention center will generate more than $700 million annually. Critics say such revenue projections are unrealistic, however, and that the state would have difficulty recouping its investment. These critics favor smaller casino operations. In any event, no one doubts that big-time gambling is coming to the bayou.

The Rise of the Reservation Casinos

The public hunger for gambling grew throughout the final quarter of the twentieth century. In those states that did not permit gambling beyond lotteries, one group saw an opportunity to make some money: Native American Indians.

The roots of the current boom in reservation casinos lie in a mega-Bingo hall, with prizes in the hundreds of thousands of dollars, opened in 1979 by the Seminole Indians on their reservation land near Hollywood, Florida. In the 1987 landmark case *California v. The Cabazon Band of Mission Indians,* the U.S. Supreme Court ruled that tribes have a sovereign right to sponsor gambling on their own reservation land. This was followed by the Indian Gaming Regulatory Act, passed by the U.S. Congress in 1988, which basically authorized recognized Indian tribes with treaty relationships to the U.S. government to run full-fledged casinos on their land, the revenue of which would not be taxable. The tribes were authorized to offer any game permitted to be played in the state surrounding their land. As a result, reservation casinos in California, such as Cache Creek Indian Bingo and Casino in Brooks, can only offer Poker card games and not Craps, Roulette, or Baccarat, because these are the restrictions in California generally. The federal law, not popular with established gambling impresarios such as Donald Trump, withstood two legal challenges before the U.S. Supreme Court.

Within a few years of the passage of the Indian Gaming Regulatory Act, elaborate, professionally run casinos began to spring up on reservation land in Arizona, California, Colorado, Florida, Wisconsin, Minnesota, Louisiana, Maine, Oregon, South Dakota, Washington, and other states. Now, there are more than one hundred Indian-run casinos in nineteen states. At least one third of the 545 federally recognized Indian nations have gambling in some form on their land.

In prim and proper Connecticut, for example, the sovereign nation of the Mashantucket Pequot tribe, which has only 179 members, opened the enormously profitable Foxwoods megacasino with 2,300 employees and 179 gaming tables. The casino, an enormous 1.3-million-square-foot complex, cost a staggering $240 million to build, but that investment was paid off the very first year of the casino's operation. According to a report in *The Economist,* the Foxwoods operation sells around $2 million worth of chips every day and has long since made each member of the tribe a multimillionaire.

It's little wonder that other Native American tribes from Maine to California have decided to get in on the action. Until gambling reached the reservation, approximately one third of America's two million Indians lived in poverty and sixty-two percent were unemployed. Now, many are able to find jobs at gambling establishments owned and run by their own people. Among the largest of the Indian-run casinos are the Mystic Lake Casino, run by the Shakopee Mdewakanton Sioux near Prior Lake, Minnesota; Turning Stone Casino, run by the Oneida Nation near Oneida, New York; the Grand Casino Mille Lacs and Grand Casino Hinckley, run by the Mille Lacs Band of Chippewa in Wisconsin; the Fantasy Springs Bingo Palace and Casino, run by the Cabazon Band of Mission Indians in El Cajon, California; and Seminole Bingo, run by the Seminole Indians in Hollywood, Florida.

The old Indian businesses of selling untaxed cigarettes and illegal fireworks just don't compare to the new gambling enterprises, which are veritable money-making machines. To understand just how popular the Indian casinos are, consider this: state officials in New York now concede that the Oneida Nation's Turning Stone Casino, which hosts 7,000 people each day, is now the state's biggest tourist attraction, drawing more people each year than Niagara Falls or the Statue of Liberty.

All of those people mean big money. According to New York-based *International Gaming and Wagering*

Business, a journal of the industry, tribal gaming revenues nationwide were estimated to be around $4 billion in 1995.

New Megacasinos and Resorts

The old casino operators were not about to lose out on the new action on the reservations. In the early 1990s corporate casino enterprises poured hundreds of millions of dollars into reinventing the casino concept for the twenty-first century. The dingy old rug joints of the Vegas Strip and the Atlantic City boardwalk have gone the way of the Treasury tickets and mechanical slot machines. They still exist, of course, but they are being edged out by the new "family entertainment" megacasinos.

The MGM Grand in Las Vegas is in many ways typical of this new type of casino, one in which gambling is only one of the many activities offered. When it was completed in the early 1990s, the MGM Grand became the largest hotel in the world, with 5,005 rooms and 751 suites of up to 6,000 square feet each. Adjacent to the hotel and casino stands a 33-acre theme park that includes rides, shows, and "theme areas," such as "Casablanca Plaza" and "Tumbleweed Gulch." The casino itself covers an incredible 170,000 square feet.

Nor is the MGM Grand alone. The Luxor, a self-proclaimed "unique resort destination," features a 30-story pyramid-shaped hotel, a 10-story replica of the Sphinx of Giza, and an obelisk that towers 191 feet into the Nevada sky. Inside the hotel, there is the world's largest atrium, a second obelisk (120 feet high) and an indoor "Nile River" that carries guests on special boats past elaborate murals illustrating the history of the Egyptian empire. Created by special effects wizard Douglas Trumbull, designer of the "Back to the Future" ride, the "Secrets of the Luxor Pyramid" attraction features 3-D effects and a state-of-the-art, interactive virtual reality program provided by Sega. As for gambling, the Luxor casino is "only" 100,000 square feet, but has an enormous Race and Sport Book area with 17 large screen TVs and 128 personalized monitors. The restaurants all have Egyptian themes, of course, with names such as Tut's Hut, Nefertiti's Lounge, Isis, and Papyrus.

New Games

Not only are the casinos today nothing like their forebears, many of the games are different as well. As mentioned above, gamblers from the 1950s or even 1970s would be a bit confused by the games in many casinos, card houses, and riverboats today.

These games are variations on traditional card games and most require at least an elementary knowledge of Poker. Most of these newer games are modifications of games in which players once played against one another—such as Stud Poker—and in which all players now play against the house. For example, in Caribbean Stud, a popular game in the card casinos of California, players sit around a Blackjack-like layout and all play against the dealer. Another of the new games, Poker Pai-Gow, a card variation on the Asian domino game, also allows all participants to play against the dealer.

In addition to the new card games, there are also new ways to play old games—principally the new video versions of Poker, Keno, and Blackjack. Video Poker, in particular, has enthusiasts all its own and in many locations rivals the traditional slot machines as the most popular form of gambling. Video Keno is also gaining popularity. As with traditional and popular Keno, gamblers like the possibility of relatively high payouts from inexpensive bets.

High-Tech Gambling in the Twenty-first Century

At least in the minds of many science fiction writers, gambling will not die out in a future world of super-computers and space travel. In the U.S. television and movie franchise *Star Trek,* a feral race of cutthroat businessmen and inveterate gamblers called the Ferengi operated a game named Dabo that appeared to be part Roulette and part Poker. And while Dabo was merely the creation of a television writer, casino executives are doing everything they can to bring the same high technology it employs to the real world of gambling. Many hope to make gambling completely electronic so that money can be transferred from ATM and credit cards directly onto a casino-issued credit card, which is used for all different types of gambling. Others hope to see on-line gambling through computer networks, or the placement of electronic Poker and Blackjack games in hotel rooms.

The casino debit card concept already exists in some establishments. At casinos such as the Trump Castle in Atlantic City gamblers use a debit card to play the slot machines. The card, called a slot club card, works exactly like a debit card. A gambler puts the card into a special card-reader connected to a slot machine or video Poker machine and the reader credits, or more likely deducts, money electronically from the card. The use of the slot club card serves another purpose than simply convenience for the gambler. They allow the casinos to track, down to the last nickel, how much money a given customer has spent. The casinos have found that players who use the cards spend three times more on the slots than those who do not (at the Trump Castle, $101 per player using cards compared to just $31 for those using coins).[7]

Even governments are getting into the high-tech gambling business. The state of South Dakota, for example, pioneered what some believe will be the most popular form of gambling in the twenty-first century—Video Lottery Terminals (VLTS). These machines, which have been in bars in South Dakota since 1989, are not really lotteries at all but really nothing more than video slot machines. They are, however, owned or licensed by the state lottery commission, which shares in the profits (which are, of course, enormous). Eleven states have legalized these machines thus far, and others are expected to do so shortly.

Interestingly enough, technology is eroding the legal barriers to gambling in many nations. In Europe, for example, many nations ban most forms of gambling except, of course, the state-run lotteries, but the advent of low-cost international telephone calls, credit cards, and fax machines have made national gambling laws a farce. It is fairly easy, for example, for a French businessman in Paris to call his favorite bookie in London and place a bet on a football (soccer) game. The development of computer bulletin boards, data encryption technology, and the use of modems make the long-held dream of computerized bookmaking a reality. It is now a simple thing to log a completely illegal bet on the Internet that is, for all intents and purposes, undetectable by national governments. A company called Internet On-line Offshore Electronic Casino, operating in the tax haven of the Turks and Caicos Islands, in May 1995 opened a World Wide Web site where gamblers can place bets, using either real or play money, on Blackjack. The owner set up the system this way so that U.S. government wiretappers can't trace the winnings of gamblers who use the service.

Technology is a two-edged sword, however, for the gambler. The big casinos have long used the results of sophisticated psychological testing and a variety of technological gimmicks to keep gamblers spending money. These techniques include having slot machines emit a special scent, Odorant 1, developed by a Chicago neurologist, which allegedly keeps slot addicts at the machines longer. The psychological manipulation is endlessly creative. Casinos routinely give out low-denomination chips for cash, for example, because they know that the average gambler will hesitate to bet a fifty-dollar chip but won't think twice about betting a series of ten chips worth five dollars each. For a similar reason, slot machines today are now wired to pay out frequent small wins, as low as a single coin, to keep gamblers excited and feeling that they are not simply throwing their money away. In the past, the slots did not pay out frequently, and the casino owners noticed that gamblers quickly grew discouraged and gave them up entirely.

In 1980 a mathematician named Jess Marcum discovered that the longer a gambler stayed in a casino, the lower his or her odds were of winning. Given the built-in odds advantage of the house—from 1.5 percent to 25 percent, depending upon the game—it is only a matter of time before a gambler loses. But Marcum was able to show precisely how the time curve works. For example, he demonstrated that a gambler who bet one-dollar chips on the Craps table for two whole months would have only one chance in 2 trillion that he would win $1,000 before losing $1,000. On the other hand, if this same gambler limited himself to just 25 minutes at the Craps table, and wagered $200 every other bet, his odds of winning $1,000 went from 1 in 2 trillion to . . . 1.15 to 1.[8]

Big difference!

As a result of this information, the casinos have intensified their longstanding efforts to keep gamblers in the gaming areas as long as possible. This includes the tried-and-true techniques of offering free drinks and food to the more subtle efforts, such as posting attractive female shills, complete with casino-provided chips, at the Baccarat tables. Indeed, the major casinos will go to great lengths to keep their customers happy and comfortable. One of the reasons why so many casinos are now offering family entertainment instead of, or in addition to, the topless showgirls of the past is so gamblers can take their families with them to the casinos and, as a result, stay longer. As mentioned above, the advent of electronic money and ATM-like slot club cards have enabled the casinos to keep detailed database records on customers, including how much money they have won or lost. The casinos study this information precisely so they can offer added inducements to keep people gambling. These inducements range from RFBs—complimentary rooms, food, or beverage coupons—to all-expenses-paid junkets.

Gambling Strategy for Absolute Beginners

Gambling games are games of chance in which the player may or may not be able to improve his chances of winning by skillful play. Some games, such as the slot machines, are completely games of chance in which there is no element of skill involved whatsoever (despite what the systems books claim). Other games, such as Craps, are purely chance in their execution but involve an element of skill or knowledge in the manner in which bets are placed (that is, some bets are smarter than others to make). Still other games, such as Poker and Blackjack, are largely games of skill with an element of chance included. A good Poker player will almost always beat inexperienced players over the long term. And Blackjack is the only casino game in which a highly skilled player actually has a slight edge over the house—which is why casinos put so much effort into quickly identifying and actually banning such players.

The odds in most forms of gambling can be calculated, thanks to the science of probability theory, with exact precision. In other words, I can tell you, with mathematical certainty, that the odds of winning a flip of a coin are precisely 50/50 or dead even. If I bet you $10 a coin will be heads, with an even money bet, then that is a completely fair bet. If I win, you pay me $10; if you win, I pay you $10.

But professional gambling establishments don't operate that way. They can't. They have enormous overheads to pay for—including all of those flashing lights, free shrimp cocktails, and cheap booze. In order to make a profit, therefore, all professional gambling establishments, from casinos to state lotteries, rig the games so that the odds are in their favor. They do this in a variety of ways, from special rules that favor the house to the manner in which they pay off bets. A casino *builds in* its advantage by paying off its bets in a manner that does not reflect the true odds. Put more simply, in casino games there is a difference between the payoff odds and the correct or "real" odds.

The great gambling expert and amateur mathematician John Scarne used to give the following example to illustrate the difference between betting odds and real odds. Let's say you're at a carnival and are playing the Big Wheel, which has 15 numbers on it. You pick a number and spin the wheel. If your number turns up, the operator pays you 10 to 1—or $10 on a one-dollar bet. Sound like a fair bet? It's not. The problem with this arrangement is that it does not reflect the "real" odds. Since there are 15 numbers on the wheel, that means you will win, according to the laws of probability, one time and lose 14 times for every 15 spins of the wheel. If this were a fair bet, therefore, the real odds would be 1 in 14—much means that when you did win, the operator should pay you $14 plus the original one-dollar bet. Over the long haul, you'd just break even (i.e., you would have bet $1 fourteen times and lost, and bet $1 once and won $14). But the operator does not do this in real life. He or she pays only 10 to 1, not 14 to 1, and thus has a built-in advantage of 26.66 percent in his or her favor.[9]

This is precisely how the major casinos, lotteries, and card rooms operate, although usually the house advantage is smaller and not so obvious. In Roulette, for example, there are 18 red numbers, 18 black numbers, and two zero numbers for a total of 38 possible numbers. To bet on any one number coming up, therefore, your "real" odds would be 37 to 1. But the house does not pay off at 37 to 1 on a single number bet, but rather at 35 to 1 (on a one-dollar bet, if you win you get back $35 plus your one-dollar bet). The house also has this same percent advantage if you bet on, say, any red. With 18 red numbers out of a total of 38 possible numbers, the real odds are 20 to 18 or 1.11 to 1—but the house pays off on any red bet 1 to 1 or even money ($1 bet, and won, gets back $1). This works out to a 5.3 percent advantage for the house. Over time, therefore, the house picks up, on average, a little more than a nickel on every dollar bet at Roulette.

The most basic lesson that an absolute beginner must learn is that no matter what friends or books about systems say, it is a mathematical fact that the odds are against the player in all forms of professionally managed gambling.

However, these odds do vary considerably from game to game. The house advantage in line (pass/don't pass) bets in Craps, as we'll see, is only 1.4 percent. Compared to other games, Baccarat has relatively good odds with its 1.17 percent house advantage. On the other hand, your chances of winning the jackpot in the California Super Lotto drawing are 18 million to 1. It is important to know that some games are better than others in terms of your likelihood of winning.

The second principle of gambling that absolute beginners should never forget is that gambling, because the odds are weighted against you, should be viewed as a form of entertainment and not as an investment. Always keep in mind that if you play long enough, you *will* lose when gambling. The only question is when . . . and how much.

Therefore, the smart gambler views his or her money spent gambling as merely the cost of having a good time. Never bet money you're not prepared to lose. When going out gambling, take a certain amount for food and drinks, another amount for lodging, and a third amount that you plan on losing. If you happen to win, that should be seen as gravy, an unexpected bonanza, not something that can be repeated. It used to be said, when novice gamblers set out to Las Vegas, that the worst thing that could happen to them was for them to win. The rationale was that if a novice gambler wins, he or she might actually come to believe that winning is the norm—when, in fact, it is the exception.

The third principle that absolute beginners must learn is a corollary of the first two and reflects what we touched on in the section above on high-tech gambling. That principle is this: Time is *not* on your side when gambling. The longer you stay in a casino, the more money you will lose. A smart gambler knows when to quit—both when winning and, equally important, when losing. You must know when to back off a winning streak and when not to throw good money after bad.

This is known in the argot of gamblers as ''money management.'' The casinos and card houses do everything in their power to undermine this basic principle. They will wine and dine you, parade beautiful women in front of you and make you as comfortable as possible. They will take your credit card faster than you can say Visa Gold. It is always a good idea, therefore, to leave your credit cards behind when gambling and to take only as much money with you, in cash, as you plan on losing. If you insist on taking a credit card with you, for hotel and dining purposes, take one with a spending limit you're comfortable with.

All You Need to Know About Systems

A final word about so-called systems. Absolute beginners hear about allegedly foolproof systems for beating casino games, and the most gullible believe what they hear or what they read. When people talk about systems, they are not referring to actual attempts at cheating, such as using crooked dice, or legal but difficult gambling methods like card counting in Blackjack. A system in gambling usually refers to a method of betting that is alleged to guarantee winnings no matter what. Systems invariably fail over the long haul. But they can work in the short term, at least in games over which the house has only a small advantage. This is what gives systems their illusion of legitimacy.

Nearly all systems are variations on the so-called Martingale or Progressive System in which the gambler simply doubles his bet at each loss and starts over in the cycle with each win. For example, on the first bet the gambler bets $1 and loses. On the second bet, therefore, he bets $2 and, if he loses again, on the third bet he wagers $4, and so on. The theory is that eventually he will win and by that time his bet will be so large that his winnings will cover the previous losses with a little profit to spare. Here is how it looks in theory on an even money (1 to 1) bet:

Bet No.	Amount Bet	Amount Won	Amount Lost	Total
1	$1	0	$1	($1)
2	$2	0	$2	($3)
3	$4	0	$4	($7)
4	$8	0	$8	($15)
5	$16	$16	0	$1
Totals:	$31	$16	$15	$1

Sounds great, right? It takes five bets and a total of $31 wagered, but this fellow picks up $1 for his efforts. What's wrong with that? Actually, nothing. Systems can and do work—for a while. As in anything in gambling, you can buck the odds for a time and end up a winner. Many a systems player will try out a new system, get ahead a few hundred dollars or so, and be utterly convinced that it will keep working. But the problem with systems is that eventually the odds catch up with you—only by that time the system has you betting extremely large sums for very little actual profits, sums no one in his or her right mind would risk losing.

Let's take a look at what happens if we continue this table a few more steps. You'll notice that the bets become very large, very quickly.

Bet No.	Amount Bet	Amount Won	Amount Lost	Total
6	$1	0	$1	0
7	$2	0	$2	($2)
8	$4	0	$4	($6)

Bet No.	Amount Bet	Amount Won	Amount Lost	Total
9	$8	0	$8	($14)
10	$16	0	$16	($30)
11	$32	0	$32	($62)
12	$64	0	$64	($126)
13	$128	0	$128	($254)
14	$256	0	$256	($510)
15	$512	0	$512	($1,022)
16	$1,024	$1,024	$0	$2
Totals:	$2,078	$1,040	$1,038	$2

Now, this table reflects a fair—that is, an even money—bet and still the sums involved become quite large. Not too many gamblers have enough faith in their ''proven'' system to lay down $1,024 on a single bet just to make $1. In fact, the casinos add two monkey wrenches into the systems works. First, they have those payoff odds that do not reflect the true (even) odds. And second, they have limits on the amount of money someone can wager on a single bet—$500 or $1,000 or even $5,000. In other words, long before a system can, in theory, pay off—given even a modest string of bad luck—the gambler hits the ceiling of the casino's maximum bet limit.

There are other systems even more complex than the progressive one. There is the double plus one system, the cancellation system that's used frequently with Roulette, and a variety of even more complex ones. But each of them bumps up against the maximum bet limits. Remember, the point is not that systems always fail; they don't. With enough luck, even a systems player can win. The point, however, is that even with good luck the systems player would have to bet staggering sums to win small amounts and eventually, when his luck changed, would end up losing big money.

Besides, there are more cost-effective ways for an absolute beginner to have an edge while gambling. Now that we have taken a brief look at the overall gambling scene at the turn of the millennium, we'll turn to the specific games and discover the key principles that will help save you money over the long run—and even win. Although there are no surefire systems, there are right ways and wrong ways to play almost every gambling game. We'll start off with a game almost everyone has played at one time or another—the lottery.

1. *U.S. News and World Report,* March 14, 1994, pp. 42–45.
2. Ibid.
3. *International Gaming and Wagering Business,* June 5, 1994, p. 1.
4. Australian Associated Press, November 17, 1994.
5. *McLean's,* May 30, 1994, p. 27.
6. *The Economist,* April 11, 1992, p. 23.
7. Ibid.
8. Ibid.
9. John Scarne, *Scarne's New Complete Guide to Gambling* (New York: Simon & Schuster, 1961, 1974), p. 19.

What Every Absolute Beginner Should Know About Lotteries

Even the queen of England plays the lottery.

In late 1994, when Great Britain reintroduced a national lottery for the first time since 1826, Queen Elizabeth did her part to promote the betting frenzy, collecting a pool of money from her family members and purchasing one of the 25 million tickets bought in the first round. Her Royal Highness was among the 1.1 million winners—although, like most of the other winners, her take was small, just ten pounds (then about $15.69). When split among the members of her royal "syndicate," the total winnings per person was less than fifty pence each.

Actually, it was Queen Elizabeth's great predecessor and namesake, Queen Elizabeth I, who introduced the first Lotterie Generall into England in 1566. The money raised was to be used "towardes the reparation of the havens [harbors] and strength of the Realme and towardes such other publique good workes."[1] National governments all over the world, then and now, recognize that lotteries are a form of voluntary taxation and use them to produce revenue for many worthwhile causes—such as the settlement of the American colonies, the British Museum, Harvard University, and the Syndey Opera House.

Lotteries, at least in the sense of drawings for prizes, have been around for more than 2,000 years, with Caesar Augustus (c. 63 B.C.–14 A.D.) organizing the first Roman lottery to raise money to pay for public works. In 1530, the Italian National Lottery, *Lo Giuoco del Lotto,* became the first lottery to award cash prizes. This lottery, the Lotto, is the forerunner of other national lotteries and the inspiration for such games as Bingo and Keno. It has been in constant existence, taking place each week, since its inception in 1530. Players pick numbers for each of ten Italian cities, and the results of drawings are published in newspapers all over Italy. A typical summary of the results appears on page 29.

From Italy, the lottery idea spread to France, Great Britain, and eventually all over the world. Throughout history the lottery has been accompanied by cycles of public enthusiasm, corruption, and then legal prohibition. The number of lotteries in England grew from 1566 until they were banned by Parliament in 1826. That year British Treasury officials ran off with the lottery proceeds, prompting the government to ban lotteries outright for more than 150 years. They weren't reinstated until 1994. The same dynamic of enthusiasm followed by prohibition occurred in the U.S. Lotteries

Giuoco del Lotto

Bari	60	10	43	21	14
Cagliari	15	42	65	89	18
Florence	4	19	21	74	10
Genoa	38	7	71	45	1
Milan	89	40	5	74	27
Naples	28	83	79	65	19
Palermo	82	74	47	61	3
Rome	77	37	85	4	2
Turin	19	72	66	86	15
Venice	90	8	52	46	33

were such a stable source of income to the American colonies that the Continental Congress actually proposed financing the Revolutionary War through the sale of lottery tickets in 1776. The plan collapsed when members of Congress realized that there were not enough colonists rich enough to play. Lotteries were enormously popular throughout the eighteenth and nineteenth centuries, but as the number of lotteries, both public and private, increased, so did corruption and abuses of them. In 1823, three years before the British Treasury scandal, the organizers of the so-called Grand National Lottery collected millions of dollars in lottery ticket sales and then vanished without a trace. They were never caught. Eventually, Congress and the states passed more and more laws limiting the distribution of lottery tickets until finally, in 1895, Louisiana became the last state to outlaw lotteries. Americans who wished to play a lottery badly enough participated in foreign lotteries—such as the Irish

Sweepstakes, British soccer pools, or the Puerto Rican lottery—or spent money on an enormous underground numbers operation estimated to gross $10 billion in 1973.[2] The growth of legal state lotteries put the old "numbers rackets" largely out of business just as the repeal of Prohibition put an end to liquor smuggling.

Beginning in 1963, public approval for lotteries was on the rise again when New Hampshire became the first state to once again authorize a statewide lottery. Led by New York in 1976 and New Jersey in 1970, most other states soon followed suit. Today lotteries are legal in 37 out of the 50 states. They are still illegal in Alabama, Alaska, Arkansas, Hawaii, Mississippi, New Mexico, North Dakota, North Carolina, Oklahoma, South Carolina, Tennessee, Utah, Wyoming, and Nevada, strangely enough. A full 80 percent of all Americans now live in states that authorize lotteries, and it is estimated that each week one third of all adults in the United States—57 million people—buy lottery tickets.

One reason for greater public acceptance of lotteries is that they are all run by state governments, presumably free of corruption, and are seen by many as a viable alternative to higher taxes. State lotteries are usually authorized to pay for some public good, such as schools or roads. After years of declining state tax revenues and cutbacks in federal spending, the states have become dependent upon the money that lotteries bring in. It is estimated that state governments make between $8 and $10 billion on their lottery operations each year, which has led critics to charge that government is now the biggest promoter of gambling in America.[3] Another reason given for the popularity of lotteries is that, in an era when middle-class Americans believe it is harder and harder to make ends meet, the large size of lottery jackpots makes playing the game almost irresistible since a chance at the big money only costs a dollar or two.

The U.S. is not unique in its growing addiction to lotteries. For years, Britain was one of two European nations—the other being Albania—not to have a national lottery, but then it authorized one, as we've seen, in 1994. In France televised lottery drawings are enormously popular. And experts estimate that Spaniards spend upwards of $1 billion on lottery tickets during each Christmas season alone.[4]

How Lotteries Really Work

There are a number of ways to run a lottery. One of the most ancient forms of the lottery is a raffle, a still-popular method for raising money for charities. In a raffle, an organization will sell tickets for a small amount, each of which gives the buyer a chance at a large prize or a number of prizes. Most raffles use a two-part ticket, both of which have serial numbers on them. The buyer keeps one part of the ticket and the other part, with the same number, is placed in a large drum. At a specified date, often with much ceremony, the tickets in the drum are drawn out and the winner, or winners, are announced. For some raffles, winners must be in attendance at the drawing; at most, they do not.

Lotteries operate on the same basic principle, except for one important difference: buyers of the tickets are allowed to pick their own numbers or, in a modern twist, have a computer pick them for them.

In the early years of U.S. state lotteries final lottery numbers were selected by a strange combination of drawings from a drum and the results of a specific horse race. The horse race element was purely a tax dodge to get around a 10 percent federal gambling tax (winnings from horse racing, for some mindless congressional reason, were exempt). The idea was that the winner of the lottery was actually a winner at the horse races and, thus, did not have to pay the tax. Today state governments have eliminated the horse racing loophole and have turned, instead, to a variety of other methods.

The California lottery, one of America's most ingenious, has at least half a dozen different ways to play. California's system is in many ways typical of state lotteries, so we'll take a close look at it as an example of how the game works in other states.

Winning at Super Lotto

The most popular state lottery is the Lotto, which is similar to Keno and patterned after Lo Giuoco del Lotto. It includes a betting system based on the parimutuel system at horse tracks.

In California it works like this. All over California, individuals purchase tickets for one dollar each. A typical California Super Lotto play slip, found in bars and grocery stores, has ten separate "plays" on each slip that are marked from A to I. (See the play slip sample on pages 34–35.) Each play consists of a box filled with six rows of nine numbers from 1 to 51. The first row is 1 to 9, the second row is 10 to 18, and the sixth and final row has only six numbers, 46 to 51. These bracketed numbers look similar to the circled numbers used in tests such as the Scholastic Aptitude Test or the Graduate Record Exam. Using a pen or pencil, players make a dark mark in the brackets of the six numbers they wish to pick in each box, which is why the game is also called Pick Six. To the right of each box of numbers are two other brackets, one with the words Quick Pick next to it and the other with the word Void. If you do not want to pick your own numbers, you can simply mark the Quick Pick, and the computer will generate a random number for you—we'll get to the computer in a moment. If you make a mistake, you do not cross out or try to erase the number(s) but simply fill in the Void circle and go on to another play on the play slip.

You can fill out more than one box of numbers (six numbers to each box); each is a separate play and costs an additional $1. You can use the same numbers for between one and eight future drawings simply by marking a spot called Advance Play. When you're finished marking your numbers, you take the play slip to the clerk at a grocery store or bar, and he or she then enters your numbers into the lottery computer and collects your money. The clerk gives you back a computerized ticket that shows your chosen numbers (or the computer's own generated Quick Pick numbers) and the draw date(s). Players are encouraged to sign the back of their computer ticket, because once it has been signed, only the person who signed the ticket may cash it in. Lotto tickets can be bought between 6 A.M. and 10 P.M. up to five minutes before the twice weekly drawings. Every Wednesday and Saturday night the winning six numbers are selected in a special drawing broadcast on television. Players can find out the winning numbers by watching TV on the draw dates, by calling a special telephone number, or by reading the results in newspapers.

The total amount of money raised in ticket sales is split in two. Half is taken out by the state of California

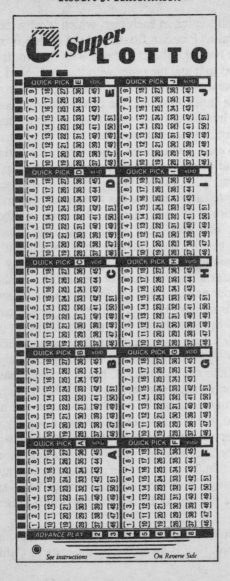

WHERE THE LOTTERY MONEY GOES

Education 34%
Prizes 50%
15%
Retailer Commissions & Operating Expenses

In the first eight years, California Lottery players contributed $6 billion to public education. This is equivalent to, 2 to 3 percent of total school budgets.

PLAY SUPER LOTTO

- Mark 6 numbers from 1 to 51 for each play. Do not use red ink.
- Or mark Quick Pick® for randomly selected numbers.
- Pay $1.00 for each set of 6 numbers played per draw date.
- Play the same numbers for future draws by marking Advance Play® Play up to 8 draws in a row ($1.00 per play per draw).
- If you make a mistake, mark the void box. DO NOT ERASE.
- Your ticket will show your numbers and draw date(s).
- Winning numbers are selected Wednesday and Saturday nights.

PRIZE CATEGORIES AND ODDS

MATCHING NUMBERS	ODDS
All 6 of 6 Winning Numbers	1 in 18,009,460
Any 5 of 6 Winning Numbers	1 in 66,702
Any 4 of 6 Winning Numbers	1 in 1,213
Any 3 of 6 Winning Numbers	1 in 63
Overall Odds of Winning	1 in 60

- Super LOTTO 6 of 6 Jackpot winners shall be paid in equal annual installments for up to a 20 year period.
- Super LOTTO 3 of 6 pays $5.00; all other payouts are calculated by a pari-mutuel formula.

For winning information on Super LOTTO call:
976-4CSL (English) or 976-5CSL (Spanish)
(25¢ per call plus long distance charges if required)

TO CLAIM YOUR PRIZE

- All winning tickets must be validated at any Super LOTTO retailer and claimed no later than 180 days from the winning draw date.
- Special Lottery promotions may have variable claiming periods. Contact the California Lottery for details.
- All winning tickets under $600, per play, may be claimed from any participating cashing Super Lotto retailer.
- Or, after validating your winning ticket at any Super LOTTO retailer, you can submit a claim form, claim receipt, and your original validated ticket to the Lottery. These three items must be submitted to the Lottery no later than 180 days from the winning draw date printed on the ticket.

- Your ticket, not the playslip is your only valid receipt. Check your ticket immediately to ensure the information is correct. Sign the back of the ticket to indicate ownership.
- Super LOTTO is subject to Federal and California State laws and California Lottery regulations.
- State law prohibits the sale of a lottery ticket or payment of a prize to any person under 18 years of age.

12/1/93   A7

for its profits (34 percent said to go to education and 16 percent to commissions and operating expenses). The second half of the money is divided into various prize pools. Forty percent of the money raised goes into the jackpot and the rest is placed into the smaller prize pools. If someone managed to pick all six of the winning numbers, he or she would win the jackpot, which can be in the $5 to $25 million range. Any jackpot over $700,000 is paid off in equal annual installments for up to a twenty-year period. If someone else also picked the six winning numbers, he or she would have to split the jackpot with the other winner. Prizes under $600 can be claimed directly from a participating Super Lotto retailer.

In addition to the jackpot, however, there are other cash prizes. You can win if you have five of the six numbers, any four of the numbers, or any three. Each of these winning categories usually has more than one winner, and the various winners must split the pot for each winning category. For example, if you have five out of the six winning numbers, you split the prize with people who also had five out of six numbers; and if you had four out of six, you split the prize with those who had four out of six. Three out of six wins $5 automatically.

On page 37 is the breakdown, by percentages, of the cash prizes for a sample win and the percentage of the total pot that went to each category.

The amount of money in the total pot covering the various prizes depends upon how many people have played. If there is no winner for the big jackpot in a given week, that money is carried forward for the next drawing, which is how jackpots can build up to enormous amounts quite rapidly. The actual amount of

Sample of Super Lotto Cash Prizes and Percentage of Total Money for Each Prize Category

Category	Number of Winners	Amount Won by Each	Total for Category	% of Prize Money
6 of 6	1	$13,600,000	$13,600,000	89.5
5 of 6	138	$1,706	$235,428	1.5
4 of 6	7,490	$81	$606,690	3.9
3 of 6 ($5)	147,222	$5	$736,110	4.8
Totals:	**154,851**		**$15,178,228**	**100.0**

money won by individuals, therefore, depends both upon how many people have bought lottery tickets and how many winners there are in a given category. Winnings over $600 must be certified by a Lotto retailer who will present the winner with a claim form, a claim ticket, and the original ticket. The winner must submit these three items to the California State Lottery for payment. The form and the receipt must be postmarked or received by the CSL within 180 days after the draw date on the ticket.

What are the odds of winning the jackpot? The mathematics are quite simple for calculating the straight odds of picking six out of six correct numbers in a field of fifty-one. What is more difficult, because of the number of variables involved—different number of tickets bought each week, and so on—are the precise odds on specific winnings. Because multiple winners split the pots, and the amount in the pot varies from week to week, the real odds for a given amount are impossible to calculate with accuracy. However, here are the straight odds of picking a certain match of winning numbers.

California Super Lotto Odds

Matching Numbers	Odds
6 of 6	1 in 18,009,460
5 of 6	1 in 66,702
4 of 6	1 in 1,213
3 of 6	1 in 60

Players are attracted to the Lotto because of the enormous amounts of money in the jackpots and because you can have a chance at winning the jackpot by putting up very little money. But, according to statistician Mike Orkin, most people can't fathom what their real chances are like. "To put these odds in perspective, if you buy fifty Lotto tickets a week, you'll win the jackpot about once every five thousand years," he says. Put another way: To have just a fifty-fifty chance of winning the jackpot, you would have to buy a lottery ticket twice a week for 110,372 years.

The New Fantasy 5 Games

At first the California lottery was once a week with the Pick Six system. The lottery raised so much money, however, that soon the lottery commission began a twice-per-week drawing with Super Lotto. Next it introduced a separate lottery, the Fantasy 5, that is played simultaneously with the Super Lotto. A Fantasy 5 play slip has five separate plays per slip, marked Play A to Play E. Each play consists of columns of circled numbers from one to thirty-nine. The Quick Pick and Void circles are found below the column of numbers. Players mark five, not six, numbers for each play and each play costs $1. Participants take the play tickets to a clerk, as in Super Lotto, and get back a computerized ticket. As in Super Lotto, players may also use the same numbers for future drawings—up to twelve consecutive drawings, in fact. See the sample Fantasy Five play slip on the next page.

There are a number of important differences between Fantasy 5 and Super Lotto. First, the winning numbers in Fantasy 5 are selected five days per week, on Monday, Tuesday, Thursday, Friday, and Sunday nights. Also, unlike Super Lotto, Fantasy 5 pays its jackpot winnings in a single lump sum, not in installment payments over a number of years. The reason for that, however, is that the jackpots are much smaller. In one instance at the same time that the 6 for 6 Super Lotto jackpot was $13 million, the jackpot for Fantasy 5 was only $104,165—which two players each won. In addition, another 248 players each won $283. Fantasy 5 has better odds than Super Lotto:

California Fantasy 5 Odds

Matching Numbedrs	Odds
5 of 5	1 in 575,575
4 of 5	1 in 3,387
3 of 5	1 in 103
2 of 5	1 in 10

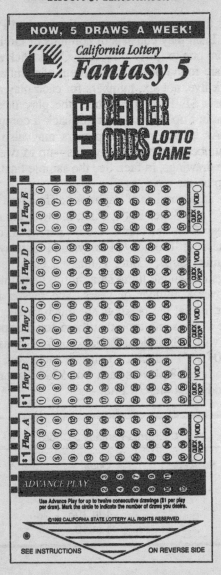

WHERE THE LOTTERY MONEY GOES

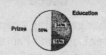

Prizes 50%

Education 34%

16%

Retailer Commissions &
Operating Expenses

In the first eight years, California Lottery players contributed
nearly $6 billion to public education. This is equivalent to
about 1.5 percent of total school budgets.

PLAY FANTASY 5!
"The better odds Lotto game"

- Mark 5 numbers from 1 to 39 for each play. DO NOT USE RED INK.
- Or mark Quick Pick® to have your 5 numbers randomly selected for you.
- Pay $1.00 for each set of 5 numbers played per draw date.
- Play the same numbers for future draws by marking Advance Play®. Play up to 12 draws in a row ($1.00 per play per draw).
- If you make a mistake, mark the VOID spot. DO NOT ERASE.
- Your ticket will show your numbers and draw date(s).
- Winning numbers are selected Monday, Tuesday, Thursday, Friday and Sunday nights.

PRIZE CATEGORIES AND ODDS

MATCHING NUMBERS	PRIZES	ODDS
All 5 of 5 Winning Numbers	Pari-mutuel *	1 in 575,757
Any 4 of 5 Winning Numbers	Pari-mutuel *	1 in 3,387
Any 3 of 5 Winning Numbers	Pari-mutuel *	1 in 103
Any 2 of 5 Winning Numbers	Free Replay Ticket (see below)	1 in 10
Overall Odds of Winning		1 in 9

All Fantasy 5 prizes will be paid in a single payment.

* Prize amounts will vary depending upon sales levels and number of winners.

For winning information on Fantasy 5:
Check your local newspaper or television news, or
Call 976-6CSL (English) or 976-7CSL (Spanish).
(25¢ per call plus long distance charges if required).

TO CLAIM YOUR PRIZE

- All winning tickets must be validated at any Fantasy 5 retailer and claimed no later than 180 DAYS after the winning draw date.
- Winning tickets for prizes under $600 per play may be claimed from any retailer participating in cashing Fantasy 5 tickets.
- Or, after validating your winning ticket at any Fantasy 5 retailer, you can submit a claim form, claim receipt, and your original validated ticket to the Lottery. These three items must be submitted to the Lottery no later than 180 DAYS from the winning draw date printed on the ticket.
- Follow the instructions on the claim form when submitting your winning ticket to the Lottery.
- Special Lottery promotions may have variable claiming periods. Contact the California Lottery for details.

TO CLAIM YOUR REPLAY TICKET

- A ticket with a correct match of two of five numbers is eligible for a Replay ticket. A Replay ticket is a free Fantasy 5 Quick Pick ticket valid for one draw.
- To claim a Replay ticket, a ticket with a two-number match must be validated at any Fantasy 5 retailer within 60 DAYS from the winning draw date on the ticket.
- A ticket with a two-number match can only be redeemed for a Replay ticket by a Fantasy 5 retailer.

- Your ticket, not the playslip, is your only valid receipt. Check your ticket immediately to ensure the information is correct. Sign the back of the ticket to indicate ownership.
- Fantasy 5 is subject to Federal and California State laws and California Lottery regulations.
- State law prohibits the sale of a lottery ticket or payment of a prize to any person under 18 years of age.

RFGS 613 5/2/94

B1

Decco

Decco is yet another gambling operation similar to but separate from Super Lotto and Fantasy 5. As with those two games, a chance still costs $1. The game is played based on a 52-card deck and players pick one card from each suit. During the Decco drawings, which are also broadcast on television, players see the winning numbers. There are currently six drawings per week, one on each day except Sunday. The newspapers publish the results daily. It is very simple and the results look like this: Thursday—Hearts: **8.** Clubs: **5.** Diamonds: **King.** Spades: **Ace.**

If you pick four out of four correctly, you win $5,000. Three out of four wins $50. Two out of four wins $5. And one out of four wins another free Decco ticket.

The odds of winning at Decco (for example, picking three right) are worse than for Fantasy 5.

California Decco Odds

Matching Suits	Odds
4 of 4	1 in 28,561
3 of 4	1 in 595
2 of 4	1 in 33
1 of 4	1 in 4

The Truth About "Instant Win" Scratch-Off Games

In addition to the Super Lotto and Fantasy 5 games, California and many other states also have a number of popular "instant win" scratch-off type games. You buy a ticket for one of these games for $1, $2, or $5 and then scratch off a metallic silver coating to see if you've won. The actual combination of numbers and the prizes vary from game to game (see the samples of scratch-off games on pages 44 and 45). For example, Bank Roll, bought for $1, features prizes of $40 to $500 and players win when they have three like amounts. For example, three $40 on one ticket means the player wins $40. In contrast, the game "In-Between," which also costs $1, features three three-card hands, each with a unknown prize. When the player scratches off the metallic coating, the middle card in each hand must be lower than the "Dealer's" high card to the left and higher than the Dealer's low card to the right. The amount of the prize won if this happens is also revealed by scratching off the coating. In Royal Casino, a two-dollar game, players can win prizes from $100 to $300 directly from lottery retailers and prizes of between $1,000 to $10,000 by mailing winning tickets in to the main lottery office in Sacramento. To win, players scratch the coating off five "chips," which must match a "house chip" also printed on the card. The amount of the prize is under the "house chip" as well. The odds of winning any cash prize, according to the California lottery, are 1 in 9.38—or about double the odds at winning in Roulette.

A popular subcategory of scratch-off type games involves a subsequent element of chance, the so-called big wheel. In games such as Winning Combination and The Big Spin, players have a chance at both an instant win for small prizes, between $40 and $500, as well as a chance at bigger prizes in the $1,000 to $1,500 range. If players satisfy certain conditions on their cards—such as unveiling a little TV set and three letters in Winning Combination—then they send in their tickets and have the right to participate in The Big Spin TV drawing. For The Big Spin game, a player scratches off the coating over a little TV set. If there are three spin symbols under the coating, he or she gets to spin the Big Wheel. If there are three TV show symbols under the coating, he or she gets to go to The Big Spin show in person and win either $1,500 in cash or a chance to spin the Big Wheel. The grand prize in all of these games is the chance to spin a wheel-of-fortune-type big wheel that allows a player the opportunity to win prizes between $10,000 and $1 million. There is a "double" section on the big wheel, and if a player lands on the double in his or her first spin, the amount of the next spin is doubled. Experts calculate the odds of winning a chance at the Big Spin to be one in 1 to 2 million.

According to Mike Orkin, chairman of the Department of Statistics at California State University, Hayward, and author of the book *Can You Win? The Real Odds for Casino Gambling, Sports Betting, and Lotteries*, the original "Win and Spin" game sold 135 million tickets with 22,766,623 winners.[5] The total amount of cash prizes given out was $68 million, and the breakdown was as follows:

Sample of Prizes for "Win and Spin" Type Games

Instant Prize	Number of Winners
$1	10,800,000
$2	8,100,000
$5	3,240,000
$10	540,000
$50	54,000
$100	27,000
$500	6,073
$1,000	1,350
$10,000	150
Chance at Big Spin	50

How to Play New Closed-Cast Keno

California is paving the way into yet another lottery frontier: closed-cast Keno.

Unlike video Keno, which is played on individual video monitors, the new lottery Keno is like regular Keno but the winning numbers are displayed on TV monitors set up in bars and liquor stores in California.

Draws are held on a regular basis, usually about every five to ten minutes.

Players fill in a play slip, just like with Lotto, and take it to a cashier in a liquor store or bar. The play slip features the standard eighty numbers, as in regular Keno, and players may select the number of "spots" (or numbers) they wish to select, from one to ten, as well as the amount of money they wish to bet (from $1 to $20). While players may use the same numbers for consecutive draws, up to 100 times (or a possible total amount of $2,000 wagered), they may not make the various combinations possible in regular Keno. The lottery Keno also features a Quick Pick feature for those who do not wish to pick their own numbers. Players may collect up to $600 directly from the lottery retailer; amounts above that must be collected by filling out a lottery claim form as in Super Lotto.

The payout schedule for Keno is as follows:

10 Spot Game	
Match	*Amount Won*
10	$250,000
9	$3,000
8	$250
7	$50
6	$5
5	$2
4	$4

Odds of winning: 1 in 9.1

9 Spot Game

Match	Amount Won
9	$25,000
8	$250
7	$100
6	$10
5	$4
4	$1

Odds of winning: 1 in 6.5

8 Spot Game

Match	Amount Won
8	$10,000
7	$400
6	$40
5	$10
4	$1

Odds of winning: 1 in 9.8

7 Spot Game

Match	Amount Won
7	$2,500
6	$100
5	$10
4	$2
3	$1

Odds of winning: 1 in 4.2

6 Spot Game

Match	Amount Won
6	$1,000
5	$25
4	$4
3	$1

Odds of winning: 1 in 6.2

5 Spot Game

Match	Amount Won
5	$250
4	$10
3	$2

Odds of winning: 1 in 10.3

4 Spot Game

Match	Amount Won
4	$50
3	$4
2	$1

Odds of winning: 1 in 3.9

3 Spot Game

Match	Amount Won
3	$20
2	$2

Odds of winning: 1 in 6.6

2 Spot Game

Match	Amount Won
2	$8

Odds of winning: 1 in 16.6

1 Spot Game

Match	Amount Won
1	$2

Odds of winning: 1 in 4.0

What these tables of payouts and odds reveal, obviously, is that there is a wide range of odds and possible winnings from different Keno picks. The odds range from a low of just 1 in 4.2 with a seven-spot ticket to as high as 1 in 16.6 with a two-spot ticket. Also, the top prize in a ten-spot game, shown above as $250,000, can vary. The rules stipulate that no more than $10 million will be paid out for the top prize in any one draw. The prize will be divided and distributed based on the amount wagered.

Systems for Beating the Lottery

There is a lottery subculture in America, no doubt about it. What is less known is that there is also an entire industry that exists merely to serve this subculture—offering books, tapes, charts, newsletters, and even computer programs that promise to help customers "beat the system." One popular lottery book shows players how to win lotteries by following their astrology and biorhythm charts. A 900 telephone number service, Network Solutions Unlimited in Costa Mesa, California, offers the "latest/hottest winning numbers" as well as the "coldest" numbers for $1.75 per minute, $3.50 maximum. Professor Darrell Dolph markets a program he calls the Lottery Number Advisor (LONA), which selects "ranges" of numbers to be used—for example, from 38 to 40 and from 55 to 57.

A publication called *Lotto Edge,* published in Los Angeles by the Edge Media Group, features detailed computer analysis charts of past lotteries, loading tube charts, and lists of numbers to be used in a given week's games. For example, one week it recommended using numbers ending in 2, 6, 7, or 9. For Fantasy 5, the publication came up with a list of "most hit numbers" (the number 18 one week had 15 "hits" or 21.7 percent), "most paired numbers" (03 and 04, four times), "most probable numbers," and so on. The amount of data lottery enthusiasts have at their disposal is almost as staggering as the amount of data avid horse players keep track of.

A company in Portland, Oregon, offers an IBM-compatible program featured in *Lotto Edge* called the Versa-Bet Management System. It features "complete lottery analysis and database management'' for lotteries and Keno games. "The Gaming Management System includes over 100 Lotto wheeling systems of every kind to match any budget, and also includes game databases for every 5- and 6-number lottery in the U.S.,'' an advertisement for the system boasts. The company also has a Versa-Bet Bet Maker program and a Versa-Bet Daily 3/4 program. Customers can buy the software for $159.95 for two programs and $199.95 for all three. The Bet Maker program will spit out a list of fifty "most probable" numbers for many state lotteries.

What do the experts say about "computer analysis" of past Lotto wins and numbers? Only this: that because Lotto numbers are selected randomly, past data is utterly useless in picking future numbers—which is, after all, what counts. "The real truth about Lotto systems is that the Lottery Commission monitors the randomness of the selection methods, and there's no way to predict randomly selected numbers," says Orkin, the statistician. "Put simply, trying to predict Lotto numbers is a waste of time."[6]

What about buying more than one lottery ticket? Doesn't that increase your odds? The short answer is that, yes, it does, but the increase is so infinitesimal that it is almost statistically irrelevant—unless you buy a lot of tickets. And even then, the amount of money you have to spend to increase your odds significantly is more than offset by other factors, such as inflation and taxes on jackpot winnings. For example, in 1992 a "syndicate" in Australia raised $7.5 million from 2,500 "investors"—who contributed $3,000 each and bought 5 million out of the 7 million available tickets in the Virginia State lottery. The syndicate won the jackpot of $27 million—but because the winnings will be paid out over twenty years, and be taxed 34 percent in state and federal income taxes, the individual "investors" will only get back $7,128 over twenty years. It hardly seems worth the risk when you consider that investing the same amount in a top-performing mutual fund could return ten times that.

1. John Scarne, *Scarne's New Complete Guide to Gambling,* op cit., p. 144.
2. Ibid., p. 186.
3. *The Economist,* April 11, 1992, p. 23.
4. Ibid.
5. Mike Orkin, *Can You Win?* (New York: W. H. Freeman and Company, 1991), p. 98.
6. Ibid., p. 106.

Bingo Basics

One form of gambling almost everyone is familiar with is Bingo.

Although it is scorned by hard-core gamblers because of its relatively poor odds, Bingo is still amazingly popular in the United States, Canada, and many other countries. Currently forty-four out of the fifty U.S. states permit some type of charitable gaming, including Bingo. The six that do not are Arkansas, Hawaii, Idaho, Kentucky, Tennessee, and Utah.

When you count all of the Indian reservation Bingo parlors and the myriad church concessions, Bingo in America is big business. It is estimated that at least $10 billion is wagered each year at 75,000 charitable gaming operations in the U.S., which include both Bingo parlors and so-called casino nights at various charities, such as the Boys and Girls Clubs. According to *Money* Magazine, that amount is triple what the 2,100 chapters of the United Way managed to collect each year.[1]

Both Bingo and its close cousin, Keno, are derived from the Italian national lottery, *Lo Giuoco del Lotto*, which has been in existence each week since 1530 (see the chapter on lotteries). As in Bingo and Keno, the Italian lottery, or Lotto for short, features a card with a series of numbers on it. In Lotto there are numbers from 1 to 90; in Bingo, the numbers are generally from 1 to 25. In this, Keno, which was originally played with ninety numbers, is closer to Lotto than Bingo. Players pick numbers on the Lotto card and then wait for the results to be published in newspapers or broadcast on TV.

Bingo, of course, is played slightly differently.

In its standard form, Bingo is played by people who purchase cards each with a different combination of twenty-four numbers on it. The card has the word Bingo written at the top, and beneath each letter in that word is a column of five numbers. The first column of numbers, beneath the letter B, has five numbers from 1 to 15. The second column, beneath the letter I, has five numbers from 16 to 30. The third column, beneath the letter N, has five numbers from 31 to 45. The fourth column, beneath the letter G, has five numbers from 46 to 60. And the fifth column, beneath the letter O, has five numbers from 61 to 75. In the middle of the card, under the letter ''N,'' there is a free space.

The card looks like this:

B	I	N	G	O
5	20	36	54	73
2	21	38	50	69
11	23	FREE	60	74
3	17	42	55	65
10	25	33	49	71

A game manager, usually known as a caller, calls out numbers from a special hopper (originally borrowed from Keno games) filled with seventy-five numbered and lettered Ping-Pong balls. For example, there are balls numbered 1 through 15 and each bearing the letter B, balls numbered 16 through 30 and each bearing the letter I, and so on. The hopper looks like a wire cage through which is blown air, which makes the balls fly around and produces, at least theoretically, a purely random selection of numbers. The caller pulls out one of the balls and announces, say, "B-8," and the player who has, or players who have, an 8 under the B column mark that on the Bingo card through a variety of methods—by using a special inker, for example, or by placing a token on top of the space. The balls are always set aside in a special display rack for future examination, in case of disputes, and are often displayed on an electronic bulletin board as well.

The object of the game, in the simplest form of Bingo, is to cover all of the 24 numbered squares (and the one free square). This is called a blackout. When a player manages that, he or she yells "Bingo!" and wins. The amount won varies from a low of just $100 to as high, at illegal and Indian reservation games, of $200,000 or more.

To play, either at a local church or in Las Vegas, you need to buy a Bingo card, which can cost anywhere between $1 and $10, depending on the game. Many hard-core Bingo fans will purchase numerous cards and play them simultaneously, hoping to increase their odds of winning.

Popular Bingo Variations

Over the years, variations on the basic Bingo pattern developed. In the 1970s it became common to have a special colored ball in the hopper that acted as a kind of wild card, allowing players to cover any square they chose. Some games are played so that you can win a Bingo merely by covering a row (horizontal Bingo), a column (vertical Bingo), or even a diagonal (diagonal Bingo) of numbers, albeit for a smaller pot than the total blackout.

Diagonal Bingo, for example, looks like this:

B	I	N	G	O
●	20	36	54	73
2	●	38	50	69
11	23	●E	60	74
3	17	42	●	65
10	25	33	49	●

Other variations include wins when a player can cover:

- the four corners of a card (four-corner Bingo)

- all eight squares around the free square in the center

- all of the squares around the entire Bingo card

- all of the squares in different separate lines (double Bingo)

- all of the squares in the top, middle, and bottom row (layer cake Bingo)

and so on.

Double Bingo, for example, looks like this:

B	I	N	G	O
5	20	●	54	73
2	21	●	50	69
11	23	●FREE	60	74
3	17	●	55	65
●	●	●	●	●

Progressive Bingo

At many Bingo palaces today, especially those on Indian reservations, the pots can be truly enormous, reaching tens of thousands of dollars, and occasionally even hundreds of thousands of dollars. Competition for a $200,000 prize, however, comes with a catch: players must make not only a "blackout" Bingo, they must do it within a specified number of calls. In other words, in ordinary Bingo the caller keeps calling out numbers until someone wins. For the big prizes in progressive Bingo, the caller only calls out fifty numbers, for example, and usually no one wins.

Calculating Bingo Odds

There is a reason why Bingo parlors put up such huge prizes, which of course attract huge crowds to vie for them. The Bingo operators know the odds. The late, great John Scarne, perhaps the foremost expert on gambling ever to appear in America, calculated the odds of winning the typical progressive Bingo "bet" years before the advent of personal computers. He wanted to figure out the odds of winning a Bingo "blackout" in fifty calls or less. The mathematical formula he used for discovering the number of combinations of n things taken r at a time was this:

$$\frac{n(n-1)(n-2)\ldots(n-r+1)}{r!}$$

Scarne simply substituted the 75 Bingo Ping-Pong balls for n and the 24 possible spaces on the Bingo card for r. That gave him the number of possible combinations that 75 balls could make in 24 spaces, or

$$25,778,699,578,994,555,700.$$

To find out the possible combinations using only the first 50 balls, he substituted 50 for n instead of 75. The result was only 121,548,660,036,300. He then divided the first number above by the second and arrived at the odds of covering all 24 spaces in 50 balls or less: 1 in 212,085.

$$\frac{25,778,699,578,994,555,700}{121,548,660,036,300} = 212,085$$

That's for each individual player, however. A Bingo operator may sell about 3,000 Bingo cards in a given session, so he or she has to divide 212,085 by 3,000, which works out to 70 to 1 odds in his or her favor. Not bad, when you think about it.

Scarne took this calculation of probability one step further. He wondered what the odds would be if a shrewd Bingo promoter sold Bingo cards for just one penny apiece and offered a prize of $1 million to whomever covered a Bingo card in just twenty-four calls. The odds of doing that, Scarne calculated, would be 25,778,699,578,994,555,700 to one—not impossible, to be sure, but a bit daunting nevertheless.

Calculating Bingo odds at ordinary games is difficult because there are so many variables involved—the number of players, for example, or the number of Bingo cards sold. It's important to remember that in ordinary Bingo games, unlike in progressive games, numbers are called out until someone wins. What that means is that you are not playing against the general Bingo probabilites shown above but against the other players. This gives you much better odds. For example, let's say you're playing ordinary blackout Bingo in a church hall with 500 people playing. On a single game you have one chance in 500 of winning. The more variations that are played, the better your odds (because sometimes more than one player can win).

Some states strictly regulate Bingo operations; others are more lax. The Bingo operators usually figure out how much money they have to pay back in prizes to keep people coming. Obviously, if they are selling cards at $1 each and the prize is $50, not too many people will be interested in playing.

What about buying multiple cards? Does it improve your chances of winning?

Well, the answer is: yes. But . . . and this is a big but . . . the improvement in the odds is not necessarily significant. It all depends on how many players are involved. Obviously, if you're playing blackout Bingo for a $1,000 prize and there are only five players, buying more than one card makes sense. If there are 3,000 players engaged, multiple cards improve your odds, but less significantly.

Bingo is primarily a social activity used to support worthy causes. When you compare the odds in Bingo with some other popular gambling games, such as Blackjack or even Baccarat, it's apparent that Bingo has more to do with charity than with making money.

How to Spot Crooked Bingo

The first thing you must know about Bingo, at least the kind used for charity, is that a very small percentage of the whole pot actually goes to the charity involved. In December 1992 the South Carolina Tax Commission reported that just 1 percent of the state's $272 million in Bingo revenues actually benefited the charities sponsoring the games.[2] Many experts insist that, on average, about 10 percent of money bet in Bingo parlors actually go to the church or charity that is sponsoring the game.

A good chunk of the money, of course, between 50 and 80 percent of the total, comes right back out in prizes. Another sizable portion goes to the concessionaires who run the games—the people who own the equipment and sell the Bingo cards. Some charities are forced to give up a third of the total income, or more, to the promoters. Some charities have discovered too late that the promoters who run the Bingo and charity "Las Vegas" nights are really crooks or mobsters, attracted to the money-laundering possibilities of legitimate gambling and more than willing to skim profits right off the top. According to *Money* magazine, the Pennsylvania Crime Commission reported that "the operation of fraudulent charity Bingo is a near-perfect form of white-collar crime."

These problems only affect players, at least monetarily, from the point of view of the prizes offered. Charity Bingo nights that have high upfront costs obviously cannot afford to offer larger cash prizes.

A more serious problem for Bingo enthusiasts is outright cheating on the part of either the Bingo operators or experienced gamblers in the crowd. Charity gambling, in general, is an easy target for professional gamblers, because often the people running them—even experienced operators—are no match for even a mediocre card counter or even an outright cheat. The Bingo operators themselves can cheat very easily, although, with most church events and certainly in the major Las Vegas Bingo places, it is very rare. The most common way Bingo operators cheat is by using a stooge in the audience. The caller has a copy of the Bingo card used by the stooge, and sometimes even an extra series of balls. The caller calls out most of the numbers legitimately, but at crucial moments he or she simply calls out one or more of the numbers that the stooge needs and switches one of the balls taken out of the hopper with a ball that has the stooge's needed number. The stooge wins the big prize, which of course he or she simply gives back to the Bingo operator in exchange for a hefty fee.

1. *Money* magazine, October 1993, p. 130.
2. Ibid., p. 132.

The Inside Story of Slot Machines and Video Gambling

I grew up with slot machines.

My father, a small-town attorney and later a judge, collected antique slot machines from the early 1900s—beautiful polished wood and brass machines that were, in their own way, works of art. We had about a dozen of these "one-armed bandits" down in our basement rec room. They were just for our own use, obviously, but over the years I would see my parents' friends in our basement during parties dump fistfuls of nickels, dimes, and quarters in the machines, despite numerous warnings from children and adults alike. Some would win, but most would lose. Even those who won, however, usually ended up losing their winnings and then some.

The slot machine was invented in 1887 in San Francisco by a twenty-nine-year-old mechanic named Charles Fey. His mechanical machine was very similar to the ones in my parents' basement and was called the Liberty Bell. It featured three windows each displaying different wheels covered by ten ordinary card symbols, such as diamonds and clubs, as well as bells and horseshoes. The three wheels were spun by pulling a long arm on the side of the machine—which is, of course, where the machines got their name "one-armed bandits." Although you could see about nine symbols through the window on Fey's machine, only the three symbols that landed on the "pay line" were the ones that counted. Fey had a monopoly on his slot machines and they were an immediate hit. But then a Chicago manufacturer named Herbert Stephen Mills designed his own machine with the typical layout we associate today with slots—three windows with wheels covered by twenty symbols, oranges, cherries, lemons, plums, as well as bars and bells.

Most of the early mechanical slots were very straightforward: players put in nickels, dimes, quarters, half-dollars, or silver dollars and were paid back according to a fixed schedule shown on the front of the machine. On Charles Fey's original machine, for example, three bells paid out "ten drinks"—or ten times the nickel inserted for each pull of the handle. His original payout schedule was as follows:

Three Bells	10 drinks
Flush of Hearts	8 drinks
Flush of Diamonds	6 drinks
Flush of Spades	4 drinks
Two Horseshoes and Star	2 drinks
Two Horseshoes	1 drink

In later years slot designers came up with the concept of the "jackpot," in which the machine automatically added coins to a special box in the middle of the machine, seen through a clear glass window. The jackpot kept getting bigger and bigger until someone finally won it, generally by having three bars appear on the pay line.

In the 1960s and '70s slot machines went through a revolution in development through such changes as multiple-coin slots, "hold and draw" features, progressive slots, and, most important of all, the substitution of electronic components for the mechanical wheels and gears of the older machines. Today's slot machines hardly resemble the simple single-coin machines of the early years.

For one thing, there are very few real mechanical slot machines left—and they are mostly for show. Players have always liked the feel of the mechanical slots, however, so machine manufacturers, such as Bally Manufacturing and International Game Technology (IGT), have continued to simulate the mechanical slots even though there is no practical reason to do so. For example, the new electronic machines don't need to have an arm to pull—play could easily be initiated with a simple push of the button—but players *like* pulling the arm, and so most machines have them. Designers have even attempted to simulate the dragging feel of the arms. In the 1950s, '60s, and early '70s, manufacturers developed a hybrid between a mechanical slot machine and a strictly electronic machine called the electromechanical slot, which still had mechanical mechanisms but enhanced these through such refinements as electronic coin meters and lots of bells and whistles. In the 1970s some manufacturers experimented with completely electronic machines with simple video screens to display the results. They found that players mistrusted them and wanted to see those wheels spinning around, and so the manufacturers kept the wheels as well.

But while most manufacturers today keep the mechanical feel of the old machines through the spinning wheels, the actual guts of the modern-day slot machine are completely electronic. The modern slots are totally computerized machines that utilize microprocessor chips to control all parts. The heart of the microprocessor machines is the so-called Random Number Generator (RNG), which guarantees that the play is "random." It is not really random, in a precise mathematical sense of the term, but only simulated random, because the numbers which the Random Number Generator turns up are generated according to a fixed formula. But because the range of numbers is so large, between 0 and 5 billion, for instance, it is random for all intents and purposes. The Random Number Generator spins out a series of numbers, which the microprocessor then translates into symbols from two different sets of symbols—winning symbols and losing symbols. These symbols, displayed on the turning wheels inside the slot machine, are what appear in the display case on the front of the machine.

Today in the casinos there are no longer any single-coin, single-line slot machines. Instead there are a variety of multiple-coin, multiple-line machines with a dizzying array of possible winning combinations. There are still nickel slots in some casinos in the Midwest, but there is a trend toward bigger and bigger denominations—multiple-coin 50-cents, one-dollar, and five-dollar machines. Some casinos, such as

Caesars Palace, now even use special $100 tokens for their biggest slot machines. Many casinos now feature slot machines with four wheels instead of the traditional three. There are even some specialty slots, such as the so-called Big Berthas, that have eight reels and are designed for more than one player.

Different Types of Slot Machines

Slot machines come in a wide variety of sizes, shapes, colors, and designs, but, despite their outward differences, there are basically only three major types in use today.

One very popular type is the "progressive" slot machine, which allows you to increase your possible jackpot by adding more coins. In essence, this type of machine lets you multiply your bet by inserting more money. The company International Game Technology (IGT) produces progressive machines with names such as Quartermania, High Rollers, and Fabulous 50s. A fifty-cent wager on the Quartermania, for example, allows a player a shot at winning up to $200,000; Fabulous 50s allows a player to win up to $500,000 on a two-coin bet.

One of IGT's most famous machines, Megabucks, allows players a shot at winning jackpots totaling more than $6 million! This type of slot machine is not a stand-alone unit but is, in fact, linked electronically to many others of the same type in more than one casino. In other words, players attempting to win a Megabucks jackpot are, as in a lottery, actually competing with other players at other locations.

It works like this. Say you play on a four-reel machine that requires $1. The jackpot is won by lining up four sevens. The first dollar allows you to play on the middle line for a $5,000 jackpot. The second dollar you put in allows you to play on the second line for a $10,000 jackpot. The third dollar allows you to play on the third line for the progressive jackpot that varies but never is below, say, $1 million.

In addition to the super jackpots, some Megabucks machines also feature "multi-mini" or "mega-mini" jackpots with smaller wins in the range of hundreds of thousands of dollars. The mega-jackpots are paid out, like lotteries, over time. For example, a $5 million jackpot would be paid out in ten annual installments of $500,000 each. Some slots also feature lottery-like special prizes such as cars or all-expenses-paid vacations.

A second type of slot machine is the "multiple-line" machine that allows you to win with different configurations of symbols, such as matches straight across or crisscrossing across nine symbols shown in the windows. In addition to the standard three-line machines, there are also now five-line and even eight-line machines. The machines are electronic, and each of the possible lines of play will light up when enough coins have been inserted to win if that line "hits." For example, if you insert one coin, then you can win only on the middle line straight across. A second coin allows you to win also on the top line. A third coin allows you to win on the bottom line, and so on.

A final type of slot machine is the "name your play" machine in which inserting one coin allows you to win on one level of play, such as cherries, while inserting two coins allows you to win on another, higher level, like oranges.

More changes are on the way for slot machines.

Many casinos have already begun to experiment with devices that accept dollar bills and simply credit the machines. The technology allows players to avoid having to ask for more coins from a change person, but it also allows him or her to spend more money. The MGM Grand in Las Vegas is leading the way in this coinless technology. The giant casino now has bill acceptor units on all of its 3,500 slot machines, about 500 of which are completely coinless.[1] The way these 500 coinless slots work is that a player inserts a given number of bills into the bill acceptor and then is issued credits for that particular machine. When the time comes to "cash out," with either winnings or the amount of money remaining from that originally put into the machine, the slot issues a special voucher that can then be redemmed for cash or used on another coinless machine. Some experts foresee that the paper voucher now being used will eventually become a full-fledged debit card that is similar to the ones used on college campuses today for copy machines. Players would buy a debit card at a casino with a certain amount of money encoded in it, and use that card on any of a variety of electronic games in a casino—from slots to video Keno and video Poker. If depleted, the card could have more money put into it—either by means of a machine that accepts bills directly or through a casino representative. Some experts even propose that these casino debit cards could be used at a variety of casinos in a given area, such as Las Vegas, and would eliminate such clumsy mainstays of casino gambling as coin buckets or chips.

This trend may continue even further. Unless barred by state legislatures, it is likely that innovative casinos will soon introduce some form of cashless money collection—such as tying the slots or debit cards directly to ATM or credit card machines. Most people proposing this realize, however, that limits would have to be established, out of the fear that a gambler might drain his or her entire bank account. Still, proponents insist that there is no real difference between (1) someone going to a bank ATM, withdrawing $200, and converting the cash to coins or chips and (2) simply having that same $200 placed directly onto a debit card or into a slot machine credit account.

Strategies for Winning at Slots

In the early 1940s, a number of sharpies who called themselves the Rhythm Boys, many of whom were women, figured out a way to beat the slots by timing the pulls of the handles. In the old mechanical slots a component called the clock fan controlled the amount of time each of the wheels spun, but the clock fan went dead seven to eight seconds after the wheels stopped spinning. The Rhythm Boys took advantage of this fact. By observing the symbols that appeared in the window and knowing the order of symbols on each wheel, a rhythm player was able to manipulate the wheels by timing when he or she pulled the handle.

To make a long and very complicated story short, these players were able to make at least some of the winning symbols appear more consistently and, given enough time, were able to empty the slots of all their money. It's estimated that the casinos lost at least half a *billion* dollars in one year, between 1948 and 1949, because of this system—which was entirely *legal*. Just as they were to do with card counters, however, the casinos quickly figured out a way to sabotage the winning system. They simply added a device to the slot machines that would vary the amount of time it took the clock fans to make the wheels spin.

Today, of course, the electronic components, specifically the Random Number Generator, effectively eliminate all skill and most cheating from slot machines. There are two traditional cheating methods still common: they are ''slugs,'' the use of fake or low-value foreign coins in slot machines, and ''stringing,'' which is the continual use and reuse of a special coin with a thin nylon string or wire attached to it. Player Instigated Action, another electronic factor in slot machine design, actually increases the randomness to such a degree that no two players would win the same amount—*even if theoretically they could play each other's turns!* With the old mechanical machines, a given unit was set up so that no matter who pulled the next turn, the same result would ensue. But this is no longer true. By designing the slot machines so that the Random Number Generator is only activated when a player performs a certain action or combination of actions—for example, when the first series of coins is dropped in the slot or when a player starts to pull a lever—each player will have a different result. Because each player drops his or her coins in the slot at different speeds, even if just a fraction of a second different, the Random Number Generator kicks into gear at different times with different players giving different results.

What does all this high technology mean, then? It means that the idea that a certain machine is ''due'' to win no longer holds true. The Random Number Generator enforces the laws of probability with utter ruthlessness. While it is true that there must be a certain amount of wins over the long term—all predetermined by the slot's computer program and the percentage of wins the casino allows—the time those wins occur is now totally random. It's also true that this randomness, over the short term, can work against a casino. It's not uncommon for there to be a remarkable winning streak on a given slot after which the casino actually has to restock the coin-drained machine with more money. But the basic axiom is the same: predicting this winning streak is impossible—one slot may produce two mega-jackpots one right after another and then not deliver another big win for years. It's now just luck, pure and simple.

That does not mean, however, that all slot machines are created equal, or that there is not a certain amount of skill that will pay off when choosing which machines and which type of slots to play. Most states require that the machines return a minimum amount of money in winnings, but individual casinos set these return percentages at different levels. In the early years of the slots, most of the legal machines kept half of the money put into them, which was why they were called one-armed bandits. Gradually, however, the twin forces of competition and government coercion forced most slot owners to raise the percentage the machines kicked back. In New Jersey, by state law, the slots must pay back 87 percent of the money put into them. In Nevada, they must pay back 75 percent. Most of the casinos in Nevada and Atlantic City fix the percentage between 90 and 95 percent, however. Some casinos advertise their "loose" slots to attract players to them—some claiming winning percentages as high as 97 percent. Harrah's in Vegas, for example, likes to advertise its "97-percent Blazing Sevens."

The monthly magazine *Casino Player* regularly publishes a chart of the slots and their percentages at various casinos. For example, in a recent issue the magazine reported that Harrah's in Atlantic City had 993 quarter-slots with an average win ratio of 90.7 percent, 257 fifty-cent slots with win ratios of 91.8 percent, 505 dollar slots with a win ratio of 92.6 percent, and 80 five-dollar slots with a ratio of 95.3 percent. Some experienced players mistakenly believe that the casino owners merely flip a switch and electronically alter the winning percentages or change the percentages from different times of day. Most experts insist that this is simply not so. For one thing, the Gaming Control Board prohibits the use of remote control devices to change the percentages and, secondly, it is simply impractical to do so. Most casinos make so much money from their slot machines even with payouts in the 87 to 95 percent range that for them to tinker with the winning percentage on a day-to-day basis would be counterproductive.

So what is an absolute beginner to do? Well, we began this book with the basic notion that gambling is, in essence, a form of recreation, a way to have fun. When you combine that idea with the absolute, unshakable fact that slot machines are purely a game of chance, with the odds unmistakably in favor of the machines, then a number of inferences can be drawn.

First, do try to find the machines with the higher winning ratios—either by looking around for signs that advertise them, by reading gambling magazines, or simply by asking around. Be selective. Don't grab the first machine you see open. Some experts advise what is called the "three-pull rule"—play three times on a given machine and, if it doesn't hit, move on to another.

Second, the key to winning at slot machines, which I learned quite literally as a teenager in our basement rec room, is to *quit when you're ahead!* The house has a built-in advantage of between 3 and 25 percent, and so you will certainly lose over the long haul. On a typical three-line machine with twenty symbols on each wheel, programmed to pay back 94.4 percent of the money put into it, your chances of hitting the jackpot are only 1 in 421. If you get lucky after an hour or so of playing and win $25, quit. I repeat: Quit! Go have a good steak, or see a show. Don't put that $25 back in the machines.

Third, don't bother trying to play the minimum number of coins in each machine. While it is true that your money might last longer that way, most statisticians who have studied the slots insist that by taking away the chances at the bigger jackpots—with progressive or multiple-line machines—you actually end up hurting your odds in the end.

Fourth, if your goal is not to lose too much money—as opposed to winning the jackpot of your life—stay away from the big-money progressive machines and concentrate instead on the machines that deliver smaller but more frequent payouts.

Fifth, don't play more than you can afford. If you want to have a good time and not burn through all of your money too quickly, don't overreach. Unless you have a couple of hundred dollars to throw away, stay away from the dollar machines and head for the quarters instead. Set a limit of how much you are prepared to lose and stick to it.

Winning at Video Poker

In addition to the ever-popular slot machines, casino owners and gaming manufacturers have invented a large variety of new stand-alone products featuring video technology. These devices are known in the industry as specialty machines, and basically they are just computer simulations of traditional casino games—from Poker and Blackjack to Roulette, Craps, Keno, and even Bingo—but with the added attraction of real gambling. For players who are intimidated by the Craps table, for example, they can stand quietly in front of a video simulation of one, electronically throw the dice, and place real bets.

Video Poker is perhaps the most popular of the specialty machines. In some areas of the country, video Poker is even outstripping such old standbys as slot machines and Bingo as the game of choice. Some states that do not permit full-fledged gambling, such as Montana, have nevertheless legalized video Poker for bars (with certain restrictions).

The video Poker machine obviously has its roots in slot machines—as we saw above, the early slots featured card symbols on the reels. Some early designers figured out clever ways for slot players to "hold" certain of the "cards" and then take another pull on the slot machine, but that type of Poker-based slot machine never really gained in popularity. Full-blown video Poker, however, has definitely caught on. For one thing, the video machines insert an element of skill into the slot machine world—where, as we saw, blind chance usually rules supreme. There is definitely a skill factor in Poker, even when you take away the psychology of bluffing. There is a calculus of probability involved in Poker, and players who know how to play the odds—such as not drawing to an inside straight—will usually best players who do not. Another major attraction is that video Poker allows absolute beginners to learn the game without the embarrassment and intimidation of a Poker table. The hierarchy of hands—which hand beats which—is printed right on the front of the video Poker machine allowing players to quietly learn the rules and gain confidence before venturing out in front of the Poker sharks.

Video Poker machines are easy to spot in any casino. People usually still stand in front of slot machines, but most video Poker players sit in front of the machines on chairs provided by the casinos. Also, they push buttons instead of pulling the side handle of a slot. It's all self-explanatory, even if you don't know much about Poker (see the chapter on Poker for more details about the rules).

The typical setup for video Poker is as follows. On the front of the unit there is a small video screen on which are displayed facsimiles of cards. Below or at the right are a series of buttons. A player first puts in some coins, from one to five depending on the machine. A player then pushes the Deal button and five cards appear on the screen. Under each of the cards is a button to ''hold'' that card. If a player wants to hold two out of the five cards dealt, therefore, he or she simply pushes the Hold buttons under those two cards. (To make matters somewhat confusing, some machines use a Discard button to select cards you don't want, instead of cards you want to keep, so it's important for you to pay attention to the way each machine you play on works.) Also, some machines have a Stand button for players who do not want any more cards. Once the hold cards are picked, the player pushes the Draw button and receives more cards (from one to four). If the player has a winning hand, then the machine pays off according to a chart usually placed immediately above the video screen. Payouts are on a sliding scale and, obviously, a full house pays off more than does three of a kind.

Below is a typical payout schedule for quarter and dollar machines. Remember that there are different payout schedules for progressive machines, which hold the promise of enormous jackpots, as well as for machines that feature wild cards.

Payout Schedule for Video Poker Non-Progressive Machines

Hand	1 Coin	2 Coins	3 Coins	4 Coins	5 Coins
Royal Flush	250	500	750	1000	4000
Straight Flush	50	100	150	200	250
4 of a Kind	25	50	75	100	125
Full House	9	18	27	36	45
Flush	6	12	18	24	30
Straight	4	8	12	16	20
3 of a Kind	3	6	9	12	15
2 Pair	2	4	6	8	10
Jacks or Better	1	2	3	4	5

There are many different types of video Poker machines, featuring a variety of Poker games. Most play straight Draw Poker, but some have double-down features as well as Joker Wild or Deuces Wild features.

Some machines offer players a second chance or sixth card—for additional money, of course. Still others have an electronic voice that calls out the cards as they are dealt and tells beginners what their options are.

The important thing to remember in video Poker is that you are competing against a fixed schedule of winning hands, not against an electronic dealer or "house." Strategy in video Poker can be enormously complex, but for an absolute beginner it should be limited to one basic rule: knowing which hands to keep and which to reject. You should always keep a "pat" hand, which is an automatic winner without drawing more cards. The pat hands in video Poker are a royal flush, a straight flush, five of a kind, four of a kind, a straight, a flush, and a full house. The only exception to this basic rule is in those circumstances when, while holding a straight or a flush, you are one card away from a royal straight or a royal flush or one card away from a straight flush. Because the potential payout is enormous, many experts in video Poker insist you should discard the one card and go for it. Also, as in regular Poker, you should never hold a "kicker," an extra card with a pair. The odds are better that you'll draw three of a kind than an additional pair with the kicker.

According to Dwight and Louise Crevelt, two of America's foremost experts on electronic gaming, video Poker players should also observe these additional rules—which are, in fact, part of basic Poker strategy:

☛ Hold a High Pair and draw three cards on a straight Poker machine . . . even if you have to break up a Four-Card Flush or Four-Card Straight.

☞ Hold only one of a High Pair if you have any of the following potential winners:
  • Four cards to a Royal Flush
  • Four cards to a Straight Flush (open both ends)
  • Four cards to a Straight Flush

☞ Split a Low Pair in favor of a Four-Card Flush.

☞ Hold a Low Pair rather than a Four-Card Straight even if it is open-ended.

☞ Draw one card to a Four-Card open-ended Straight.

☞ Hold a High Pair or a Low Pair rather than a Three- or Four-card inside Straight.

☞ Hold only one high card unless you have two or more of the same suit for a potential Royal Flush. Otherwise hold the suit with least cards dealt.

☞ All other hands—get a new deal. You might be dealt a Royal Flush or other winner.[2]

Playing Video Keno

Video Keno is another popular specialty machine. To play video Keno, of course, you have to know how to play regular Keno. Keno is easiest to understand when compared to Bingo. In Bingo, you get a card marked with numbers and then a game manager draws numbers, usually marked on Ping-Pong balls, out of a machine, and players mark on their cards when they have the numbers that are drawn out. The player who gets the right grouping of numbers wins. Keno is played in exactly the opposite manner. On a card with eighty numbers, players first select which numbers they want to bet on, in advance, and then the game manager draws numbers from a Bingo-like hopper. If one or more of the numbers a player selected is also drawn out of the hopper, then that player wins.

Video Keno, then, is played according to the same principles. Typically, there is a video display of eighty numbers and players mark from two to ten numbers, either with a light pen or by pushing numbered buttons. The players then initiate play by pushing a Start button. Twenty of the possible eighty numbers light up. If any of the numbers a player selected in advance light up, he or she wins. The more "hits" a player makes, the more is won. For example, ten hits out of ten selected numbers obviously wins a bigger payoff than one hit. A player can also increase the possible jackpot by putting in more coins. Some casinos now also feature mini-Keno machines that display only forty numbers instead of the usual eighty.

Video Keno machines usually have a chart on the front that displays the payout schedule. Some of the machines indicate the payout in coins, others in dollars, and it is important, obviously, to know the difference. A win of 50 would be $50 if in dollars, but only $2.50 if in coins and the coins happen to be nickels. A typical payout schedule looks like this:

	Spots Marked									
Spots Hit	1	2	3	4	5	6	7	8	9	10
1										
2	14	2	2	—	—	—	—	—	—	—
3		40	3	2	2	1	—	—	—	
4			100	14	4	2	1	1	—	
5				800	92	15	12	3	3	
6					1500	348	112	47	28	
7						7760	1500	352	140	
8							8000	4700	1000	
9								9000	4800	
10										10000

Other Video Games

Video Poker and video Keno are the two major specialty machines now in use in major casinos, but there
are many others as well. Video 21 was actually introduced before video Poker but is now not as common
as it once was. It is played exactly like regular Blackjack, with the video screen displaying both the player's
cards and those of a dealer. Players can bet between
one and five coins, and the machine pays off even
money (that is, will pay $5 on a $5 bet). As in regular
Blackjack, the video 21 machine will take another card
on 16 but stand on 17. Some machines now allow players to make use of such refinements as insurance (see
the section on Blackjack) and splits.

Video Craps and Roulette games also exist but are

not nearly as popular as the games listed above. Some experts insist it is because these games, Craps especially, are so complicated, but it may also be the psychological factor of fearing the video game is rigged. Players simply insert money and then the machine tells them whether they won or lost. To many players an electronic throw of the dice or spin of the wheel does not seem as reliable as seeing the real thing.

Video Bingo games, in contrast, have a few more fans, mostly because there are a lot of hard-core Bingo players out there. There are played exactly like regular Bingo, but the machine "calls" out the numbers when a player pushes a Start button or pulls a lever. The machines feature video "cards" that are then filled up with the numbers called.

1. *Casino Player,* August 1994, p. 18.
2. Dwight and Louise Crevelt, *Slot Machine Mania* (Grand Rapids, MI: Gollehon Books, 1989), pp. 235–37.

4

Casino Gambling for
Shy People

In the past twenty years, there has been a veritable revolution in the casino business. The seedy casinos of the Vegas strip and Atlantic City, with their topless showgirls and suspect management, have given way to glitzy new entertainment meccas designed for entire families. Casinos such as Luxor, the MGM Grand, Excalibur, and many more have reinvented the way people enjoy themselves in the major gambling centers.

The problem for absolute beginners, of course, is that casinos can still be very intimidating. Anyone can play the slots and the video Poker machines, but many people have a hard time working up the nerve to try Blackjack, Craps, or any of the other popular table games. While this is very understandable, it is also a shame. Games such as Blackjack, Craps, Roulette, and Baccarat are what the casinos are all about. They are a lot of fun and much more social than playing a slot machine. With the exception of Craps, which is a bit complicated, the casino games are not that difficult to learn. If you're willing to memorize a few key principles for each game, you can learn how to play any casino table game in a few hours. You won't be an expert, of course, and you'll still end up losing money over the long haul, but you'll have a good time and at least will know what you're doing. Moreover, the beginner can enjoy these games without facing a huge wager since most of the casinos have small-stakes tables where you can bet as little as $1 to $5.

The best way to learn is to study the principles outlined in this book and then observe some of the games in action. The dealers are always very helpful, and you can ask as many questions as you want—but they do not always have time to give you detailed answers. This is because the dealers in major casinos have "productivity" quotas, just as workers do in any assembly line factory. For example, the casinos expect their Blackjack dealers to deal anywhere from sixty to seventy-five hands *per hour* and be able to shuffle six decks of cards in less than eighty seconds. As a result, the action at the Blackjack tables is mighty fast. The reason for this emphasis on speed is that the casinos have calculated that each shuffle of the decks can take up to eight rounds of Blackjack per hour. That adds up to big money. The Aladdin hotel in Las Vegas calculated that it could earn an extra $1.2 million per year if it could figure out some method so that its dealers never shuffled the cards.[1]

But just because the casinos maintain a hectic pace, that's no reason why you should. Take your time. Learn the games as well as you can. Observe everything and then play a little at the low-stakes tables. In no time at all, you'll feel like an experienced pro.

The Secrets of Playing KENO

Keno, like its cousin Bingo, was for a time a declining attraction in the major casinos in Las Vegas and Atlantic City. It was slowly being replaced by the easier video-type Keno games. But in recent years, full-fledged Keno parlors have been making a comeback. Brand-new Keno establishments have opened in ten of Atlantic City's casinos, for example, and more are on the way at other gambling locations.[2] Because of Keno's rising popularity, an absolute beginner at gambling should be familiar with the rules. It also helps to understand traditional Keno when playing its video counterpart.

Keno, like Bingo, is a variation on the Italian national lottery, *Lo Giuoco del Lotto*. As in Lotto, Keno players choose a series of numbers, generally ten, on a card holding a total of eighty numbers. They then wait until a game operator chooses some numbers from a special Keno hopper. If a player picks the right amount of correct numbers, he or she wins. In Bingo you buy your picks in advance because you have no say about which numbers appear on your card. Each Bingo card has twenty-four numbers, from 1 to 75, arranged under the five letters in BINGO. In Keno, on the other hand, all of the cards are identical, consisting of numbers from 1 to 80. Each player picks his or her own numbers and then waits to see if they are the ones pulled at random from the Keno cage. In each game of Keno, twenty numbers are called.

As with traditional Keno, Keno as it is currently played in Las Vegas allows players to play against the house and not against one another for a fixed prize. In contemporary Keno as played in the casinos, players set their own bets and play against the house as banker.

How Keno Works

Keno is now played in Keno parlors or, more typically, in special rooms in the major casinos. The old Keno palaces featured Bingo-like hoppers with balls and electric boards that showed the numbers. Contemporary Keno parlors, however, are much more modern. They usually contain upholstered chairs in rows arranged facing a large display board of some kind. Many places now also use large video monitors posted all over the room to display the numbers drawn from the hopper. In the front or off to the side, there is a line of cashiers behind cages who take bets.

The standard, or straight, Keno ticket is very simple and looks much the same all over the country. The only major difference is that each casino's Keno ticket displays the casino's name and some information about the jackpot prizes available. Some Keno tickets are square, others are narrow and look a lot like concert tickets, but on all of them the numbers are usually arranged like this:

MARK
PRICE
HERE

KENO

1	2	3	4	5	6	7	8	9	10
11	12	13	14	15	16	17	18	19	20
21	22	23	24	25	26	27	28	29	30
31	32	33	34	35	36	37	38	39	40

KENO LIMIT $50,000   TO AGGREGATE PLAYERS EACH GAME

41	42	43	44	45	46	47	48	49	50
51	52	53	54	55	56	57	58	59	60
61	62	63	64	65	66	67	68	69	70
71	72	73	74	75	76	77	78	79	80

All cards have the same information. All a player does, therefore, is decide how many numbers he or she wants to pick—from one to fifteen—and the amount of money he or she wishes to wager. The most popular Keno bet, historically, is to pick ten numbers but you may pick one to fifteen. The numbers are marked on the card with a big X, as in the example below. The amount of money the player wishes to wager, which is referred to as the price, is marked in the box that says Mark Price Here. Once you have filled in your ticket, you take it up to one of the cashiers in the Keno parlor. He or she will take the ticket you filled out and give you back a duplicate ticket. This has all of the information on it you filled out as well as some specific information about the date and time of the game, and so on.

KENO

1	2	✖	4	5	6	7	8	9	10
11	12	13	14	15	16	17	18	19	20
21	22	23	24	25	✖	27	28	✖	30
31	32	33	34	35	36	37	38	39	40

KENO LIMIT $50,000   TO AGGREGATE PLAYERS EACH GAME   **7**

41	42	43	44	45	46	47	48	49	50
51	✖	53	54	55	✖	57	✖	59	60
61	62	63	64	65	66	67	68	69	70
71	72	73	74	✖	76	77	78	79	80

VERY IMPORTANT: You *must* collect your winnings immediately after the specific Keno game you played.

Notice the warning printed very clearly on your ticket regarding when winnings are to be collected. *If you snooze, you lose.* Keno parlors will pay off on winning tickets only before the next game begins. Once the next game begins, you cannot collect your money—even if you won $50,000! There are some bizarre legal reasons for this—states distinguish between Keno and a lottery on the time frame of the collection—but the important thing to remember is that the Keno parlors follow this rule to the letter.

In some of the snazzier casinos, there are employees known as Keno runners who will literally do all of your work for you—take your tickets to the cashier and collect any winnings. You don't actually have to wait around the Keno parlor to play, although many people do. The Keno runners will place your bets while you do other things, such as play slot machines or eat your dinner.

The Payoffs

The Keno parlor pays off according to a fixed schedule. Here is a typical payoff schedule for marking ten numbers:

Mark 10 Spots			
Winning Spots	$1.00 Ticket Pays	$3.00 Ticket Pays	$5.00 Ticket Pays	$1.40 Ticket Pays
5	2.00	6.00	10.00	2.80
6	20.00	60.00	100.00	28.00
7	136.00	408.00	680.00	196.00
8	960.00	2,880.00	4,800.00	1,400.00
9	4,000.00	12,000.00	20,000.00	5,320.00
10	25,000.00	50,000.00	50,000.00	25,000.00

The payout schedule varies from location to location, however, and savvy Keno players will definitely shop around. Here is an example of the jackpots on a five-dollar bet at various Keno parlors in Las Vegas:

Payoffs on $5 Keno Wager in Las Vegas					
Mark 5	10	10	15	15	15
Hit 5	9	10	13	14	15
Caesars	$2,500	$19,000	$200,000	N/A	N/A	N/A
Bally's	$2,750	$20,000	$100,000	$100,000	$100,000	$100,000
Luxor	$4,000	$25,000	$100,000	$100,000	$100,000	$100,000
MGM Grand	$3,500	$40,000	$100,000	$100,000	$100,000	$100,000
Excalibur	$4,000	$20,000	$100,000	$100,000	$100,000	$100,000
Harrah's	$2,400	$19,000	$100,000	$100,000	$100,000	$100,000
Sahara	N/A	N/A	N/A	$100,000	$100,000	$100,000
Hilton	$5,500	N/A	N/A	$100,000	$100,000	$100,000

With one look at the payout schedule, the attraction of Keno becomes immediately apparent. For a mere $5, anyone can have a shot at $100,000. Of course, for a similar amount anyone can have a shot at a $6 million lottery, as well, and so the question becomes: What are the odds in Keno? We'll get to that in a moment.

Other Bets

Beyond the standard, or straight, Keno ticket, there are a number of other ways to play the game. One of the most popular is the so-called split ticket, in which you play combinations of numbers. Players mark up a standard Keno ticket, then circle those numbers they want to use as specific combinations or draw a straight line separating two groups of numbers. They also mark on the sides a special notation that looks like a fraction to show how many combinations are being made—for example, 2/5 means that there are two combinations of five numbers marked on that ticket.

When you play a split ticket you are, in effect, playing more than one game on the same ticket. You could just as easily fill out two or more Keno tickets. Using one card just saves time. You can wager different amounts on different combinations by making a notation on the side of the ticket for the amount of each, although you must write the total amount bet for that card in the Mark Price Here box. This is what a split ticket looks like:

```
MARK
PRICE
HERE

10-
```

KENO

1	2	3	4	5	6	7	8	9	10
11	12	13	14	15	16	17	18	19	20
21	22	23	24	25	26	27	28	29	30
31	32	33	34	35	36	37	38	39	40

2/5

KENO LIMIT $50,000   TO AGGREGATE PLAYERS EACH GAME

41	42	43	44	45	46	47	48	49	50
51	52	53	54	55	56	57	58	59	60
61	62	63	64	65	66	67	68	69	70
71	72	73	74	75	76	77	78	79	80

$5

Besides the split ticket, there are what are called combination tickets, which are really just more elaborate split tickets. In a combination ticket, players pick numbers, group them together in different combinations by circling them, and note in the white space on the side what those combinations are and what the bets are that should be applied to them. Let's say a player marked up a Keno ticket by picking 3, 13, and 23 together, 65, 66, 67, and 68 together, and 61, 52, 43, 34, and 25 together. That would be three different combinations of three, four, and five numbers. The player would circle the appropriate groups, write 1/3, 1/4, and 1/5 in the margin and then write the bet and circle it on the side. The player would then write in 3 in the space Mark Price Here, indicating the entire wager for that ticket is $3. It would look like this:

MARK PRICE HERE
3-

KENO

1	2	X	4	5	6	7	8	9	10
11	12	X	14	15	16	17	18	19	20
21	22	X	24	25	26	27	28	29	30
31	32	33	X	35	36	37	38	39	40

1/3
1/4

KENO LIMIT $50,000 TO AGGREGATE PLAYERS EACH GAME

1/5

41	42	X	44	45	46	47	48	49	50
51	X	53	54	55	56	57	58	59	60
X	62	63	64	X	X	X	X	69	70
71	72	73	74	75	76	77	78	79	80

1-

There are numerous other ways to write up a Keno ticket bet—combinations known as "way tickets," "three-way eight tickets," and "high-low combinations"—but this is more than enough for an absolute beginner. Most casinos and Keno parlors have little pamphlets that explain all of the myriad variations that are all similar, in concept, to the combination ticket.

Keno Odds

The mathematics involved in determining Keno odds are even more complex than those for Bingo, but the final results are similar. The edge the casino or Keno parlor has over the players, depending upon which combination is being played and the amount of money paid on each win, ranges from 25 to 35 percent. This is obviously much higher than the 1.4 percent house edge on pass/don't pass bets in Craps or the 6 percent advantage casinos have on a straight bet in Roulette.

Keno seems fairly cheap to play and the prizes offered are large. As we saw, a three-dollar bet on a ten-spot ticket can potentially earn $50,000 if the player managed to pick all ten numbers correctly. The odds of someone picking ten out of ten, however, are one in nine million. These odds are better than those for state lotteries, which are about one in 14 million, but then again the jackpots in state lotteries are typically much larger: in the multimillion-dollar range.

BACCARAT AND CHEMIN DE FER

When I think of classy casinos in Monte Carlo or Latin America, I always think of Baccarat or its variant, Chemin de Fer. It's the game of choice for high rollers and the one you see Sean Connery play in all of those James Bond movies.

The contemporary game is a French variation on the Italian game of *Baccarà*, which means zero. Historians believe the game was played as early as the fifteenth century in France during the reign of Charles VIII. It became popular in the seventeenth century in the age of the Sun King, Louis XIV, but then was periodically banned by subsequent monarchs. All gambling was prohibited in France from 1837 until 1907, when the prohibition against gaming was finally lifted and Baccarat once again became popular in trendy French casinos at Deauville, Monte Carlo, and Cannes. The game came to the United States illegally in the 1920s and was known by the nickname "shimmy." When gambling was legalized in Nevada, a legal form of Baccarat was introduced in the late 1950s.

The only major difference between Baccarat, as played in American casinos, and Chemin de Fer, as played in European and British casinos, is that in Baccarat the house is the banker and everyone bets against the house. In Chemin de Fer the casino takes a fixed cut, usually 5 percent of the pot, and the players play against each other. In other words, Baccarat is more like Blackjack and Chemin de Fer is more like Poker.

Baccarat remains a very intimidating game for absolute beginners, mostly because of the mystique surrounding the game at casinos and because of the generally high stakes associated with it. In truth, however, the rules of the game are remarkably simple. Also, the odds in Baccarat are better than those of almost any other casino game, similar to line bets in Craps or to Blackjack played by an experienced player. Baccarat is still perceived as a game for high rollers, though, and the casinos continue to cultivate that image. You still see tuxedoed men and elegant young women gathered around the Baccarat tables, which are far from the noise of slot machines and the Craps tables. The casinos still hire attractive young women with ample cleavage, called "starters," to lure players in and "get the action going" with chips provided by the casino (which the shills never cash).

The Baccarat Table

A Baccarat or Chemin de Fer table is shaped like a barbell—there are two semicircles at either end of a rectangle. The two dealers stand in curved indentations on both sides of the rectangle. The Baccarat layout is printed on the table, and there are chairs for between nine and fourteen players grouped around the semicircles at each end of the table. Each player sits in front of a large number on the Baccarat layout. There are fourteen such large numbers—one through fifteen with the number thirteen omitted because of gamblers' superstitions—seven on each end arranged in a semicircle. One end has one through seven and the other end eight through fifteen. The Baccarat layout on the semicircular ends consists of four concentric rings—the large outer ring, nearest the players, is made up of the large numbers for each player. The next ring features the word Players written in it, and the next smaller ring has the word Bankers. The ring inside that contains the players' numbers written again and then, finally, as a kind of hub, is a small horseshoelike space with the word Tie and 8 to 1 written in it. Bets are made by placing chips on one of these three areas—Players, Bankers or Tie.

In the middle rectangular area two words are written—Bankers and Players. The dealers place the cards in these two areas for the two imaginary players in Baccarat, Player and Banker. Above the printed words Players and Bankers are three slots in the middle of the

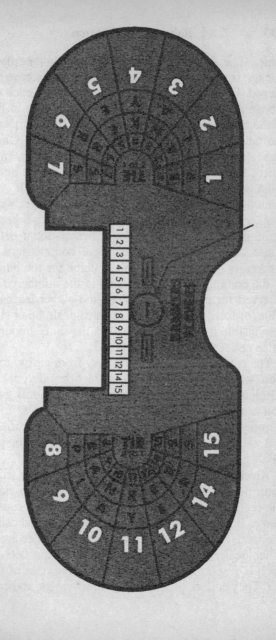

table. The center slot, also known as the discard bucket, is where cards are dropped after they have been played. Dealers put cash in the two slots on each end. Above the three slots on the edge of the table in front of the two dealers are a series of small boxes drawn on the table and numbered from one to fifteen. One of these little boxes is reserved for each player and is where the dealers mark the commissions that players must pay when they win a Banker hand (we'll get to commissions in a moment). Whenever a player wins a Banker hand, he or she must pay the house a 5 percent commission—for example, on a twenty-dollar bet the house collects $1. The way these commissions are marked is that the dealers place chips for the amount of the commission on each hand in the numbered box reserved for each player. When the player leaves the table, or there is a new shoe of cards dealt, he or she is responsible for paying the dealers the same amount of chips collected in his or her box.

The rules of Baccarat never vary from casino to casino, which is one of its many attractions. If you, as an absolute beginner, take the trouble to learn this game, you can play it anywhere in the U.S. The rules for its European variant, Chemin de Fer, are slighty different and will be discussed in the section beginning on page 110.

American casinos usually have three, sometimes four, people running a Baccarat table. On one side of the rectangle stands the caller, who basically runs the game. It is his or her job to supervise play and call out the totals of the hands. Across from the caller are two other dealers. Together they handle all the bets, and each is responsible for one of the semicircles of players. They collect all losses, pay all winnings, and calculate commissions on hands that the banker wins (we'll get to that in a moment). A fourth casino official sometimes watches over all of the proceedings to make sure everything is done correctly. He or she is the final authority in any and all disputes and used to sit up high on a ladder and was called a "ladderman," but today this official usually just sits off to the side on a high stool or chair.

The Rules of American-Style Baccarat

There are two characteristics of Baccarat which should make it very attractive to absolute beginners.

The first is that the odds are very good. Overall, the casino has only a 1.5 percent advantage over each individual player. If a player bets only on the Banker, the house has just 1.17 percent advantage. These odds are much better than those in, say, Roulette, which favor the casino by 5.26 percent.

Baccarat also is very, very simple to play. The rules about drawing or not drawing cards are a little complicated at first, but these are fixed and are known by the dealer. Players can pick them up as they go along.

The individual players themselves really only have one decision to make: to bet on the Player, the Banker, or a Tie. That's it. There really is no reason to be intimidated, because all you do is place your chips in the Player or Banker box—the Tie is a long shot and is rarely played—and then wait to see what happens. You'll either win or lose. It's that simple. Of course, it helps to know the rules a bit, so you know what's going on. But these, too, are really not that complicated and can be learned in a few moments.

Baccarat is played with eight decks of 52 cards for a

total of 416 cards. No jokers are used. After the cards have been shuffled, with elaborate ceremony, they are placed in a special dealing box, known as a *shoe* in the U.S. and as a *sabot* in Europe. Each player is allowed the opportunity to deal from the shoe, beginning with player number one. Each player is also allowed to pass the deal, with no shame, but it really is fairly simple.

Only two imaginary players receive cards in Baccarat—the Player and the Banker. As we noted above, the actual players, the people who sit in the chairs, play only by betting on one or the other of these two imaginary players—or, if they wish, by betting on a tie. Although each of the players in the chairs may take turns dealing from the shoe, they still only deal cards to the two imaginary players. The caller places two sets of cards, which he or she gets from the player dealing the cards out of the shoe, on the areas of the table marked "Player" or "Banker."

The game, therefore, is remarkably straightforward: the dealer deals cards to the imaginary Player and the imaginary Banker, and whoever ends up with the highest hand wins. If the individual players in the chairs bet on the Player, and the Player wins a given hand, then those who bet on the Player win their bets. And vice versa.

All bets in Baccarat are even money: that is, if you bet $20 and win you get back your $20 plus another $20.

The easy thing to learn in Baccarat are the rules concerning how the cards in each hand are added up to determine whether the Player or the Banker won. There are three simple rules:

Rule No. 1: In Baccarat, unlike most other card

games, all face cards (king, queen, jack) and the tens of all suits count for zero, zilch, whereas in most card games they count for ten. The rest of the cards, one to nine, count for their face value—a two of spades, for example, is worth two. Cards in a given hand are added up just like in Blackjack—a two of spades and a four of diamonds, for example, are worth six. A queen and an ace of spades are worth only one because the queen is worth nothing.

Rule No. 2: In those cases when the totals of the cards exceed nine, you drop the first digit. This is the truly unusual twist in Baccarat and the one that makes it so exciting. Two eights, for example, which would normally count as sixteen in Blackjack, are worth only six points in Baccarat since you drop the first one. Two fives and a seven, which add up to seventeen, are only worth seven in Baccarat.

The goal is to have a hand worth nine points or as close to that as possible. In fact, Rule No. 2 makes it impossible to have a hand worth more than nine. Nine is the highest hand, and eight is the second highest. These two scores are called a natural in the U.S. In Europe, a hand worth nine points is called *la grande* and one worth eight *la petite*.

Rule No. 3: A given hand of Baccarat can never contain more than three cards. We'll discuss this in more detail in a moment.

These three simple rules make for some amazing reversals. As in Blackjack, the addition of a single card can easily make a strong hand go "bust," exceeding nine and ending up with a very low score. For example, let's say the Banker has a four and a two for a total of six points. The rules require the Banker to draw another

card, and let's say that card is nine. That would result
in a hand worth fifteen, which in Baccarat is only worth
five.

Here is a little table to give you a better idea of what
Baccarat hands are worth:

Cards	Regular Total	Baccarat Total
9, Q	19	9
A, 5	6	6
10, K	20	0
K, Q, 5	25	5
9, 9	18	8
3, 7	10	0
1, 2, 3	6	6
K, K	20	0
A, 10, K	21	1

The only really tricky aspect to Baccarat is learning
the rules concerning when the Player or the Banker
must draw an additional card. These rules are absolutely inflexible, which means that individual players
do not have any decisions to make. The caller will announce the situation and the applicable rule, and you
either win or lose.

In some ways, Baccarat is very much like Blackjack.
At the start of each hand, both the Player and the
Banker receive two cards. As in Blackjack, the Player
must confront his cards first. But unlike Blackjack, the
Player has no choice whether to draw a card or not.
This is determined by a fixed set of rules. If the two
cards given to the Player are worth between one and
five—or worth ten—points, he must draw an additional

card. If the hand is worth six or seven, he must stand. And if the hand is worth either eight or nine, it's a natural and an automatic win.

In a chart, the Player Rules look like this.

Player's Rules	
Having	
1-2-3-4-5-10	Must Draw a Card
6-7	Must Stand
8-9	Natural. Automatic Win.

After the Player confronts his cards, it's the Banker's turn. Whether the Banker gets to draw an additional card or not also depends on rigid rules, but these are a bit more complicated. Whether the Banker gets another card is determined both by the total value of the Banker's hand and by the card that the Player drew. Confusing?

Here are the Banker's Rules. They are usually

	Banker's Rules	
Having	*Draws When Giving*	*Does Not Draw When Giving*
3	1-2-3-4-5-6-7-9-10	8
4	2-3-4-5-6-7	1-8-9-10
5	4-5-6-7	1-2-3-8-9-10
6	6-7	1-2-3-4-5-8-9-10
7	Stands	
8-9	Natural. Cannot Draw.	

printed on special cards on or near every Baccarat table.

All you need to know to read this chart is that the word Giving simply means that the Player drew that card. If the Banker "gave" a four, for example, that simply means that the Player drew a four.

Let's say that the Banker has a two of clubs and a three of hearts, worth five points, and the Player just got through drawing a six of diamonds. Does the Banker get a card? The answer is: Yes. The chart says that the banker "draws when giving" a four, five, six, or seven.

These rules sometimes force a tie. For example, if the Player has a two and a three, worth five points, and draws another three, that is worth eight points. Had the Player had eight points in the first two hands, that would have been a natural and an automatic win, but if it is achieved with an extra card, the play must continue. Now, let's say the Banker gets two fours in his original two cards. According to the rules, that is a natural and the Banker cannot draw. It's a tie. No one wins unless he or she bet by placing chips in the Tie box.

Playing the Game

Okay, you're all dressed up for a show. You've put on some nice clothes, but you have an hour to kill while you wait for your spouse, who is upstairs getting ready and is taking his or her sweet time. You've played all the slot machines you can stand, are not in the mood for Blackjack, and can't figure out all those complicated bets in Craps, no matter how hard you try.

You decide to gather up your courage and check out

the Baccarat table. Depending upon which casino you're in, the Baccarat tables may be cordoned off from the general casino area or may even be in another series of rooms. The entire ambience is different. For one thing, it's quiet. For another, there seems to be a dress code—the dealers all wear tuxedoes, as do many of the players. Baccarat is already living up to its up-scale image.

You wander over to a low-stakes table. There are lit-tle signs on the tables indicating the minimum bets, and you find one for $20. You then place some casino chips you have on the table or buy some there. You sit down at one of the plush chairs and a pretty waitress immediately asks if you'd care for a drink. The atmo-sphere, for all of the elegance, is remarkably relaxed, even casual. Players nod a greeting. You keep expect-ing to see Omar Sharif or Sean Connery walk by.

You watch for a while, reading over the plastic chart that has the rules printed on it. You wait while the shoe is finished off and the dealers reshuffle the decks. There is a special procedure for all of this, and you realize at once that Baccarat is a game of tradition with its own unique rituals and customs. This is part of the charm. Players like Baccarat because of its relaxed style of play and because they have a good chance to actually win.

The casino dealers finish shuffling, cut the cards with a special plastic card, place all eight decks into the shoe, and then "burn off" a few cards from the top. The casino employers shove the shoe to the player sit-ting at chair number one, but he declines to deal and pushes the shoe gently over to you, sitting next to him at chair number two. You're horrified, as you don't know what to do, but everyone seems friendly enough and so you accept the deal. The caller asks for bets and you place a twenty-dollar chip on Banker.

You rather awkwardly push down on the first card exposed at the bottom of the shoe and you find it slips easily out. The caller directs you to push it over to her, facedown, and you do that. She places it, still face-down, on top of the word Player on the table in front of her. Next you push out another card, for the Banker, but the caller explains that you should slide that card under the shoe for now. Then you push out a third card, this time for the Player, and you slide this one over, again facedown, to the caller, who places it next to the other card in the Player area. You push out another card for the Banker and slip it facedown under the shoe.

The caller then passes the two Player cards to the player with the largest bet on the Player. This bettor has the honor of flipping the cards over. (I told you Baccarat is a game of ritual.) The bettor returns the cards to the caller, and then the caller asks the dealer to give her the Banker's cards. These are then placed, faceup, on the spot marked "Banker" above the spot marked "Player."

At this point, the caller calls out the totals of the two hands and summarizes the situation: whether the Player must draw another card, stand, or has an automatic win. If the Player gets another card, you, the dealer, push out another card and give it to the caller.

Let's look at an actual pair of hands. The Player has a four and an ace, for a total of five. The Banker has a queen and a three, for a total of three. According to the fixed rules of Baccarat, the Player must draw with a five—you deal the card and the Player receives a nine of spades. Five plus nine equals fourteen, which in Baccarat is worth only four. Now, because the Banker had a three, and gave the Player a nine, he must draw another card. This card turns out to be a three of hearts. Thus, at the last minute the Banker wins, because his total of six points beats out the Player's total of four. That's how it works.

The two casino employees standing in front of the chips quickly go about their business, taking chips off of the Player boxes and placing chips onto the Banker boxes. You notice, to your satisfaction, that the casino worker on your side of the table places a twenty-dollar chip on top of your original chip. You've doubled your money! You also notice that this same casino employee places a chip marked "$1" on the little box in front of him with a number 2 in it. This is the marker for the 5 percent commission, or $1, which you owe the house for winning on the Banker. Had you bet on the Player, and won, you would not have had to pay this commission. When you leave the table, the casino employee will count up all the chips in your little box and you will have to pay him or her that amount in chips. It is also customary to give the casino employees a small tip, especially if you were lucky and won.

You, as the temporary dealer, continue to deal cards until the Banker loses, in which case you slide the shoe over to the player next to you at chair number three. And play continues from there.

What are your real chances of winning in Baccarat? The great John Scarne, gambling mathematician extraordinaire, first caluclated the odds more than thirty years ago when Baccarat was first being popularized in Las Vegas casinos. He calculated that the Player wins 49.33 percent of the time and the Banker wins 50.67 percent of the time. This works out to the house having a 1.17 percent advantage on Banker bets and a 1.36

percent advantage on Player bets. These are remarkably good odds for casino games and more than make up for the higher stakes you bet at Baccarat.

Chemin de Fer

If you are ever in Europe and decide to visit one of the fabulous casinos in France or Monte Carlo, you may want to know how to play the European version of Baccarat known as *Chemin de Fer* (French for "road of iron" or railroad). It is very similar to Baccarat except

(1) the players bet against *one another* instead of against the house, and

(2) they have *a few limited options* concerning whether to draw cards or not.

(3) only six decks, or 312 cards, are used.

Players take turns being the Banker and dealer combined. At first, the players bid for the right to be Banker, with the player putting up the most money, under the casino's table limits, winning that right. This player is the Banker until the bank hand loses, at which time the right to be Banker moves around the table to the right, counterclockwise, along with the *sabot* or shoe. Every player has the right to pass up being Banker, but the Banker must also be the dealer. When a player no longer wishes to be Banker, the croupier holds an informal auction to determine who is willing to put up the amount of the previous bank or as close to it as possible. The casino or house has no actual stake in the game; it merely provides the equipment and charges a flat five percent commission on all wins by the Banker, as in Baccarat.

In a sense, the Banker in Chemin de Fer takes on all of the other players at once. As in Baccarat, there are only two hands, for the Player and the Banker. But unlike Baccarat, only the real Banker can bet on the Banker cards, and all of the other players *must* bet on the Player.

The way it works is like this. The player who is the Banker decides how much money he or she is willing to risk on a given hand and places it in the center of the table. The bet is counted by the croupier who acts as the game manager. This entire amount becomes the pot or bank and is at risk. The amount of wagers by the other players is limited by the amount in the bank. Any player may bet against the entire amount of the bank by simply saying "banco." If this happens, then no one else may bet. If no one says "banco," then each player, beginning with the player to the Banker's immediate right, makes his own individual wager against the bank by placing chips in front of him on the table. This is called, in American lingo, "fading" the bank. When the total amount of the bank has been wagered against, the bank is said to be "faded," and no one else at the table may place a bet. For example, let's say the Banker puts up $500. The player at his immediate right bets $100 and the next two guys each bet $200. That means the entire $500 bank is covered, and everyone else at the table has to sit out this hand, called a *coup* in Chemin de Fer.

If the person who calls out "banco" loses the *coup*, he or she has the right to *banco* the next hand, and announces the acceptance of this right by calling out *"banco suivi"* (French for "the following banco"). If two or more players call out "banco" at the same time, the player closest to the Banker's right has the right to this banco. This is known as *banco prime*.

If the entire bank is not covered by bets, by the way,

that portion not bet against is set aside by the croupier and is not at risk. Only the amount faded is at risk. However, a Banker *cannot* remove money from the bank after winning, skimming some profits, as it were. All of the winnings must remain in the bank until the Banker surrenders the deal and the *sabot*. Of course, the entire amount of the bank, as stated above, is not necessarily covered by bets—but it *can* be! In other words, if the Banker keeps winning, and the bank grows larger and larger, all of the money is at risk until the Banker decides it's time to quit and surrenders the *sabot* or until the amount in the bank exceeds the casino's own table limits. However some casinos allow the Banker to reduce the bank by half after three wins. Chemin de Fer can be an extremely exciting game because oftentimes the bank just keeps growing and growing and there is the chance that at any moment, any player can yell out "banco" and take a shot at the whole pot. A $500 bank can quickly escalate to $10,000, $20,000, or more. That's why Chemin de Fer has always been viewed as a game for high rollers.

After the bets have been wagered, it is time to play. The use of the *sabot*, and the order of cards dealt, are exactly the same as they are in American Baccarat—except that there is greater care that the cards remain facedown. In American Baccarat, as in Blackjack, it really doesn't matter if anyone sees the cards, because there are no options. But in Chemin de Fer there are one or two options, and so secrecy is more important. The Banker deals out first one card to the Player, represented by whomever has the largest bet, and then one to himself or herself. The Banker then deals another to the Player and himself. At first, therefore, both the

Player and the Banker have two cards, both facedown, which they may look at. The croupier, by the way, manipulates the cards with the help of a special palette that looks a lot like a cricket bat.

The Player, as in Baccarat, looks at his cards first. If the Player has a natural, either *la grande* (nine) or *la petite* (eight), then no further cards are drawn, and the Player and the Banker must immediately compare hands. Whoever has the highest hand wins. If the Player and Banker are tied, then no money changes hands and a new *coup* begins. Note that, unlike in Baccarat, having a natural does not result in an automatic win for the Player. If the Banker has a higher hand, say a nine to the Player's eight, he or she wins.

If the Player does not have a natural eight or nine, he or she says "pass" and the Banker gets to look at his cards. If the Banker has a natural, then he turns his cards faceup and the croupier collects all bets for him. If he does not, then a second phase of play begins— that of drawing or not drawing additional cards.

The rules for whether the Player must draw an additional card are exactly the same as in Baccarat with one important exception: If the Player has cards worth five, he or she has the option of drawing an additional card or standing pat. If the Player has less than five, a card *must* be drawn, and if the Player holds six or seven, he or she *must* stand. Thus, the Banker knows if a Player draws another card that he or she did not have a natural and had five or less. This allows for a tiny amount of strategic thinking. Here is a chart of the Player's Rules:

Chemin de Fer—Player's Rules

HAVING	
0–1–2–3–4	Must Draw a Card
5	Option: May Draw or Stand
6–7	Must Stand
8–9	Natural. Show cards.

Next it's the Banker's turn.

Whether or not the Banker must draw an additional card is, of course, also governed by fixed rules, but the Banker has two options instead of just one. As in Baccarat, these rules concern both the totals in the Banker's own hand and the value of the card he or she gave to the Player. Below is the table of Chemin de Fer Banker Rules:

Chemin de Fer—Banker Rules

		Draw When Giving	*Stand when Giving*		
H	3	1-2-3-4-5-6-7-10	8	9	O
A	4	2-3-4-5-6-7	1-8-9-10		P
V	5	5-6-7	1-2-3-8-9-10	4	T
I	6	6-7	1-2-3-4-5-8-9-10		I
N					O
G					N
					A
					L

The optional numbers refer not to the Banker's hand but to that of the Player. In other words, the Banker has the option of standing or drawing an additonal card if he or she holds a hand worth three *and* the Player drew a nine. The Banker also has this option when holding a hand worth five if the Player just drew a four as his or her third card. Chemin de Fer experts say that the exercise of the option to draw in the first case reduces the Banker's odds of winning by 1 percent, from 60 to 59 percent. In the second case, the Banker's chances of winning actually increase by one half of one percent (0.5%) if he or she exercises the option of taking an additonal card.

Luckily for the Banker, he does not have to actually pay off and calculate all of the bets. If he loses, the croupier immediately pays off the bets from the money or chips in the center of the table.

The play moves at a relatively even pace because of the rituals involved in Chemin de Fer. For this reason, it's not only enjoyable to play but also a lot of fun to watch.

BLACKJACK

Blackjack is the only casino game in which a skillful player actually has a slight edge over the house. While this makes it one of the most popular games you'll find in a casino, it is also true that an absolute beginner has a hard time taking advantage of the player's edge. Advanced methods, such as card counting, are out of the reach of the average player. The good news, however, is that there are a few simple principles that, once memorized, will make you an above-average player in a short time.

Blackjack is played with multiple decks of fifty-two cards shuffled together and placed into a dealing box called a shoe. In the past, casinos used only one deck but players gradually learned how to capitalize on their built-in advantage against the house through the practice known as "card counting," and the casinos quickly adopted multiple decks as the standard.

In Blackjack all players play against the house, represented by the dealer. Each player, followed by the dealer, is dealt two cards. Traditionally, the dealer deals out one card, facedown, to each player sitting at the Blackjack table, moving from left to right. He then deals himself one card, also facedown. The dealer then deals a second card, facedown, to each player from left to right and then deals himself a card, this time faceup. Some casinos deal all the cards faceup. A few even trumpet this fact as though they were giving a special advantage to the players. Because the dealer has no options on what he does with his cards, it actually makes no difference, but many people find the faceup deal distracting at first.

The official object of the game is for you to get a hand in which the face value of the cards adds up to 21 or as close to 21 as possible without going over. The real object of the game, however, is different: It is to beat the dealer. There is a big difference between these two objects, one which dramatically affects your basic strategy. We'll discuss all this in a moment.

Now, you can either keep the original hand dealt to you by the dealer, which is called standing pat, or ask for more cards, one at a time, until you either go over 21 points, called going bust, or decide to stand pat. In

Blackjack suits have no value whatsoever, and all face cards and ten cards are worth 10 points. A queen and an eight, for example, are worth 18 points and beat a dealer's hand worth 16 points.

The ace is a kind of wild card worth either 1 point or 11 points. If you hold a card worth ten points (say, a queen) and an ace, you have the magic 21, also called Blackjack, and win automatically. Blackjack looks like this:

If you have an ace and an eight, you have a hand worth either 9 points or 19 points—it's up to you to decide. If you ask for another card and get a king, you will play the ace as one point and stand pat for a total of 19 points.

Bets are placed before the cards are dealt, which means that, unlike Poker, you must place your bets before you see your cards. This is annoying to many absolute beginners. The only major decision that you have to make after being dealt cards is whether to stand pat or take a "hit," or another card. More advanced players need to learn when to "double down," and we'll discuss this option later on. It is customary when the cards are dealt facedown to "stand pat" by sliding your cards under your chips. If you want another card, you indicate this to the dealer by scraping the cards on the felt table toward yourself a little. If a casino uses the faceup system, however, which some do, you do not touch the cards but indicate you want another card by pointing an index finger at the cards for a hit. If you want to stand pat, you just wave your hand palm down over the cards. These gestures are universally recognized signals.

If you ask for an additional card and go bust, you lose immediately. In this case, both the cards and the chips you bet are removed quickly from the table. Even if the dealer himself goes bust later on in the deal, players who went bust before him still lose. You must wait until all other players have finished before another round of betting begins.

The dealer's hand is where the action is. In order to win, you must beat the dealer's hand. If you have a five and a nine, for example, you have to guess whether 14 points will beat the dealer's hand. The dealer's one big advantage in Blackjack is that he or she gets to wait until all the players have either gone bust or stood pat before playing his or her cards. Other than this, the dealer really has no advantage over the players. You have the option of standing pat or asking for a hit, but the dealer's plays are governed by strict rules. According to the casino rules, the dealer *must* take a card if his or her hand contains 16 points or less whereas you can elect, if you wish, to stand pat on any amount under 21. In other words, even if all of the players have hands totaling just 11 points and the dealer's original hand is worth 16 points, normally a winning hand, he still has to take an extra card and risk going bust.

In most casinos, the dealer must stand pat if he has 17 points or higher and must take a card if he has under 17. If he has 17 points exactly, it depends on whether it is a "hard" 17 (without an ace) or a "soft" seventeen (with an ace). If it's a hard 17, he must stand. If it's a soft 17, the dealer must take a hit in casinos in downtown Las Vegas and northern Nevada, but in most other places in the world, including the Las Vegas strip, he must stand. When in doubt, look at the posted rules. There is always a sign of some sort, usually on the table, that says something to the effect of, "Dealer must draw to sixteen and stand on seventeen."

It sometimes happens that there is a draw—that is, both the dealer and you or another player have hands worth the same amount. This is called a "push" in casino slang, and no money is exchanged either way.

Additionally, in most casinos the dealer does not have the option, as you do, of treating an ace as either an eleven or one. He or she has to treat it as eleven. Thus, if a dealer has an ace and a seven, and draws a king, he or she would go bust, while a player could treat an identical hand as 18 points. Some casinos, however, do allow the dealer this option, and you should find out quickly what the rules are for this situation.

Casino Blackjack

When you walk into a casino anywhere in the world, from Monte Carlo to Lake Tahoe, there are dozens, sometimes hundreds, of Blackjack tables. This is because Blackjack is extremely popular with most gamblers.

Blackjack pays off even money on all hands except a Blackjack, which pays off three to two ($30 on a bet of $20). Insurance bets, discussed below, pay off 2 to 1. The table's minimum and maximum bets vary from table to table and are usually announced with a small sign on each. A table with a $1 minimum, for example, probably has a maximum bet of between $500 and

$1,000. Casinos generally allow players to bet either cash or chips, but most encourage the use of chips. If you win, though, the casino only pays off in chips. One table may have a minimum bet of $2, another $5 or $25, still others $100. The maximum wager allowed is rarely more than $1,000, although some establishments allow $3,000 or more. Why would a casino not want someone to make large bets? The reason is simple— the casinos can lose a lot of money. What's more, low maximum bets help stop people from using progressive systems, such as doubling up, because a low-maximum bet defeats such a system very quickly.

By the way, you're allowed to play more than one hand at a time, and it is not all that unusual to see a high roller alone at a table, like a slot machine junkie, playing four or five hands simultaneously. In European and Asian casinos, it is also possible to place bets on people's hands even when you yourself are not playing. These side bettors are called standees because they usually stand behind a gambler sitting at a Blackjack table.

Beyond the basic decision of whether to stand or take a hit, a few other situations may arise and present you with some options. Let's take a look at the most common.

Insurance

This is a side bet common in major casinos throughout the world but usually not permitted in smaller card houses. You make an insurance bet only when the dealer's up card is an ace. You're betting, in effect, that the dealer has a card worth 10 points, and thus Blackjack, in the hole. The insurance bet, which is half your original bet on the table, is paid off two to one. So, if you bet and win the insurance bet but lose the hand, you break even. This is how it works.

Let's say the dealer turns over his first card, and it's an ace. He'll ask if you'd "like insurance." If you say yes, you put forward half of your original bet. If the dealer does have a Blackjack, you win and the dealer pays you two to one ($40 on a bet of $20). If he doesn't have a Blackjack, you lose that side bet but the game goes on.

Most experts advise that there are some instances when an insurance bet can be a good bet. For example, it's something you might want to do when you have a Blackjack or close to it. Let's say you have bet $20 and your first two cards are an ace and a king, which means Blackjack. But when it comes time to see the dealer's cards, he, too, turns up an ace and asks you whether you want insurance. You say yes and bet $10 because there is no way you can lose the hand itself. The worst-case scenario is that you tie and the wager is "pushed." If the dealer does have a Blackjack, you win the insurance bet and he pays you double your bet or $20. If the dealer doesn't have a Blackjack, he'll take your $10 insurance bet but pay you $30 for winning the hand—which works out to a profit of $20.

Doubling Down

In most casinos in the U.S., except for those in northern Nevada, players have the option of "doubling down" on any initial two-card combination. What this means is that you can double your bet *after* you see your cards. For example, let's say you bet $10 and then receive two queens. You're feeling pretty confident. You have the option, if you want, to double your original $10 bet to $20. This can be a tremendous advantage if you know what you're doing. In northern Nevada you are allowed to double down only on cards with totals of 10 or 11. In European casinos, you can double down only on hands totalling 9, 10, or 11.

Splits

Another option available to you is that of splitting pairs. If you receive, say, two sixes in the initial deal—either both facedown or both faceup—you have the option of separating the two cards and doubling your bet. If the casino rules require that the cards be dealt facedown, you turn them over and put more chips next to one of them. If the cards are dealt facing up, you separate them, add an additional amount of chips next to the card you wish to bet more on and ask for another card.

Let's say on the first six you get a king. You have 16 points on that card and can elect to stand or ask for a hit. Let's say you stand. Now the dealer gives you another card. Let's say that new card is also a six. Yes, if you wish to, you can even split that hand, so you will have three hands going simultaneously. But let's say you do not split that hand but ask for yet another card. The card dealt is a queen, and you stand pat with 16 points in your first hand and 22 points in your second. You went bust on your second hand.

The dealer begins with a four and a queen, or 14 points, and so he or she must take a hit. The card comes up a jack, so the dealer is busted and must pay on your first hand. The major restriction on splitting is that if you have two aces and split them, you are only allowed a single draw card on each ace, even if the next card is very low. In Atlantic City the casinos allow you to split pairs but you may not, as in Las Vegas, resplit the split hand in the event you receive another card of the same denomination (for example, another four after having split a pair of fours).

Blackjack Strategy for Absolute Beginners

Blackjack is essentially a game of skill with an element of chance thrown in for fun. It is, as we've noted, the only casino game in which a skillful player can actually win consistently.

To do this, however, requires that you learn a little

strategy. Card counting, which is a complex but fairly effective way to win at Blackjack, is too difficult to explain in this book and is beyond the abilities of absolute beginners anyway, especially given the numerous distractions present at a casino (free drinks, sexy waitresses). However, with basic Blackjack strategy outlined below you can actually have a significant edge much of the time. Card counting is only for experts who have mastered the basic strategy. Also, increasingly nervous pit bosses in the big casinos, and some spectacular recent losses, mean that dealers are frequently reshuffling the decks in their shoes whenever they suspect that a player is a "counter." Card counting is perfectly legal, by the way, because there is nothing that a casino can do to prevent you from counting the cards. What the casinos can do, however, and do a lot, is to reshuffle the decks as many times as they think necessary. This effectively shuts down even the most advanced card counting operation.

The most fundamental strategy you must learn when playing Blackjack is when to take a hit and when to stand pat. There are fixed rules of thumb to help you make this crucial decision, and you should follow them, at least at first, with absolute obedience. These rules are dictated by the insight that the real object in Blackjack is not to get as close to 21 as possible but to beat the dealer.

Here is the recommended Hit/Don't Hit strategy that experienced Blackjack players use. You should memorize it before you even go near a Blackjack table. The table assumes that the cards are dealt facedown and none of the totals involves an ace. We'll deal with aces in a moment.

Player's Total	Dealer's First Card	Strategy
17–20	Any card	Stand
14–16	7–10 or Ace	Hit
14–16	2–6	Stand
13	7–10 or Ace	Hit
13	2–6	Stand
12	7–10 or Ace	Hit
12	4–6	Stand
12	2 or 3	Hit

As you can see, there are some general rules reflected in this table. These are the principles you should live by. There are three main ones:

1. Always stand pat with 17 points or higher.
2. Never take a hit on a hand worth 13 to 16 points if the dealer shows low cards (two through six).
3. Always hit a hand worth 12 points unless the dealer shows a four, five, or six.

An astute absolute beginner might wonder why a player should take a hit, and therefore risk a bust, when he or she has relatively high cards (15 through 16) and when the dealer shows high cards. It's a good question, and the answer is very simple. A card worth 10 points is the most common in the deck, which means that there is a very good chance that a dealer showing a seven, eight, nine, ten, face card, or ace already has a ten in the hole card and, therefore, a player with a hand of 16 has already lost. A hit increases the odds of beating the dealer.

Now, what do you do about aces? Aces are, of course, the wild cards of blackjack. The strategy for playing them is somewhat more complex.

Player's Total Ace Plus A ...	Dealer's First Card	Strategy
2–5	2 or 3, 7–10, Ace	Hit
2–5	4–6	Double Down
6	2–6	Double Down
6	7–10 or Ace	Hit
7	2, 7–8, Ace	Stand
7	9, 10	Hit
7	3–6	Double Down
8	Any card	Stand
9	Any card	Stand

Let's take a close look at this table. You'll notice, first of all, that on totals below 17 points that include an ace (that is, a "soft" hand), you should always take a hit. The reason is because you cannot go bust even if you get a card worth 10 points (5 plus 1 plus 10 equals 16). Secondly, you should never stand pat on a "soft" 17 (one made with an ace). But, and this is equally important, you should always stand pat with a soft 19 or 20 (an ace with an eight or nine). If you have an ace plus a card worth 2 through 7 points, always double down if the dealer shows a four, five, or six card as his up card.

You ask: What about splitting pairs? When should you split? The best rule of thumb is this: split any pair except fours, fives, or tens. Always split aces.

That's it. These rules must simply be memorized;

there are not that many of them and, besides, it will help you learn the game. If you do memorize them, however, you'll be ahead of 90 percent of the people who play Blackjack in the casinos. Most people are casual players, strays from the slots, and they're just taking a stab at it. This is especially true on the lower stakes tables, which is where you should be anyway. It's true that at some of the bigger-limit tables, the players do have a certain intimidating savoir faire about them, but you don't have to play on those tables. Moreover, as we've mentioned, Blackjack dealers are among the friendliest people on the planet. That's their job. They are there to make sure you have a good time, relax, drink lots of drinks, and lose your money. Don't ask them for advice, of course—there's nothing worse than some neophyte player whining "What should I do?" to the dealer—but they'll explain the rules to you in a professional, courteous manner.

So give it a shot. Have some fun. Get away from those slot machines. If you're not up for Poker, my personal favorite, Blackjack gives you some of the best odds available in casino gambling.

CRAPS

If Blackjack makes absolute beginners slightly nervous, Craps makes them break out in a sweat. It is perhaps the most intimidating game in a casino, which is understandable because it is also the most complicated. But whereas Blackjack is largely a game of skill, Craps is entirely a game of luck—albeit a fast-paced and exciting game of luck. It is also a game for high rollers, although you can also enjoy the action with small bets.

In Craps, as in Blackjack, all the players bet against the house. This is true whether they are betting with or against the dice. That is a cardinal rule of Craps that you should remember. Many players seem to believe that if they are betting *with* the dice, they are betting *with* the house. That simply isn't the case. You are still betting against the house, even if you bet with the dice.

But we're getting ahead of ourselves. You may not even know what Craps is or where it is played. A Craps table is a rectangular table with curved edges about ten feet long, about five feet wide, and about three feet off the floor. The surface of the table is covered by green felt upon which is painted a complex diagram (see page 131) made up of every sort of bet imaginable. There are spaces for bets on each combination of the dice—such as 4, 5, 6, and so on—as well as for the basic pass/don't pass bet and the come/don't come bet.

Four casino employees run a Craps table. Two of the employees are "dealers" who place bets for the players and collect and pay off after each throw of the dice. Off to the side and in the middle of the table sits a "boxman," who actually runs the game. He watches the action, collects all of the cash, and deposits it into a special slot located in the table. Finally, at one end of the table stands an employee known as the "stickman," who holds a wooden stick that is used to push the dice to the players. The stickman also "calls" the game and takes various side bets that are sometimes made on the action.

How Craps Is Played

Craps is played with standard six-sided dice, now usually made out of hard red or green plastic. On each of the six sides are dots representing the numbers 1 through 6. What this means, therefore, is that with two dice the lowest number possible is 2 (one dot on each die) and the highest possible is 12. There are thirty-six possible combinations of the dice. There may be a number of different sets of dice at the table, but a player uses only one pair at a time.

The player who throws the dice is called the shooter. The other players crowd around the table in those areas not taken up by the stickman, the dealers, and the boxman. The turn to be the shooter usually moves clockwise around the table, but a player may decline the honor of throwing the dice if he or she chooses.

A shooter throws the dice until a combination lands that equals 7, at which point he or she loses his or her turn. Bets must be made before the dice are thrown, and this is done by placing chips on the proper spaces on the table (we'll get to the betting in a moment). Oral bets are not permitted, and all bets are collected, or paid off, immediately after the dice are thrown.

Now, the following is a bit confusing to absolute beginners and is one of the reasons why so many people shy away from Craps. It's one of those things that simply must be memorized.

Each time the dice are thrown, different combinations result. The combinations equaling the numbers 2, 3, and 12 are called Craps. For example, a 1 and a 2 equals 3, or Craps. It looks like this:

The combinations equaling the numbers 4, 5, 6, 8, 9, and 10 are called point numbers and must be repeated in another throw before a shooter throws a 7.

The way it works is like this. Let's say you're the shooter. The stickman pushes the dice to you and you pick them up and do your best to throw them down toward the other end of the table. If you throw a combination that equals 2, 3, or 12, that's Craps. That doesn't mean you lose, because losing all depends on which bets you made (bear with me). What it means is that you didn't get a point number, which you must repeat before you get a 7.

The reason Craps is so complicated is that winning and losing all depend upon what the bet is. So let's take a brief pause to look at the bets.

The most basic bet in Craps is called a line bet, which pays even money. A line bet is made by placing a chip on the Pass Line on the felt. If you place bets on the Pass Line, you are said to be betting "with" the dice or "right." If you place a chip on the Don't Pass Line, you are said to be betting "against" the dice or "wrong."

You win on the Pass Line if (1) on the first roll of the dice, a 7 or an 11 comes up, or (2) if the shooter rolls a 4, 5, 6, 8, 9, 10 on the first roll and then repeats that initial number again before he or she rolls a 7. In other words, let's say a shooter rolls a 9, like this:

The casino employee controlling the bets will place a special marker, called a puck, onto the number 9 on the felt diagram so everyone will know that 9 is the number to get, or the "point." A pass bet, made by placing a chip in front of you on the Pass Line, is that the shooter will get another combination of dice that adds up to 9 before he or she rolls a 7. If the player rolls a 10, then a 5, then a 6, then a 9, he or she (and everyone else who bet on the Pass Line) wins. If he or she rolls a 10, then a 5, then a 6, and then a 7, he or she loses. Also, if the shooter throws 2, 3, or 12 on the first roll, that is known, once again, as Craps and he or she loses.

Everyone who bets on the Pass Line is betting the same way, and everyone is bound by the roll of the shooter.

If the shooter and the other players make a bet on the Don't Pass Line, the opposite of the above applies. In other words, on a Don't Pass bet, you are betting that the shooter *won't* repeat his or her first (point) number before getting a 7. You can also win if the shooter gets Craps on the first roll. Even though Craps is actually 2, 3, or 12, some casinos do not allow players to collect on either a 2 or a 12, depending on the location, when making a Don't Pass bet. The casinos do this simply to increase their odds. Many casinos in Las Vegas bar 12, and those in other places, such as Reno, bar 2.

Now, each of the various combinations of dice have different odds of appearing when the shooter rolls. Ob-

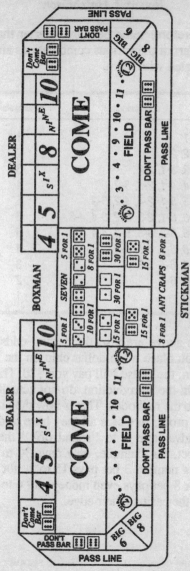

viously, therefore, some bets are smarter than others. Here is a chart of the various combinations and the real odds associated with them.

Number	Combinations	Ways to Make	Odds
2	*1-1*	1	35:1
3	*1-2, 2-1*	2	17:1
4	*1-3, 3-1, 2-2*	3	2:1
5	*1-4, 4-1, 2-3, 3-2*	4	3:2
6	*1-5, 5-1, 2-4, 4-2, 3-3*	5	6:5
7	*1-6, 6-1, 2-5, 5-2, 3-4, 4-3*	6	—
8	*2-6, 6-2, 3-5, 5-3, 4-4*	5	6:5
9	*3-6, 6-3, 4-5, 5-4*	4	3:2
10	*4-6, 6-4, 5-5*	3	2:1
11	*5-6, 6-5*	2	17:1
12	*6-6*	1	35:1

The odds above are also the betting odds. In other words, if you place a ten-dollar chip on the number 4 spot and win, the house will pay you $20. The casinos, as we saw in the Introduction, do not actually pay off according to the real odds. That is how they make their guaranteed profit. In Craps all they have to do to have a built-in advantage is to "round off" the odds—a number 2 bet, for example, only pays 30 to 1 instead of 35 to 1; a number 3 bet pays 15 to 1, not 17; and a number 6 or 8 bet pays even money, not 6 to 5. This is what gives the casinos their edge.

Other Bets in Craps

Besides the Pass/Don't Pass bet, the most basic bet in Craps, there are a variety of other bets that can be made. In addition to the line bets (Pass or Don't Pass), a player can back up his line bet by placing what is called an odds bet. Only experienced players know how to do this, because, unlike the other bets in Craps, there is no sign on the table indicating how this is done. An odds bet is placed by putting a stack of chips *behind* the original bet on either the Pass or Don't Pass Line. Generally, the casinos only allow you to bet an amount of money on an odds bet equal to your original bet, but some casinos, such as those in Reno, allow you to place up to double your original bet. This second bet is paid off at the actual odds shown in the table above. So, let's say you place $10 on the Pass Line. The shooter throws a 6—which means, for you to win, the shooter has to throw another 6 before he throws a 7. You put another $10 in chips (two five-dollar chips) behind your original bet on the Pass Line. The odds on the shooter throwing another 6 are 6 to 5. The shooter throws a 5, and then a 4, but finally throws a 6. You win $10 (even money) on your original ten-dollar bet, but also an additional $12 (6 to 5) on your odds bet.

In addition to odds bets, which most beginning players don't know about, there are what are called Come bets. A Come/Don't Come bet, which is marked on the table felt, is basically a side bet on the precise outcome of the next throw of the dice. It is actually an independent bet on the throw of the dice. If a player puts $10 in the Come box, he's betting on the outcome of the next roll, not on the original line (Pass/Don't Pass) bet.

I realize that all this sounds very complex; that's because it is. Many Craps players simply place line bets for that reason. But it's possible to lose a line bet and win the Come bet, which is why people place Come bets. Let's say a player puts $10 on the Pass Line, and the shooter throws a 5. Now the player places $10 in the Come box. The shooter rolls a 7. The player loses the line bet but collects on the Come bet, because you win if the shooter throws a seven on the initial roll and in a Come bet the next roll of the dice is considered an original roll.

An even more complicated bet is a place bet. Big bettors love this type of bet because the winnings can be substantial though the odds are against you. At the top of the Craps table you see a series of numbers surrounded by rectangles. These are the spots for place bets. Basically, you're betting that the shooter will turn up each of the numbers you bet on before he throws a 7. The place bets pay out at the odds for each of the numbers (see chart page 132), and players frequently place bets on different combinations or even on all of the numbers. Unlike other bets, place bets can be increased or even removed, at any time before the 7 is rolled. Once the 7 is rolled, all the place bets on the table are lost. Here is how it works. You place $10 each on number 4 and 10, both of which pay at 2 to 1 odds. The shooter throws a 6, then a 4. You win $20 on your place bet on the 4. But then the shooter throws a 7, and you lose your $10 on the number 10 place bet.

There is another type of bet that looks like a place bet but is not. It is called a field bet and is made by placing chips on the numbers in the middle of the craps table. The word *field* is prominently displayed on the felt with the numbers circled below it. The field numbers, unlike the place numbers, are paid at even money—if you bet $10, and win, you collect $10 plus your $10. Also, the field numbers win or lose with each toss of the dice, while with place bets you don't lose until a 7 is thrown. Put simply, if you place a bet on number 4 in the field, you're betting that the next throw of the dice will come up as 4. On a place bet, you're betting that a shooter will throw the number you're betting on before he throws a 7. There's a big difference. Next to the field numbers are special boxes for Big 6 and Big 8. With these numbers, a player is betting that either a 6 or an 8 will appear before the shooter throws a 7. The house pays off these two bets at even money.

Finally, you can bet a number of other bets that are called out by the stickman—such as "any crap" or "hardways." Most of the time, these bets pay out at 7 to 1 odds, which make them attractive until you realize that the real odds of winning are 8 to 1. That gives the casino an 11 percent advantage. The standard Nevada layout for this bet is confusing for beginners because it says "8 *for* 1," which is the equivalent of "7 *to* 1." With an 8 for 1 bet, the casino pays $8 for your bet of $1, which it keeps. With a bet 7 to 1, the casino pays $7 in winnings plus your original one-dollar bet. Now, any crap is pretty much what it sounds like—the player is betting that a crap number, 2, 3, or 12, will come up on the very next roll of the dice. Hardways refers to pair combinations—2-2, 3-3, 4-4, etc.—like this:

When you bet a hardway 8, for example, you're betting that two fours will appear before the shooter throws a 7.

Strategy in Craps

Is there any skill at all involved when playing Craps? You might think that because Craps is purely a game of luck, there is absolutely no skill involved. That is only partially true. The skill in Craps comes from knowing the odds and which bets to place. Some bets in Craps are better than others and a few are downright suicidal.

There are some general principles that will make life much easier for an absolute beginner. First, know which bets to avoid completely—such as any craps and hardways bets. The casino has too much of an advantage with these. Also, don't bother placing Big 6 or Big 8 bets, and if you want to make a place bet, do so only on the 6 or 8.

Everyone agrees that the best Craps strategy, especially for absolute beginners, is to make Pass/Don't Pass bets that you back up with odds bets. Once you gain some confidence, you can also begin to make Come bets. At least with Pass/Don't Pass and Come/Don't Come bets, the casino's advantage is only 1.40 to 1.41 percent—certainly enough to beat you over the long haul, but far better than the odds playing the field or in most place bets.

ROULETTE

Roulette is a very popular game in Europe. In America, however, it lags behind Craps and Blackjack. There are a variety of reasons why Roulette is not as popular in America as it is in Europe, but the most basic reason is that it is more difficult to win at Roulette in U.S. casinos. In the States, the house has a built-in advantage ranging from 2.7 to 5.26 percent. The game can be a lot of fun, however, which is why many people are willing to give it a spin.

The standard American Roulette wheel is approximately three feet in diameter and features thirty-eight numbers in grooved pockets—1 through 36, which are alternately red and black, plus the numbers 0 and 00, which are usually green. The European-style wheel only has one 0. The extra 0 in the American wheel *doubles* the U.S. casinos' house advantage, making it

5.26 percent as compared to Europe's house advantage of 1.35 percent.

Above each of the numbers on a Roulette wheel is a small pocket, separated by metal dividers, into which the Roulette ball falls. The wheel is turned and then a small plastic ball is sent around a track in the opposite direction of the wheel's rotation. Small metal buffers slow down the speed of the ball until it eventually falls down into the wheel's inner bowl and into one of the pockets. The number of the pocket the ball falls into is the winning number.

There are 150 different bets possible in Roulette, and they are all made by placing chips on a special diagram, or layout, of the numbers that is printed on the table next to the Roulette wheel (see page 139). The numbers on the layout are arranged in three long columns. The numbers start from 1, and, proceeding left to right in rows of three, go all the way to 36. In other words, left to right, the top row of numbers (three across) is 1, 2, 3. The second row is 4, 5, 6. But the first column, running top to bottom, is 1, 4, 7, 10, 13, etc. At the base of each column is a box with the words *2 to 1,* which is where you make a bet for all of the numbers in that column. To the immediate left of the columns are three rectangles. The first says *1st 12,* the second says *2nd 12,* and the third says *3rd 12.* This is where you place bets for the first, second, and third dozen numbers on the Roulette wheel, respectively (see letter E on diagram).

To the left of these rectangles there are some more boxes indicating other possible bets. Obviously, the red and black diamonds are for bets on any red or black number (letter J). The same is true for the spaces for odd and even numbers (letter I). Finally, at the top and

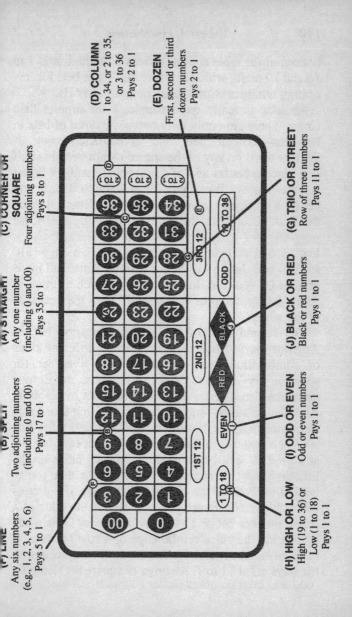

(D) COLUMN
1 to 34, or 2 to 35, or 3 to 36
Pays 2 to 1

(E) DOZEN
First, second or third dozen numbers
Pays 2 to 1

(C) CORNER OR SQUARE
Four adjoining numbers
Pays 8 to 1

(A) STRAIGHT
Any one number (including 0 and 00)
Pays 35 to 1

(B) SPLIT
Two adjoining numbers (including 0 and 00)
Pays 17 to 1

(F) LINE
Any six numbers (e.g., 1, 2, 3, 4, 5, 6)
Pays 5 to 1

(G) TRIO OR STREET
Row of three numbers
Pays 11 to 1

(J) BLACK OR RED
Black or red numbers
Pays 1 to 1

(I) ODD OR EVEN
Odd or even numbers
Pays 1 to 1

(H) HIGH OR LOW
High (19 to 36) or Low (1 to 18)
Pays 1 to 1

bottom of the table are two spaces with the words *1 to 18* and *19 to 36,* which is where you place bets for low or high numbers within those ranges (letter H).

Roulette is really quite simple, a lot simpler than Craps. There are really only two basic types of bets in Roulette—straight bets and combination bets. A straight bet is on any of the spaces mentioned above. If you place a bet on any of the specific numbers (letter A), the house will pay you 35 to 1 if you win. If you bet on a particular column of numbers (letter D) or on the first, second, or third dozen numbers, the house pays out at 2 to 1. If you bet red vs. black, high vs. low, or odd vs. even, the house pays even money ($10 for $10 bet). In the Las Vegas casinos, if the ball lands on 0 or 00 you lose. In other casinos, such as those in Atlantic City, the play is "pushed" until the next spin of the wheel.

The second kind of bet is a combination bet. In American-style Roulette there are five different kinds of combination bets—a split, a trio, a corner (or square), five numbers, and six numbers. In Europe there are also a series of special bets not available in American casinos—such as bets on the first four *(quatre premières),* the last three *(trois derniers),* the first six *(six premiers),* and so on. Let's look at each bet one at a time. A split bet is made by placing chips on the line dividing two numbers, which means that you're betting on both of the numbers (letter B). If either of the numbers comes up, you win at half the odds of a single number bet or 17 to 1. A trio (letter G) is made by placing the chips on the edge of a row (such as 1, 2, 3) of numbers and covers those three numbers. A trio pays off at 11 to 1. A corner or square bet (letter C) is made by placing chips at the intersection, or crossing lines, where four numbers converge. This bet pays 8 to 1. A five number bet can be made only by placing chips on the line above the number 2 and covers 0, 00, 1, 2, and 3. It pays 6 to 1. A six number or line bet (letter F) is made by placing chips on the outside line separating two rows—for example, between 22 and 25, which covers 22, 23, 24, 25, 26, and 27. This bet pays 5 to 1.

Finally, there are a number of special bets available only in European-style casinos. For example, you can bet on the first four numbers *(quatre première)*, 0, 1, 2, and 3, which pays 8 to 1. You can also bet on the final four *(quatre derniers)*, the final three *(trois derniers)*, or on the neighbors *(voisins)*, which refers to the two numbers before and the two numbers after the number on the wheel, not on the layout.

The chips should be placed very precisely and you should ask the dealer where to place the chips for a combination bet—or have him or her place them for you.

Also, in many casinos special chips that are different from the standard house chips are used for Roulette. These chips are a different color for each player, so everyone can keep track of who owns which chips. Casinos don't use this system in Craps because there is enough room for players to place their chips directly in front of them and, for some reason, the dealers are able to keep track of who made which bets. In any event, when you cash out of a Roulette game, the dealer will convert your Roulette chips into standard casino chips. To get real cash, you have to take these chips to the cashier's window.

Strategy in Roulette

For some reason Roulette is the favorite game for the systems player. As we saw in the Introduction, however, all systems, no matter how foolproof they look and how much they win in the short run, always end up failing over the long haul. This can be seen by one incontestable fact: unlike card counting in Blackjack, which the casinos vigilantly watch for and aggressively discourage (by kicking suspected counters out in the streets), the major casinos actually *encourage* systems players. In fact, in the old days in Las Vegas the casinos frequently handed out special record sheets to help players using various progressive systems.

There is no "scientific" way to win at Roulette. It is purely a game of chance, one at which the casino has a built-in advantage. Like slot machines and Craps, therefore, you will lose in the long run but can win, and win big, in the short term. That's the attraction of games of chance, after all. At 35 to 1, a $100 bet on Number 5 will pay off $3,500—if you win.

The best advice for absolute beginners, therefore, is to forget about systems and just have fun. Don't stay very long at a Roulette table. The longer you stay, the more you'll lose. Just give it a try, and if you win, walk away with your profits. That's the best strategy of all. Quit while you're ahead.

WHICH GAMES SHOULD YOU PLAY?

Casinos can be a lot of fun, but as we saw at the beginning of this chapter, they can also be intimidating for absolute beginners. Too many beginners huddle next to the omnipresent, omnivorous slot machines and never venture out to play the more exciting and more social casino games.

If you learn the basic rules of these games, however, you can spend many hours enjoying yourself in the biggest casinos in America. Naturally, it takes a while to really learn the fundamental principles. They have to be memorized or you will be eaten alive in the big casinos. Games such as Blackjack, which seem so simple, take a lot of time to learn really well. An absolute beginner, therefore, is advised to take things slowly, make small bets at first, and, most important of all, watch what the other players do. You learn far more watching people play these games than you do reading a book or even playing yourself. When you play, you're so wrapped up in what you are doing and in the money you're making or losing that you can't concentrate on what's really happening. Any beginning player should play a few rounds of a game and then stand on the sidelines for a time and observe.

Once you've mastered the fundamentals, you can start really playing. Each of the casino games covered in this book has its own set of special rules of thumb and its own psychology. You have to know when the dice are "cold," for example, and be astute enough to know it's time for lunch. Remember: the longer you spend at a game, on average, the more you will lose. This is a proven mathematical fact.

The most important thing to remember when you're gambling is that you are there to have fun, not walk away rich. Blackjack, Craps, Baccarat, Keno, and Roulette are all *games*. They're supposed to be entertaining. While you can play them as a business, unless you really know what you're doing, you'll probably be disappointed with the amount of money you win. On the other hand, by mastering the fundamentals—by taking your time and learning to observe—you will gain a significant edge over the vast majority of your fellow gamblers and will stretch your gambling money. You can learn to win, and when you do lose—and you *will* lose—you can learn to minimize your losses.

1. *U.S. News & World Report*, March 14, 1994, pp. 48–50.
2. *Casino Player*, September 1994, p. 30.

5

Winning Poker for People Who Don't Know a Straight from a Full House

Poker is undoubtedly the most popular card game in the United States. Everything about the game appeals to, and reflects, the American character—the one-against-all individualism, the shrewd calculation, the bluffing, and the fact that someone dealt lousy cards can still end up winning the entire pot. In Poker, as in life, you are dealt a hand that you have no control over, but with skill, street smarts, and a little old-fashioned bravado, you can win it all. You quickly learn that in Poker there are no certain losers and no sure winners. You can win an entire pot holding just a pair of threes and lose everything on a full house. This almost certainly explains why Poker slang is so much a part of American vocabulary, and why you see so many Poker games in Hollywood movies. Poker is popular because it is primarily a game of skill, not a game of chance.

Although it may be based on card games that are centuries old, such as the Persian game Ās-Nâs and the French games Ambigu and Bouilotte, Poker actually originated in the United States. In the sixteenth century, the French writer Rabelais described a game similar to Poker that was played in both France and England. However, the Poker we know and play today appears to have come into existence in New Orleans and in the early part of the nineteenth century.

The Cajuns in Louisiana, descendants of French pioneers, called the game *poque,* which was possibly derived from the French word *pocher,* which means to bluff. However John Scarne's favorite theory was that the worde *poker* came from the old pickpocket slang that called a wallet a poke, because in its earliest incarnations Poker was considered a "cheater's game" much like Three-Card Monte. In any event, Poker became vastly popular on the gambling steamboats of the Mississippi, and over time players brought the game out West to frontier saloons in St. Louis and Kansas City.

Most high-stakes gambling in the early nineteenth century was actually done with another card game called *faro* in which all of the players bet against a single banker as in Blackjack. But the riverboat gamblers soon discovered that Poker allowed a player to bet against all of the other players and thus made both more control and vastly bigger winnings possible. The game was played originally with what is called a stripped deck—which consists of only the ace, king, queen, jack, and ten of each suit. But, from about 1830 on, Poker has been most commonly played with the standard fifty-two card deck.

The Basic Structure of Poker

The basic structure of Poker is quite simple and remains constant for all of the game's dozens of variations. In all games, a standard fifty-two card deck is used and usually jokers are removed. Players make a first, and usually token, bet called an *ante,* which signifies that each player is "in" the game. Usually, each player places this bet, either in cash or in chips, in the center of the card table, saying, "I'm in." The initial antes become the "pot." The pot is the total amount of money bet during each hand and which players attempt to win, usually (but not always) in a winner-take-all fashion.

Players each take turns being the dealer, who deals out one card at a time to each player until all of the required number of cards have been dealt. Upon receiving his or her cards, each player then has an opportunity to place an initial bet. Often players will stipulate before starting the game that cards of a certain level must be possessed by a player before he or she can make an opening bet. Usually in Draw Poker this minimum value of cards is a pair of jacks, which is why this game is called Jacks or Better to Open. When playing a game such as Jacks or Better, the player with the required initial cards starts off the betting and then each player in turn, going from the initial bettor's left, has the option of meeting or raising that bet or dropping out of the game entirely.

Each variation of Poker has its own set of betting

rules. Players usually agree beforehand on maximum amounts that can be bet, the total number of raises permitted, and so forth. For example, a group might say that a game is "nickel ante," with a maximum bet of $1 and only two raises permitted. That means that on any bet or raise (which is an increase in someone else's bet), the maximum amount is $1 and only two raises are permitted. If Player A makes an initial bet of, say, 25 cents, and Player B "sees" that bet and "raises" it the maximum of $1—meaning that the next player must put in $1.25 to stay in the game—Player C may further raise to a maximum of $1 but then all raises must stop for that round of betting. Players after Player C must put in $2.25 to stay in the game but cannot raise the bet anymore. Limits on the number of raises merely keeps a certain order to the game and keeps things moving.

After the initial round of betting is completed, players have one or more opportunities to acquire cards, place more bets, or drop out of the game (called folding). The player with the best hand at the end of the game wins the entire pot.

That is the basic structure of all Poker games. Within that structure, however, are dozens of variations, the most common of which we will look at in more detail below.

Draw—In this form each player is dealt a fixed number of cards, usually five, facedown. After betting on the strength of this original hand, the players then have the option of acquiring (or drawing) additional cards (usually limited to four) or quitting the game. If a player wants more cards, he or she must discard an equal number, which are then set aside from the game. After each player has drawn more cards, kept the ones he or she already has, or quit entirely, the game continues and the players bet a second time on their new hands.

Stud—In this variation of Poker each player is dealt a certain number of cards, some faceup, some facedown. Players bet on these initial hands, and then each player is dealt an additional card (usually faceup). Betting takes place after each round of additional cards. The most common forms of Stud are Five-Card Stud and Seven-Card Stud. For Five-Card Stud, players are initially dealt just two cards, one up and one down. Everyone then bets on this initial two-card hand, and then each player receives one additional card, faceup—and everyone bets again.

Lowball—This game is simply ordinary Poker with the reverse objective—that is, a game in which the lowest hand wins. Lowball can be played in either draw or stud form.

Hold 'em—This is a variation of Poker in which a certain number of cards are dealt out on the table facedown and are eventually used by all of the players in order to form the best hand possible. Usually, players get two cards, facedown, and there is a series of betting rounds as each of the cards in the center of the table is turned faceup. It is somewhat like Stud Poker with everyone sharing certain cards.

All of these games and their numerous variations have certain features in common—the most important of which are the ranks of the various cards and of the combinations. Absolute beginners sometimes have a hard time memorizing which combination of cards beats which, but you simply must memorize the ranking of the various hands. Nothing makes an absolute beginner look like a rube more than asking, "Now, does a full house beat a flush?"

The rank of the individual cards is, from the highest, ace, king, queen, jack, 10, 9, 8, 7, 6, 5, 4, 3, and 2.

The rank of the hands, and their cards, is as follows:

1. ROYAL FLUSH
A-K-Q-J-10 all of the same suit

2. STRAIGHT FLUSH
**Any five cards of the same suit in sequence
(for example, 5, 6, 7, 8, 9)**

3. FOUR OF A KIND

4. FULL HOUSE
**Three of a kind plus a pair (for example, three tens
and a pair of deuces)**

5. <u>FLUSH</u>

Any five cards all of the same suit but not in sequence

6. <u>STRAIGHT</u>

Any five cards in sequence but not all of the same suit

7. <u>THREE OF A KIND</u>

8. <u>TWO PAIRS</u>

9. <u>ONE PAIR</u>

10. <u>HIGHEST CARD</u>
(in the absence of a pair, the highest card wins).

In those cases when players have hands of equal rank—for example, both have straights—then the hand that has the highest card wins. In other words, a straight that begins with a king high will beat a straight in which the highest card is an eight. A pair of queens will beat a pair of jacks, and three nines will beat three eights, and so on.

Some players use what are called wild cards when playing the many Poker variations. A wild card is simply a card that can used as any card a player wishes. For example, if deuces (or twos) are wild, and a player draws a two, he or she may pretend that this card is an ace, or a particular suit (say clubs or diamonds.) There are a number of different games that make use of wild cards—such as Spit in the Ocean, Up and Down the River, Michigan, Baseball, High-Low, Criss Cross, and so forth.

Many players, especially those in friendly Friday

night Poker games, stipulate that the hands will be played according to "dealer's choice." This simply means that it is up to the dealer to decide which game is going to be played as well as which cards, if any, will be wild. Some players like to declare deuces (twos) wild, while others prefer "one-eyed jacks" (only two of the four jacks have one eye), and so on.

Winning at Draw Poker

Draw poker is what Poker is all about. It is the most popular form and contains all of the psychological elements that make Poker so exciting. Two to eight players can play, and the usual form of the game consists of drawing five cards. The object is to win the entire pot, and there are usually two rounds of betting—once after everyone receives a first set of five cards, and again after everyone has discarded one to four cards and received their replacements from the dealer. A player also has the option of keeping all of his or her initial five cards and just playing those.

As with most poker games, Draw usually begins with an ante, a token bet to "buy" into the game. The ante can range anywhere from a penny to a dollar to whatever sum all the players have agreed to in advance. Once everyone has "anted up," as it is said, the designated dealer shuffles and passes the cards to the player at his immediate right to cut. After the cards have been cut, the dealer then deals out five cards one at a time, all facedown, to each player, going in a circle from his left to his right. Just to be clear about this—the dealer starts first with the player at his immediate left and deals him or her one card, then he goes to the next player, clockwise, dealing just one card to each player, and lastly he gives one card to himself. Then, after everyone has one card, he starts again and deals another card, again facedown, to each player. This cycle continues until each player has five cards.

The dealer usually determines which form of Poker will be played for this hand (Draw, for our purposes) and any additional rules that will govern this hand only, such as which cards are wild, if any, and what the "openers" are.

Openers, as we saw above, refers to the minimum hand that a player must hold in order to "open" the initial round of betting—for example, "jacks or better to open." Again, jacks or better simply means that a player must have at least a pair of jacks in order to open the betting. Usually, the dealer will proceed from his left and ask each player in turn if he or she can open.

No one wishes to open since it is a disadvantage to reveal any information about a hand to other players. A player who does have "openers," but sits far enough away from the dealer so that someone else opens before the dealer calls on him, has a built-in advantage—that is, he has a pretty good hand . . . *and no one knows it*. Little advantages like this are what Poker is all about. If no one has the minimum hand, the cards are all discarded, the dealer reshuffles, everyone throws in another ante, and the cards are dealt again. This continues until someone gets the minimum hand required to open the betting.

Once a player declares that he can open, he then makes an initial bet. As mentioned above, the bet limits are usually determined by rules agreed upon in advance—for example, a one-dollar or ten-dollar maximum bet. Some players also play what are called table stakes, which means that you can only bet the sum total of what you have in front of you on the table. In other words, you are not allowed to dig out more money from your wallet or go cash a check. Again, proceeding clockwise from this player's left, the dealer will go around to each player in turn and ask if he or she is "in." According to the ancient and sacred traditions of Poker, the dealer is the final bettor even if he is in the middle of a sequence of bettors.

Each player at this stage has three options: He may "see" (match) the initial bettor's bet, "raise" it (increase the bet), or "fold" (quit that hand). If a player calls a bet, he must place an amount equal to that bet into the pot. If he raises it, then he places the amount of the original bet, plus his increase, into the pot. The next bettor, following him, now must pay that increased amount into the pot just to stay in that hand. Of course, if the betting rules allow for two raises, the next player may also increase the bet up to a maximum amount.

After this initial round of betting, each player then has the option of discarding one to four cards and receiving a set of replacements from the dealer. The idea, of course, is that players keep their good cards and discard ones they don't believe will result in a highly valued combination. After everyone has received his or her second round of cards, then another round of betting ensues, beginning with the person who had openers. In other words, whoever opens has the first opportunity to start the betting again. This player may, if he wishes, decline to make an additional bet, and can pass, or "check," the bet to the person on his left. Proceeding from the player's left, therefore, the opportunity to make a bet continues around the table.

As stated above, each player is usually limited by a fixed maximum bet. However, the betting, with the restriction of a maximum number of raises, is cumulative—that is, by the time the betting reaches the last player, the total bet can far exceed the maximum bet allowed each player.

For example, let's pretend that the rules allow for a maximum bet of $5 with a maximum number of two raises. Player A bets $5, but then Player B sees that bet (that is, matches it), and raises the bet an additional $5. By the time the betting round meets Player C, therefore, the total cumulative bet to him is now $10. Just to stay in the game. Player C must at least match that cumulative bet of $10, although he, too, can see that bet and raise it even further—say $5, for a cumulative total of $15. By the time the betting gets to Player D, therefore, he or she must cough up $15 to stay in the game. Some players will stipulate that the maximum number of raises rule applies only to each player, not to the entire hand. In that case, each player has the opportunity to match the cumulative bet and raise it. In other words, if only two players are left in a hand, Player A and Player B, the two-raises rule is often instituted to prevent a bidding war. Player A will bet, say $10, and then Player B will see that $10 and raise it another $10. Player A now owes the pot an additional $10 to stay in the game, but he can, if he wishes, see Player B's raise and raise it (for a second and last time) yet another $10. Player B will then have to put in another $10 and "calls" (calls for Player A's cards) Player A. To get to win the pot, Player A now has to show his cards. If Player B can beat those cards, he will show his; if he cannot, he will likely fold his cards and not allow Player A to see them, conceding defeat.

As a general rule, good Poker players never let other players see their cards unless they have to in order to win a pot. You never want to give the other players an idea of how you play your hand and whether you bluff or not. If Player B had lousy cards and was simply bluffing, he doesn't want Player A or any of the other players, to know that. That's why, if he can't beat Player A's hand, he'll simply fold his cards over and mix them in with the other discarded cards. That's the origin of the popular Poker phrase "You have to pay to see 'em." The only way a player can see another player's cards is by "paying" through betting. One exception to this general rule is that the initial bettor is sometimes asked to show his openers to prove that he did, in fact, have the right to begin the betting. If he has folded, however, he does not have to show the rest of his hand.

The multiple raises in Poker explain how the pots can become as large as they do even with small maximum bets. With six to eight players in a game, even nickel ante poker can see pots exceeding $20 or more.

If there are more than two players left in a hand, everyone proceeds in order, clockwise from left to right, and either shows his hand or, if he is obviously beaten by hands already shown, he has the option, as just stated, of folding his hand over and conceding defeat without showing his cards.

Psychological Brinkmanship

The basic strategy in all Poker, but especially in Draw, is "to know when to hold'em and know when to fold 'em," as the Kenny Rogers song says. The difference between an experienced player and an absolute beginner is that an experienced player knows when to fold. He knows the odds. It is statistically possible to draw to an inside straight, for example—that is, to get the one missing middle card in a hand with, for example, 4,5,7,8—but the odds are greatly against you, 11 to 1 to be precise. A smart player knows these odds and doesn't try to go against them unless he or she feels exceptionally lucky.

As a general rule, you should stay in a hand only if you can equal or beat the minimum required openers. For example, if the game requires jacks or better to open and someone declares he has openers and you don't, fold. That may seem overly cautious, but it is just smart Poker. Some Poker experts are even more extreme, insisting that in a Jacks or Better game, if someone opens you should have at least a pair of *kings* to stay in the hand. The rationale for this is that the player holding openers will almost certainly improve his hand, or could have better than a pair of jacks (say two queens or two kings), and so to be competitive you should have at least a pair of kings.

Now, the reason why good Poker players will do a little astringent betting before the draw of additional cards is to eliminate players with lousy cards. It frequently happens that someone with a pair of threes gets lucky and draws a winning hand—another three or, even worse, a full house. A player holding a pair of aces, therefore, wants to get rid of these potential spoilers and concentrate on the players who had openers.

You must always remember that Draw Poker is essentially a game of psychological warfare in which the cards are merely the medium, the occasion, for an elaborate test of nerves. The essential elements of

Poker—an element of chance, hidden knowledge, betting, and bluffing—could theoretically be incorporated into another gaming medium, such as dominoes. The cards themselves are only a convenient mechanism for the battle of wills.

The most important part of this psychological warfare involves bluffing. You have to figure out, by considering the number of cards a player draws and his betting patterns, what kind of a hand he has. As a way of illustrating this, we'll look at a typical hand of Draw Poker. Let's say you are playing with five players and you are the dealer. The game is Five-Card Draw, dollar ante, with jacks or better to open. The maximum bet is $5 with only two raises permitted.

Everyone puts a one-dollar ante in the center of the table. You deal the cards, everyone looks at their hands, and you turn to the player at your immediate left, Player A, and ask him if he can open. He says he can and makes a one-dollar bet. Player B, the next player over, folds immediately. Player C, to everyone's surprise, sees Player A's initial bet and raises it by $5. Player D must now kick in $6 to stay in the game and he does.

Now it's your turn. You put down the deck and pick up your hand. This is what you have:

All in all, not bad for an initial hand. The pair of aces justifies staying in the game, so you throw in your $6.

This is the time to get more cards. Player A discards two cards and asks for two. You immediately consider: in all probability, Player A was holding one pair, jacks or better (because he opened), and kept a high card, known as a kicker, hoping for two pairs. If this is what he's doing, it's bad strategy, because the odds of getting two pairs are 5 to 1. On the other hand, it's entirely possible that he could have three of a kind, which is a very strong hand.

Player C discards and asks for just one card, which means he is going for a straight, a flush, or (less likely) a full house—all long shots. Of course, he, too, could be holding two pairs. You just never know. Player D asks for three cards, meaning all he had was one pair.

You're the dealer and, as we've said, are holding two aces. You're smart, don't keep a kicker, and so discard your ♠3, ♥10, and ♥6. You deal yourself three new cards and discover, much to your delight, that you picked up a second pair, two twos.

Your new hand now looks like this:

This completes the first phase in which players try to figure out what their opponents' cards are. It is the second round of betting when the real clairvoyance begins. Player A, who opened and asked for two cards, checks the bet—meaning, he bets nothing. He passes. This is a surprise—and a definite sign of weakness. It probably means he has nothing going except his original pair, but it *could* mean he's being sneaky, concealing a good hand in the hope of keeping as many people as possible in the game (and thus adding to the pot) with the plan of raising the stakes later and tricking people into believing that he is bluffing when, in fact, he actually holds a dynamite hand. This is the psychological brinkmanship that makes Poker such a fascinating game . . . and why people around the world are so addicted to it. It has obvious parallels in business and statesmanship.

Player C folds, which simply means he didn't get the card he needed for a straight or a flush and didn't have the nerves to bluff. Player D makes a modest, pro forma bet—just $1—which means he probably didn't get anything either, but doesn't want to seem completely weak. Again, though, you always have to consider the possibility that a player is deliberately *under*betting as a feint.

You, the dealer, sitting on two pairs, including a pair of aces, naturally make a bet. You see Player D's token bet of $1 and raise it the maximum, $5. This forces Player D to fold, which proves that he really didn't have anything, but Player A sees your $5 raise . . . and *raises* you an additional $5!

Now you are faced with a classic Poker dilemma. You have to wonder if Player A is (1) bluffing, holding only his openers; or (2) being sneaky, having now three of a kind; or (3) being stubborn and stupid, insisting on remaining in the game, whatever it takes. Which is it?

All three of these alternatives are possible. That is why good Poker players pay so much attention to how their opponents play, over the course of a night or over a lifetime, because you begin to know a little bit about everyone's character. You know that Player D, say, is an inveterate bluffer, that Player E is an extremely cautious bettor and only raises when he has a certain win, that Player F always folds when the bet gets too high, and so on.

In this case, you have a good hand—not a certain win, to be sure, but a strong hand. You know Player A has a habit of bluffing and is not sly enough to bet low in order to keep everyone in the game. You decide Player A is probably bluffing and so you call his raise and throw in the extra $5. "What do you have?" you ask. Player A shows his hand, which consists of nothing more than a pair of jacks and an ace high. He just has his openers.

You show your two pairs and rake in the pot—a total of $41.

At least as important as being able to gauge the psychological propensities of your opponents is a rudimentary knowledge of the odds in making the various combinations. Most players learn the odds the hard way, through years of losses, but an absolute beginner could take a short cut and simply memorize a table of odds and then stick by it. Here is a chart outlining the odds of improving a standard hand of Poker.

Initial Hand	Number of Cards	Desired Hand	Odds Against
Pair	3	Two pairs	5 to 1
		Three of a kind	8 to 1
Two Pairs	1	Full house	11 to 1
Three of a Kind	2	Full house	16 to 1
		Four of a kind	23 to 1
Four-Card Flush	1	Flush	4 to 1
Two-Sided Straight	1	Straight	5 to 1
Inside Straight	1	Straight	11 to 1

This table is self-explanatory, but a few words are in order. Obviously, drawing to an inside straight is a losing proposition—11 to 1 odds. An inside straight, of course, is when you have a sequence of four cards in which you need a middle card to complete a straight. For example, let's say you have the following:

Obviously, to complete a straight you need an eight. Should you keep your partial run and discard the ace . . . or keep the ace high and draw four new cards? Unless you're feeling very lucky, say most experts, you should keep the ace and don't bother going for the inside straight. The odds against it are just too high. There are only four eights in the deck, and with five to eight players in a game, the odds that your opponents have all or most of them are very great.

The basic lesson, then, is that it pays to learn the odds. Study the odds table above until it becomes second nature. Don't draw to an inside straight. Don't keep a kicker with a pair. And you'll do okay.

A Note on Bluffing

Bluffing, as we have seen, is what makes Poker what it is. Even the absolute beginner should learn how to bluff a little. After all, bluffing merely means that you pretend—mostly by the way in which you bet—to have better cards than you really do. The object of bluffing is to force all of the other players out of the game with bigger and bigger bets. You're trying to scare them off so that you'll collect the pot by default. This can be done quite successfully. Many experienced players sometimes will pick up enormous pots with nothing more than a pair of deuces or sometimes with just a king high. It's usually a lot easier to bluff, though, when the stakes are higher. Obviously, if you're only playing nickel ante Poker, it's harder to bluff than if you're playing $10 ante. In small-stakes games, there's always someone who is willing to pay fifty cents to see your cards. But if it costs someone fifty bucks to see if you're bluffing, that's another matter.

It pays to know your opposition. You should always study your fellow players. If they know what they are doing—meaning that they don't open with lousy cards, and they don't seem to keep a kicker with pairs—they can sometimes be bluffed. If they are lousy players, however, or very lucky ones, they are too stupid to be bluffed. You have to know the odds in order to be faked out.

Stud

In the movies, Stud Poker separates the men from the boys or the women from the girls. The reason why Stud has this reputation is clear. For one thing, the stakes are usually much higher in Stud than in Draw. After the initial two or three cards are dealt, you bet on each and every card that is dealt, which quickly raises the stakes. Also, the odds in Stud are a bit different: because you do not get to draw more cards, it sometimes happens that someone will win an enormous pot with just a jack high.

The game is very simple. There are two basic variations of Stud Poker—Five-Card Stud and Seven-Card Stud. The strategies for each are different, so we will examine them one at a time.

In Five-Card Stud each player is dealt five cards—but one at a time, with a round of betting with each card. The player with the best hand at each juncture makes the initial bet.

To begin, the players put in their antes and the dealer deals out two cards to each player, one up and one facedown. The player with the highest card facing up (let's say a queen) earns the right to make an initial bet. The betting, proceeding clockwise from the initial bettor's left, goes from player to player, with each player having the option of calling (matching) the bet, raising it, or folding. The same ranks of hands apply in Stud as they do in Draw, but you receive fewer cards to make those hands and bet more often.

After the initial bet, a second round of single cards is dealt, one card at a time, to each player, again faceup, and a second round of betting ensues. Again, the betting proceeds clockwise, beginning with the player with the highest hand showing. And again, a player is free to fold at any time. This continues until each player left in the game has five cards, the last bets have been placed, and players must show their hands. The player with the highest hand showing must show his hole card first and then each player in turn must do the same, moving clockwise from the initial player's left. The player with the best hand, including the hole card (the one facedown), wins the pot.

The strategy in Five-Card Stud is different from that in Draw Poker. As mentioned above, you have fewer cards to make a winning hand and therefore the table of odds above does not apply. You are more at the mercy of chance in Stud Poker than in Draw, and even a good player can find himself having to fold continuously because of lousy cards. This is why many good players dislike Stud and why lousy players can sometimes prosper playing it.

You can see how the pot can get very large very quickly. If you have a one-dollar betting limit with a maximum of two raises per bet, that still allows a lot of money to flow into the pot. Because you bet on each card, the raises and counterraises, can add up very quickly, especially in a game of five to six players.

The basic strategy of Stud Poker is the same as in Draw. You should never waste your time with lousy cards. If a player has a king showing, and your best card is a five in the hole, quit. Never hope that you'll get a pair or some other miracle in the final cards. Once again, the odds are against it. In Stud Poker, the basic principle is that you should stay in the hand as long as it appears that you have the winning hand (say, an ace high showing), but as soon as it appears that you do not have the winning hand, drop out and cut your losses. The beauty of Poker is that you'll get another chance at the big money. Be patient. Play smart. Don't throw bad money after good. As they say, never chase the ace.

Folding early on may cause complaints among the more inexperienced players in your circle that you're a poor sport, but you can always buy the losers a beer from your substantial winnings to make it up to them. To confuse these weaker players, however, you might occasionally make a small bet on a lousy hand, just to throw them for a loop.

Poker, and particularly Stud Poker, is really very basic. If you have an ace in the hole you should stay in the game until you see a pair or someone's overly aggressive betting leads you to believe he has a better hand and then get out.

As we've seen, Poker is a game of psychological brinkmanship. You should try to get players to do precisely the opposite of what you know to be good Poker—that is, you should try to lure them into staying in the game when they have lousy hands and you have a very good hand. To that end, never scare players away with large initial bets. Rope them in slowly. Make what appear to be merely pro forma bets—or even, sometimes, pass the bet. You want the other players to believe that you are foolishly chasing another ace but *don't have it yet*.

This is the opposite of the strategy in Draw, where it's usually a good idea to get rid of the players who hold lousy initial hands. In Stud, if you have a sure winner—say, two aces, one showing and one in the hole—you want to bet as much money as you can without scaring players off. This is why it helps to know your opponents. You know their limits and how much they'll bet on lousy cards just to stay in the game. Once you've lured these players in and they've contributed a hefty amount of cash to the pot, then you place large bets late in the hand. Your hope is that by this time most of the players have so much money already committed that they'll stay in the game in a desperate attempt to get their money back.

Now, let's say you are facing another player with a possible straight or a possible flush and you're holding two queens. What should you do? The answer is that you should stay in the game if you can. As we saw above, the odds of the other people getting the straight or flush, particularly in Five-Card Stud, are not too great. If you happen to be the one holding the possible straight or possible flush, you should fold. The ultimate secret of Poker is to remember never to bet on what you think you *might* get; only bet on what you have. If you do that, you'll end up a consistent winner over the long haul.

Seven-Card Stud is a great game, but confusing to beginners. In many ways, it's like playing with wild cards because it can throw your calculation of odds all to hell. The wild card aspect to Seven-Card Stud also makes for gigantic pots, because the extra two cards make even players with lousy hands feel that they have a shot at winning it all.

Seven-Card Stud is played just like Five-Card Stud except that the dealer deals out three cards to start— first two down and then one up—and each player receives an additional three cards faceup and the final card facedown. The final card is dealt "down and dirty," as they say. After the last card is dealt, each player has four cards showing and three in the hole.

The object of Seven-Card Stud is to make the best five-card hand out of these seven cards. As in Five-Card Stud, a round of betting follows the deal of the initial three cards, followed by another round of betting after each and every additional card dealt.

Good Poker players love Seven-Card Stud because the game has very high stakes and they can easily sucker inexperienced players. Players who don't know what they're doing are intoxicated by the possibilities a hand of seven cards holds. They foolishly believe they'll get the straight or flush even when they see a pair of aces on the table. It is precisely the wild card aspect of the game that lures so many inexperienced players to their doom. It is not uncommon for beginners to stay in a game of Seven-Card Stud with extremely lousy cards because they think that, with so many cards coming to them, they'll almost certainly get the ones they need.

The secret to winning in Seven-Card Stud, therefore, is the same as that of Draw Poker and Five-Card Stud—*bet on what's in your hand.* How you handle your initial three cards will determine over an evening whether you'll end up a winner or a loser. Most players, as mentioned above, will go with whatever they have. You, on the other hand, should stay in the game only if you have the following cards in your initial three cards: three of a kind, a medium pair (eights or better), a low pair (sevens or lower) and a high card (king or ace), and a possible straight or flush. If you have anything else—a pair of fives and a two, for example—*fold.*

What about betting? The strategy is counterintuitive. What you bet depends upon whether you have a great hand (three of a kind) or merely a good hand. If you have a great hand, you bet firmly but *moderately* so you don't scare off the other players. If you have only a good hand (say, a pair of aces), then you should *raise* the bet. If you have a potentially great hand (such as a possible straight or flush), stay in the game but *don't* raise the bet: the odds that you'll complete the series are still against you, even in Seven-Card Stud. The exception is if you have a good hand in addition to a possible flush (for example ♠A, ♠A, ♠4, ♠9, ♠6). The pair of aces justifies your added bet whereas the possible flush alone would not.

The same basic principle that applies to Five-Card Stud should be observed in Seven-Card Stud. As soon as someone has you beaten on the table, get out. Fold. Never stay in the hand with the hope that you'll get that miracle card. *Bet only on what you have, never on what you hope for.*

Lowball

Lowball, or Lo Ball, is just poker with the opposite objective—that is, the *lowest* hand wins. In other words, in Lowball a five beats a ten, a queen beats a king, and so on.

There are a few irregular rules in Lowball that you must learn. The first and most important irregular rule is that the ace is the lowest card, not the highest. The second irregularity is that there are no straights or flushes; only the value of the cards counts. The best possible hand in Lowball, therefore, is actually a straight—5, 4, 3, 2, A. Even if this hand were also a flush—which would normally make it a high hand in regular Poker—the player wins because flushes don't count.

So, a single pair beats two pairs, two pairs beats three of a kind, and three of a kind beats four of a kind. If two players have the same pair, then the player with the *lowest* remaining cards wins. Hands are evaluated by the face value of the cards, so a hand with 9, 8, 6, 4, 2 will beat a hand with 9, 8, 6, 4, 3.

This is all very confusing, of course, and more than one experienced Poker player has gone insane trying to play Lowball. It's very difficult for experienced Poker players to break up pairs, throw away queens, and pray for that magic deuce. Going against every regular Poker rule overheats the circuits of the average Poker player's brains in no time.

Except for this fundamental eccentricity, however, Lowball is played exactly like regular Poker in both its Draw and Stud forms. With Draw, however, you usually play Anything Opens and not, obviously, Jacks or Better. The bets are made in the usual fashion, and players try to bluff and outpsych each other just as they do when playing regular Poker.

One aspect to Lowball that is very disconcerting when playing Stud is that a single card can ruin a great hand. In regular Poker a single card may not advance a hand but it does not wreck it. If you hold three kings, say, in Five-Card Stud, you'll almost certainly win the hand no matter what your final card happens to be. Therefore, you can bet with aggressive abandon. In Lowball, on the other hand, you can have a simply magnificent hand (a 2, 3, 4, 5) but then get as your final card another 4—and you're cooked. Ruined. You should fold immediately. This bizarre aspect to Lowball is why Seven-Card Lowball Stud is almost entirely a game of chance. In Las Vegas this game is called

Razz and is very popular with people who like games of chance, not skill.

Another variation of Lowball is called High-Low, played either in Draw or Stud form. This is a game in which the player with the highest hand splits the pot with the player with the lowest hand. Before the showdown, when players show their hands, everyone must declare whether they are going for the high hand, the low hand, or, in the case of Seven-Card Stud, the high and the low hand (high-low). In Seven-Card Stud, you can use all seven cards to make both the highest and the lowest hand.

Hold 'Em

The final major variation of poker is Texas Hold 'Em, also known simply as Hold 'Em. It is fast becoming one of the most popular casino games and is strictly for skilled players. There can be as many as fifteen players in a game and the pots are usually huge. The game is really a variation of Seven-Card Stud in which all of the players share certain common cards laid out in the middle of the table.

At the start of the game, each player is dealt two cards, facedown. These are called the pocket cards. Next, three additional cards are then laid on the table and these are known as the community cards, or the flop. After that, another card is dealt which is known as Fourth Street, and then a fifth, known as Fifth Street. The object of the game is to form the best possible five-card hand from the two cards each player possesses and the five community cards in the middle.

In casinos there is usually a fixed dealer. Because the

order in which people bet is so important and gives those who bet last an advantage, a token is often placed in front of the nondealing players to simulate the "dealer," so that the betting can move around the table in the normal fashion and the betting order changes.

Players ante, of course, and the dealer then deals out two cards facedown, and the first round of betting begins. The person to the left of whoever has the dealer token in front of him bets first. The dealer next lays out three cards faceup in the middle of the table. These cards are used by all the players to form the best possible hand. For example, Player A has a queen and a seven of clubs, and the three cards on the table are another queen, a seven of hearts, and a four. Player A therefore has two pairs—a pair of queens and a pair of sevens. After the flop is laid out, another betting round begins, again beginning with the player to the token's left.

After this round the dealer places another card in the middle of the table next to the original three. This is Fourth Street, and once it is dealt, another round of betting follows. Next, the fifth and final card, Fifth Street, is dealt to the center, and the final round of betting begins.

As a general rule, a low pair in the pocket, or in the hole, is not worth much in Hold 'Em. The odds are that, with the community cards, other players will also have a high-card pair, such as kings. If you don't have at least a pair of eights, consider folding, especially if the betting becomes intense. If you have a couple of solid high cards, such as an ace and a king, you might stay in to see what turns up on the flop or at Fourth Street.

As with straight Poker, it's a good idea in Hold 'Em

to force out the weaker hands by betting aggressively if you hold a particularly strong hand. You don't want some clown with a pair of deuces to get lucky and make three of a kind on Fifth Street.

Position is critical in Hold 'Em, because unlike Stud Poker—where the betting position shifts according to who holds the best cards on the table—the betting moves according to a fixed course.

If you have both weak cards and are in an early betting position, consider folding. That is because you will either have to concede your weakness by pathetic bets, or even worse, you will have to bluff like hell and hope for a winning card in the flop. As mentioned above, hope is a poor substitute for good cards in Poker. Think like a conservative investor and stick with hard assets. If you see someone raising the stakes dramatically when an ace pops up on Fourth Street, assume he or she has aces in the hole. Don't waste your time hoping that you'll get an extra four on the next card to make three of a kind. Be smart. Fold.

Caribbean Stud

There are a number of new forms of Poker that have become popular in the final decades of the twentieth-century. Many of these have evolved because of the strict gambling laws in states that permit card rooms. We'll take a look at each of these.

Perhaps the most common of the new Poker games is Caribbean Stud. It got its name because it was very popular at Caribbean resorts and cruise ships in the late 1980s. The game, now played on many cruise ships as well as in most casinos and card rooms in the United

States, is a strange blend of traditional Poker and, believe it or not, slot machines. It has its own special table, like a Blackjack table, that is shaped in a semicircle with a dealer on one side and all the regular players on the other. In front of the dealer are rows of chips and usually printed on the table are the words, "Dealer Only Plays With Ace/King or Higher" (we'll discuss this in a moment). In front of each player's spot is a special box painted on the table marked "ante" and a metal slot into which you insert coins or dollars. This slot is used for an *optional* initial bet that entitles you to a chance at a progressive jackpot, which makes this game somewhat like a progressive video Poker machine with a live dealer. You don't have to play for the progressive jackpot, however.

After a regular ante, the dealer deals out five cards, all facedown, to each player. The dealer himself also gets five cards, but one is dealt faceup. As in regular Poker, players may quit if they are not happy with their initial hand. To stay in the game players have to place another bet, twice the value of the ante.

Once the bets are down, the dealer shows his cards. He must have a minimum of ace-king or all the players win automatically. After the dealer reveals his cards, so do the other players. If you can beat the dealer, you are paid according to a graduated scale. If you win with a pair or less, the dealer pays you even money ($5 for a five-dollar bet). If you win with two pairs, he pays off at 2 to 1 ($10 for a five-dollar bet). If you have three of a kind, you get 3 to 1 ($15 for a five-dollar bet). If you have a straight, you get 4 to 1 ($20 for $5). If you win with a flush, you get 5 to 1 ($25 for $5). If you win with a full house, you receive 7 to 1 ($35 for $5). If you win with four of a kind, you receive 20 to 1

($100 for $5). If you win with a straight flush, you win 50 to 1 ($250 for $5). And if you win with a royal straight flush, you win 100 to 1 ($500 for $5).

Now, if you happened to place some money in the progressive slot and win with a flush or better, then you really collect. You win 50 to 1 for a flush, 100 to 1 for a full house, and 500 to 1 for four of a kind ($2,500 for a five-dollar bet). If you win with a straight flush, you get a percentage of the total jackpot then in existence, which means you can win as much as $300,000 total. In some casinos all of the Caribbean Stud tables are linked electronically, like some of the video Poker machines, which means that the progressive pot can be quite large. The odds of winning the jackpot, while better than those of the lottery, are still quite large: better than 649,000 to 1.

Pai Gow Poker

Another poker game, enormously popular in the card rooms of California, is Pai Gow Poker. It evolved out of the Asian domino game of the same name and is, as you might imagine, widely played by Asian immigrants in the Golden State. The game is a strange mixture of Seven-Card Stud and High-Low. Each player is dealt seven cards from which he must make two hands—a five-card hand and a two-card hand. The five-card hand has to be worth more than the two-card hand (so you can have a pair of aces in the two-card hand and a nine high in the five-card hand). To win, you have to beat *both* the five-card hand and the two-card hand of the dealer. If you beat the dealer with one hand but lose with the other, you don't lose—it's a draw or "push," in gambler's slang. No money changes hands.

The deal rotates around the table, with each player given the opportunity to be the dealer.

Other Games

Casino operators are clearly intrigued by the possibilities that electronic gaming has created for live play. They especially like the idea of linking the progressive slot machine concept to table layout games. That is why there are numerous new experimental games being tried out in Las Vegas and Atlantic City—games with names like Let It Ride, Maverick Jackpot Poker, Action Poker, Strike It Rich, and so on. These games are developed by gaming manufacturers. It's too early to tell whether these new variations of Poker will really catch on—although, given the proven popularity of progressive jackpots generally, some of them undoubtedly will.

Why Poker Is the Best Game of All

This is purely personal opinion, but I happen to believe strongly that Poker is the ultimate gambling game and that all absolute beginners should take the time to learn it well. Poker is almost entirely a game of skill that has a little element of luck thrown in to make it interesting. There is no other game that allows for the same combination of excitement and cold-blooded calculation that Poker does. Craps is quite literally a throw of the dice. Blackjack is a game of skill, but difficult to learn well. However, anyone with a little patience and discipline can learn how to win consistently in Poker.

The secret to winning Poker lies in disciplined play,

shrewd observation of your opponents' weaknesses, and the courage and ability to take measured, careful risks. In essence, it is excellent training for life in general. While there is an element of chance in Poker, it is primarily a game of skill. A good Poker player will consistently beat out weaker players over the long term. What makes a good Poker player good is not the knowledge of the odds; it is his or her skill in observing and understanding human nature, the ability to detect nascent greed or quivering fear welling up in the heart of an opponent. It lies in knowing how to lay intricate traps through bets calculated to keep people in the game, not chase them away. It lies in knowing when to walk away from cards that are good, but not good enough.

My advice to absolute beginners who are interested in gambling, therefore, is to learn Poker. It will teach a lot about the psychology of gambling and about people. It is good training for almost all other forms of gambling.

6

Betting on Gin Rummy, Pinochle, Cribbage, and Bridge

People will bet on anything, of course, so it is not surprising that virtually any popular card game has enthusiastic gamblers who flock to it. Besides the many variations of Poker, there are other card games, some of staggering complexity, that people use as vehicles for betting. While it is possible to bet on almost any card game, including such simple games as Crazy Eights and Old Maid, there are a few card games outside the Poker family that are particularly popular with gamblers. These games all involve strong elements of skill combined with the basic factor of luck present in most card games. The most popular betting games, outside of Poker, are the various forms of Rummy, Cribbage, Pinochle, and Bridge, the most complex card game of all.

In this chapter, we will take a brief look at each of these other popular card games from the standpoint of gambling—although, precisely because they are so complicated, we will not be able to give a definitive account of any of them. There are entire books written about certain aspects of Bridge, for example. We will offer the absolute beginner a basic introduction to the rules of each and explain the fundamental betting strategies that will help you survive when playing a casual game with friends. When your skill increases, you can refer to guides specializing in your game of choice.

GIN RUMMY

Gin Rummy is perhaps the most common betting card game outside of Blackjack and Poker. The great John Scarne calculated in the early 1970s that Americans bet $30 *billion* each year in private gin rummy games. In wealthier circles people have been known to lose as much as $100,000 in a single evening playing Gin Rummy. Gin Rummy is actually one variation in a very large family of card games that all evolved from a Mexican game, Coon Can, once popular in the southwestern United States. This game is relatively easy to play but involves a definite amount of skill, one that is not always readily apparent.

The object of most forms of Rummy, all played with a standard 52-card deck, is to group cards in a hand together into sets of three or more cards of the same rank (three of a kind or better) or into sequences or runs (straights) of three cards or more in the same suit (for example, ♦2, ♦3, ♦4, ♦5). These groups, called melds, are then discarded from the hand. The player with the fewest cards left wins. Among the many variations of Rummy popular in the U.S. are Kalooki, Boathouse Rum, Canasta, Samba (a variation of Canasta), Bolivia, Oklahoma, Panguinge or Pan, and Hollywood Gin. Each of these has its own specific rules but are very similar in their overall structure.

How Gin Rummy Is Played

Gin Rummy is usually played by just two people using, as we said, a standard 52-card deck with the king high and the ace the low, not the high, card. The winner of each hand gets to deal. To begin, the dealer deals out ten cards facedown, alternating back and forth, to himself and to his opponent. Depending upon how the players like to play, the dealer then either deals the twenty-first card facedown to his opponent, who must then discard one of this own cards, or, alternatively, he simply deals the twenty-first card faceup and places it next to the deck. This faceup card, or the one discarded by the dealer's opponent after he looks at his hand, forms the start of what is called the discard pile. The rest of the cards in the deck, with the cards facedown, is called the stockpile.

The actual play in Gin Rummy is fairly simple. After the dealer has dealt all the cards, his opponent has the option of drawing a card from either the discard pile or the stockpile. After having chosen a card from one of these two piles, the player then looks at his or her cards and decides which card to discard. He or she places this discarded card, faceup, on top of the discard pile. The play then goes back to the dealer, who has the option of picking up the nondealer's discarded card—now resting faceup on the top of the discard pile—or selecting a new, unknown card from the stockpile. Once again, after drawing a card from either one of the two piles, the dealer must himself discard one card, and the cycle repeats itself over and over again.

The game continues like this, alternating between players, until someone either "knocks" (we'll discuss this in a moment) or draws the fiftieth card (the third to the last card in the stockpile) and discards without knocking.

As stated above, the object of the game is to form as many three of a kind or better groups (for example, three kings) and runs of three cards or more of the same suit (♠8, ♠9, ♠10) as possible. Unlike standard Rummy, in Gin Rummy these matched cards or sequences, called melds, are not laid aside immediately, but are held in the hand out of view until play is stopped by what is called a knock.

Knocking

A knock occurs when the sum total of all the *unmatched* cards in a given player's hand is 10 points or less. For example, let's say a player has three fives, a run of ♥2, ♥3, ♥4, ♥5, an ace, a two, and a seven. It would look like this:

In this case, he or she would have a total of 10 points (the ace, two, and seven) and, therefore, has a knock. When a player knocks, he or she discards one card—because players only knock after they have drawn a card and it is their turn—and says, "knock." When a player knocks, the play of the game stops and each player displays his or her cards, arranging them into the various melds, and sets the unmatched cards off to one side. Once the knocking player lays down his or her hand, however, he or she cannot rearrange the cards into different sequences. The sum total of the unmatched cards, those not in sequences or melds, is then counted out. After the knocking player has done this, his or her opponent next exposes his or her hand—only with one major difference. The nonknocking player, unlike the knocking player, has the option of forming new melds by extending melds in the knocking player's hand. For example, let's say that the knocking player has three fours. If the nonknocking player has the final four, he or she can add this card to the knocking player's meld and thus get rid of an extra card. If the knocking player has a sequence of, say, two, three, four, and the nonknocking player has an ace, a five, or both, then he or she can add cards to the knocking player's sequence as well. The unmatched cards left in the nonknocking player's hand are then counted up.

Scoring is very simple. You simply subtract the total number of unmatched cards left in the nonknocking player's hand from the total of unmatched cards left in the knocking player's hand. Let's say, for example, the nonknocking player has 16 points left (say a six and a jack), and the knocking player has 8 (two fours). The total amount of scoring points credited to the knocking player is 8. It occasionally happens that a player who knocks actually ends up with *more* unmatched cards than does his or her opponent because the nonknocking player can make new melds and rearrange his or her cards. In this case, which is called an undercut or underknock, the nonknocking player scores the points totalled from the difference between the values of their two hands.

You are not required to knock if you have 10 points or less in unmatched cards in your hand. You can keep playing with the hope that you can eventually match up more cards and get a higher score. Also, you can hold out for what is called gin, which is what occurs when a player is able to match up all of his or her cards and has no unmatched cards left. If you succeed in doing this, you simply say, "Gin!" and lay down all of your cards as though you were knocking.

The first player to reach 100 points wins and receives an additional bonus of 100 points for coming out ahead. At the end of the game, players also add 25 points for each hand (or "box") they won. If a player "gins off," he or she also receives 25 bonus points plus two bonus boxes. Players agree to play to a certain limit or for a set number of hands. The winner is, obviously, determined by whoever has the most points in the end.

You can obviously see the built-in gambling advantages of Gin Rummy. All you have to do is to agree on a set amount for each point in the spread (from a penny to a dollar), and you are set. Let's say you agree to play for a penny a point. You simply calculate the difference between the final scores and multiply the points by one cent. You can just as easily play a nickel a point or a dollar a point.

Strategy for Absolute Beginners

Strategy in Gin Rummy is very simple and consists in just a few basic principles.

There are really only two ongoing decisions you must make in this game: (1) which pile to draw from and (2) which card to discard. The latter decision is much harder than the first, and it is where good players demonstrate their skill. As a rule of thumb, you should only pick up from the discard pile if the discarded card actually will allow you to complete a potential meld that already exists in your hand. Never pick up a discard because you think you might need it later in the game. It might be very hard to get rid of later and, as in Poker, you should only play with the cards you know, not with the cards you hope for.

On the other hand, deciding which card to discard on each round can be a difficult call. For example, let's say you hold four of a kind, three twos, and ♣4, ♦4, ♦5. You draw another two, to go with your previous three. Which card should you discard now? Should you keep the 4, 4, 5 sequence, discard the extra two and hope for a gin . . . or discard the ♦5 so you can knock immediately?

What you discard depends on what your opponent has in his or her hand, and, of course, you don't know that. There are some general concepts, however, that will help you win consistently and which are based on the fundamental mathematics of the game. Out of the 96 possible three-card melds in Gin Rummy, 52 of them are formed by three-of-a-kind combinations and 44 are determined by runs of the same suit. However, it is twice as difficult to add another card to a three-of-a-kind meld as it is to add one to a run. You have a chance at both ends of a run, whereas in a three-of-a-kind meld you have to pick up that fourth card, which is statistically unlikely. What all this means in terms of strategy is that, knowing these odds, you can better calculate when to go for gin and when to knock. If most of your hand is made up of runs, you will have a better chance of adding the rest of your cards to your melds and achieving gin than if you have melds made up of three-of-a-kind combinations.

Toward the end of the game, most players begin quickly discarding their higher unmatched cards. They don't want their opponent to knock and leave them with large totals of unmatched cards—especially if they're playing for money. The problem comes, though, when you have partial sequences of matched cards (say, two jacks) and want to try for gin. That is why Gin Rummy can quickly become a test of nerves. Some players play an alternate form of Gin Rummy in which aces count for 15 points, not one, in what are called round-the-world sequences (A, K, Q or 2, A, K). In this form of the game it is more difficult to knock. As a result, players tend to play more aggressively for gin.

The central question in Gin Rummy quickly becomes: To knock or not to knock? Many players tend to knock as soon as they can because they are afraid of the other player getting gin. On the other hand, some players want to try for gin and so will postpone knocking until they think they have no other choice, especially if they have low-count hands. In general, it's a good idea to knock when you can rather than waiting for gin—particularly if you're ahead on the total score!

The game bonus is worth more than the gin bonus of 25 points plus two boxes.

PINOCHLE

Pinochle is a game that, while not as complicated as Bridge, is not nearly as easy as Gin Rummy and is, therefore, considerably less popular. However, it does have its fanatic devotees. Like Poker, Pinochle was refined in the United States in the nineteenth century, although it was inspired by the French game Bezique and uses the German ranking of cards. Pinochle is, in fact, a very complex game of strategy that does away with most of the conventions of standard card games, including the normal rankings of the cards. Also, like Rummy, Pinochle is actually an entire *family* of games that all conform to the same basic structure. The three basic forms, however, are (1) two-handed Pinochle, (2) three-handed Auction with Widow, and (3) partnership Auction Pinochle. Because it is the oldest and most popular form of Pinochle, we will first look at two-handed Pinochle, and then briefly discuss the betting possibilities in three-handed Auction Pinochle.

The Pinochle Deck

Most people know that a Pinochle deck is quite different from the standard 52-card deck. The Pinochle deck consists of 48 cards, with two each of the nine, ten, jack, queen, king, and ace in each of the four suits. In other words, there are two ♣10, not one, as in the regular deck. The rank of the cards is also different from the standard deck. From the highest (ace) to the lowest (9), the rank is as follows: ace, ten, king, queen, jack, nine.

As if Pinochle were not complex enough, there are actually two different methods used for calculating the values of the cards. The first method, the original system, counted an ace as 11 points and a jack as 2. This makes adding and subtracting a bit difficult for some people, however, and so a new, simplified system was created in which the ace counts for just 10 points and the jack for 0. Below is a chart showing the scoring for both of these two systems.

Card	Original System	Simplified System
Ace	11	10
Ten	10	10
King	4	5
Queen	3	5
Jack	2	0
Nine	0	0

The Play

In Pinochle the deal alternates between the two players. To begin, the dealer first deals out twelve cards, three at a time, alternating between himself and his opponent; that is, first three to his opponent, then three to himself, then three more to his opponent, and so on. When he is finished, and both players have twelve cards each, the dealer places the rest of the deck in the middle of the table. This becomes, as in Gin Rummy, the stockpile. The dealer also turns the twenty-fifth card faceup, which determines which suit is the trump suit, and slides it partially under or next to the stockpile. Trump is an essential concept in Pinochle as well as Bridge, and I'll describe it in detail below.

If that first card is a nine, it is called the "nine of trumps" or the *dix* (pronounced "deece," which is simply French for ten), and earns the dealer an immediate 10 points.

After the deal is completed, play then proceeds. There are two phases to playing Pinochle. The first phase continues until all of the cards in the stockpile are used up. The second phase consists of the end game, when the players use their final cards to score points.

Let's look at the first phase first. After the deal, both players have twelve cards each. As in Rummy, the players alternate laying down one card at a time from their hands. Each set of two cards laid down, one by the dealer and one by the nondealer, is called a trick, and the person with the highest ranking of the two cards wins that trick and earns the right to "lead" for the next trick. This part is really very simple.

Often it happens that the person laying down the second card loses because he or she simply does not have any card that will beat the lead. For example, if Player A lays down an ace, and Player B follows that with a king, Player A wins the trick and gets to score points on that trick.

Players score points for whatever the value of the cards happened to be in the trick, according to the above table. They agree in advance, naturally, which scoring system they will use. For example, according to the original system, a trick with a ten and a queen is worth 14 points, but according to the simplified system, 15 points. Once a trick is won, it is picked up and placed, facedown, off to the side. After a trick is won, the winner draws another card from the stockpile and so does the opponent.

The Rules of Tricks

There are specific rules for the playing of tricks. The most important rule is that to win a trick, after a player has led with a card of a particular suit, the following player *must* lay down a higher card in that suit or trump it. In other words, if Player A leads with a king of clubs, Player B *must* lay down either a ten or ace of clubs to win the trick. This is what is meant by following suit. The only other option for a player is to trump the trick. To trump the trick means to lay down any card of the trump suit indicated by the twenty-fifth card turned over at the start of the game. A player may use a trump card (for example, clubs) *only* if he or she does not have any cards of the suit led by the other player. Indeed, if this situation arises, then the player must play a trump card if he or she has any. If a player has neither the suit of the first player's card nor any trump cards, then he or she may play any card of any other suit and will lose the trick as a result. For example, if Player A leads with a ten of clubs, and Player B has no clubs and no trump cards and plays an ace of diamonds instead, Player A still wins the trick even though an ace outranks a ten.

Melding

Also during this phase of the game, players attempt to create combinations of cards, or melds, which they then lay facedown upon the table, as in ordinary Rummy. Players may lay down melds only *after* winning a trick, however, and before leading the next one. Players may also only make one meld at a time. The combinations, or melds, are as follows:

Sequences	*Points*
A, Q, J, ten of trumps (flush)	150
K, Q of trumps (royal marriage)	40
K, Q of any other suit (simple marriage)	20

Groups	*Points*

| ♠ A, ♥ A, ♦ A, ♣ A (100 aces) | 100 |

| ♠ K, ♥ K, ♦ K, ♣ K (80 kings) | 80 |

| ♠ Q, ♥ Q, ♦ Q, ♣ Q (60 queens) | 60 |

Groups   *Points*

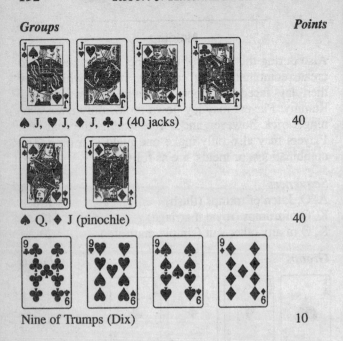

♠ J, ♥ J, ♦ J, ♣ J (40 jacks)   40

♠ Q, ♦ J (pinochle)   40

Nine of Trumps (Dix)   10

Now you can make new melds from previous melds on the table so long as at least one card is used from the cards in your hand. For example, let's say you had laid down a royal marriage (king and queen of the trump suit) and scored 40 points. Later you may add an ace, jack, and ten to the royal marriage meld, providing it is of the same suit, and thus score 150 points for the flush. However, unlike Cribbage, you may score only one meld from each combination of cards. You cannot take cards from one meld to make multiple combinations with other melds. For example, let's say you made a Pinochle (Q, J) and later laid down four kings (80 kings). You cannot then use the kings to form a royal marriage with the queen in the Pinochle.

Also, players score only the total of all the melds they have on the table at the *end* of play, not the cumulative points from melds made along the way, as in Cribbage. Finally, you can use the melds that remain faceup on the table in tricks, but you lose the points in the melds that are broken up in order to win tricks.

Play continues, back and forth, until the stockpile is exhausted—in other words, until twelve tricks of two cards each have been played and set aside and all of the possible melds have been laid faceup on the table. The winner of the final trick gets the last card in the stockpile and the loser gets the trump card. I realize that this is all overwhelming to an absolute beginner, but after playing for a little while it really does start to make sense.

This is when Pinochle gets interesting. Once all of the initial twelve tricks have been played, there is the second phase of play. To begin with, the two players calculate how many points they have made in melds that are now lying faceup on the table. Then each player picks up all the cards in his or her melds, which should be twelve cards in all, and plays them *again* in the final round as tricks. *No more melds are made.*

The same rules for tricks apply in this final round as did for the first round. Players must beat the leading suit or trump it by laying down any card of the trump suit. If a player leads with a trump card, the following player can only win by laying down a higher trump card (that is, if diamonds are trump, an ace of diamonds beats a nine). The winner of the previous trick still leads the next one.

Scoring

Scoring in Pinochle is complicated. Some players write down the scoring, especially of the melds, as they go along. At the end of the second phase of play, players add up the sum total of the melds they made during the first phase of play and add that sum to the total number of points they won playing tricks. Players can figure out their total in tricks simply by counting up the values of the cards in their pile of tricks. The player who played the last trick also gets an extra 10 points. Typically, players will agree that the first player to reach 1,000 points wins the game.

One way to simplify scoring is to figure out the difference between the value of the two players' melds before beginning the second phase of play. For example, if Player A melded a total of 180 points, and Player B just 140 points, Player A begins the second phase with a net lead of 40 points. At the end of the second phase, players then just count up the points in their pile of tricks instead of keeping track as they go along. There are 250 points total possible in the cards. If Player A has 114 points in his cards, and Player B has 136 points, then Player B has a net total of 22 points in tricks. Player A, however, had 40 points lead in the melds, so he wins by 18 points.

As in Rummy, you can see the gambling possibilities here. Players can simply agree to play for a certain amount per point.

The strategy in Pinochle is different from that of other games because of the trump factor. Many players are tempted to hang on to their trump cards to use them in a crunch, but it actually makes better sense to use them in melds as soon as possible. You can always use a melded trump card, if necessary, when playing a trick. You should meld the higher cards first—such as four aces (called 100 aces)—and should meld a royal marriage before a simple one. Most experts agree that it is vitally important for players to know how many trump cards have been played because of their importance in the end play. Your final score is often determined by how many tricks you are able to win in the final phase of the game, and a player with a lot of trumps up his or her sleeve has a distinct advantage. Good players not only know precisely how many trumps his opponent has but also most of the other cards he holds as well.

Auction Pinochle

Auction Pinochle in many ways resembles Bridge, which we will discuss below, in that both games feature tricks, trumps, and, most important of all, bidding. However, Auction Pinochle is still much easier to learn than bridge and a very popular game to bet on.

Most of the rules in Auction Pinochle are very similar to two-handed Pinochle, with a few critical exceptions. The number of cards and how they are dealt varies a bit. Whether three or four people are playing, the dealer deals out fifteen cards, three or five at a time, to each player, beginning at his left, and then to himself (if he's playing). Because of the mathematics of the Pinochle deck, many Pinochle players prefer that the dealer actually sit out the hand he deals, with the deal rotating to the left from player to player. After everyone has his or her cards, the dealer deals out three cards and places them facedown in the center of the table.

These three cards are known as the widow or the blind. Alternatively, some players prefer that the dealer deal out three cards to each player and one card to the widow pile, then three more cards to each player and another to the widow pile, and so on.

The object of Auction Pinochle is different from two-handed Pinochle. In Auction Pinochle, you have to make a bid, a declaration of how many points you think you'll get, and then you have to score that many points or higher. In each hand, the player who declares the highest bid earns the right to use the cards in the widow to help raise his score.

Beginning with the player at the dealer's left, each player is given the opportunity to bid on the widow—to declare how many points he thinks can be made with the cards in his hand and with those in the widow. A minimum bid is usually 250 points for the first two players, and 290 to 310 for the third and fourth. Raises on the bidding must be made in increments of 10 points (for example, the minimum increase to a bid of 250 is 260, not 255 or 258). All players except the one to the dealer's left may decline to bid, or pass, but if he does so is not allowed to make a bid later in that hand. The player at the dealer's left must bid, however—this is called a compulsory bid. If a player makes a bid, and everyone else passes, then the player making the only bid obviously wins that bid. (Just think of this as an auction.) If everyone declines to bid, then the cards are reshuffled and dealt by the next dealer for another hand.

Once a player has won the bid, he must collect the cards in the widow and turn them faceup on the table for all to see. Looking at the cards in his hand and at those on the table, the winning bidder then has two options: he can elect to play his hand or he can concede the hand and throw in the cards. If the winning bidder realizes that there is no way he is going to be able to score enough points to make his bid with his melds and potential tricks, then he usually folds. When a bidder folds, this is called losing *single bete*. The bidder must pay each of his opponents, and the kitty, a fixed sum according to a schedule (which we will discuss below). On the basis of what they see in the widow, the bidder's opponents can also decide to throw in their cards if they believe the bidder has a very strong hand, but this is rare.

If the bidder is able to make his bid simply with the cards in his hand and the widow, then he lays down his melds for all to see and that hand is over. If the bidder thinks he'll be able to make his bid, but needs more cards to do so, then actual play begins. He first lays down the melds he has and declares what the trump suit will be. He may change his melds and the trump suit any time before he begins playing his cards in tricks.

Now the play begins. The bidder must discard (called burying) three cards (the equivalent of the widow, to make the play even), but he may not discard any card he used to make a meld. As in regular Pinochle, Auction Pinochle proceeds by playing tricks. The bidder leads off by laying down one card, and the other players proceed, from his left, with each laying down a card on top of it. In order to win, a player must lay down a higher card in the leader's suit or a higher trump card. Whoever has the highest card wins that trick, collects the cards, and leads the next round.

When all the tricks have been played, the bidder counts up all the cards in the tricks he won and adds those points to the points in the original melds made before play began. This is his total score, and it must equal or exceed the bid for the bid to be made. If the bidder fails to make his bid, then he is said to lose *double bete,* and the penalty is that he must pay each opponent and the kitty *twice* the amount in the fixed schedule. All of the tricks won by the opponents of the bidder are collected into a single pile.

The Kitty

The kitty is an optional element of play in Auction Pinochle. It refers to a kind of pot, as in Poker, which the players may win under certain conditions. Players pay into the kitty when they lose either single or double bete. The kitty also pays out to the bidder when the players must pay out. Some players say that the kitty neither pays out nor collects on bids less than 340.

Collecting in Auction Pinochle

The way you score or make money in Auction Pinochle is determined by a fixed schedule of values. In other words, each bid between x and y has a unit value associated with it which the bidder either collects, if he makes his bid, or pays out, if he does not. If the bidder makes his bid, then all of the other players, and the kitty (if used), pay him a fixed amount. If he doesn't make his bid, then he must pay each of the other players according to this same schedule. The schedule is written according to fixed units, such as 1 or 2, which can then be set at monetary equivalents. (When the trump suit is spades, then these base values are *dou-*

bled.) In other words, players can agree that the base value is set at $1 or $10 or $100.

Here is the schedule:

Bid	Base Value
300–340	1
350–390	2
400–440	4
450–490	7
500–540	10
550–590	13

Let's say players agree that one unit is worth $1. Obviously, if a bid is 400, and a player concedes defeat before play begins, then he must pay each player and the kitty $4. If he fails to make his bid after playing tricks, and loses double bete, then he must pay each player and the kitty $8. Some players will play that a player who loses double bete with spades trump must pay quadruple value or, in this case, $16 to each player. You can see why Auction Pinochle is popular with hard-core gamblers!

CRIBBAGE

Cribbage has been around, in various forms, for hundreds of years. Sir John Suckling (c. 1609–1642) is generally credited with having invented it. Cribbage is not nearly as popular as Poker or Bridge, but the game does have its hard-core enthusiasts, who enjoy its complicated scoring system and lengthy play. More mathematical than Poker, less complex than Bridge, Cribbage is a game of skill with an element of chance thrown in.

Cribbage is usually played by two people, although there are ways to play with three or four players. The game is played with the standard 52-card deck, but, unlike Poker, the ace is the lowest not the highest card. The face cards are each worth 10 points and all of the other cards are worth their face values.

The Cribbage Board

Players keep score by means of a special Cribbage board (see page 201). It consists of a small rectangular piece of wood approximately six inches wide by one foot long with four rows of thirty small holes that are divided into two rows for each player. At the end of each of the four rows are one or two extra holes to place the pegs before starting. Players have two pegs each, which they use to count out the points they win with each hand. Generally, one player will have dark-colored pegs and the other player will have light-colored pegs. Cribbage boards can be simple pieces of wood, with toothpicks used for pegs, or elaborate works of art with inlaid ivory and ornate carvings.

To win, a Cribbage player must rack up 121 points. A player starts at the bottom of one row of thirty holes, moves up the outer row and back down the one next to it, for a total of 60 points. The player then starts over and starts back up the original row as before. Two trips up and down the rows equal 120 points. The first player to get one point over 120 wins the game. The way a player scores his or her points is by moving one of the two pegs up the row, each hole counting for one point.

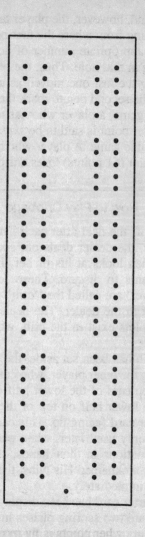

On the next hand, however, the player takes the second peg and, counting from where the first peg now stands, counts off the appropriate number of holes and places the second peg in that hole. Thus, the player alternates the pegs, using the last one moved as a guide to start counting and the second peg to mark the new score. At the end of the game, a player who has not yet reached the three-quarter point is said to be *skunked* or *lurched* and loses a double game. A player who has not reached the halfway point (61 points) loses a triple game.

How to Play Cribbage

Players trade off the deal after each hand. After shuffling the cards, the dealer deals out six cards to each player, who then looks at his or her initial hand and selects two cards to discard. These four cards (two from each player) are called the "crib" and are placed facedown next to the dealer. The dealer gets a bonus of whatever points exist in the crib, which is counted later.

After the crib has been set aside, the dealer then offers the deck to the other player, who cuts it. The dealer turns up the top card of the lower half of the cut deck and places the lower half on top of the top half, with the turned-over card facing up. This card is called the starter and is only used later, when players count the various combinations in their hands. If the card is a jack, however, nicknamed His Nibs, the dealer gets to score 2 points immediately.

After the starter card has been displayed, actual play begins. There are two scoring phases in Cribbage. The first phase occurs when the two players take turns laying down one card at a time from their hands, announcing the sum total of the cards played up to that point, and scoring points for specific combinations using the cards of both players. The second phase occurs after each player has turned over all of his or her cards and the time comes to count up the points from various combinations in each player's hand.

It's a complicated game, no doubt about it. As in Pinochle, there are various phases to each game, and we can look at each phase separately. When play begins, the players alternate turning over the cards in their hands. A player is able to score immediate points by laying down cards that, in combination with what has come before from both himself and his opponent, form certain predetermined groupings somewhat similar to the melds in Gin Rummy or Pinochle. We'll discuss these in a moment. During this first phase, each player counts out the total that his or her new card equals when added to the previous cards. For example, if Player A lays down an eight and Player B then lays down a ten on top of it, Player B announces 18. This continues until a player either has no more cards left or cannot put down a card without the sum total exceeding 31 points. When this occurs, the player says, "Go." If his or her opponent also cannot play a card without the hand exceeding 31 points, then the last person to play a card gets to take, or peg, one point. If the sum total with that previous player's final card was exactly 31 points, he or she gets to peg two points.

The Combinations

In addition to the points for Go, players get to peg points immediately during play whenever the cards they lay down, combined with the previous cards of both players, form certain combinations. These combinations are:

Fifteen—When a player lays down a card that makes a total 15 he or she pegs 2 points. For example, if Player A lays down a seven and Player B lays down an eight on top of it, Player B gets to peg 2 points for 15.

A Pair—When a player lays down a card with the same rank as one just previously laid down, he or she pegs 2 points.

Three of a Kind—If a player lays down a card that makes three of a kind in succession without any other cards in between, he or she scores 6 points.

Four of a Kind—If a player lays down the fourth card in succession of the same rank (such as four sevens), he or she scores 12 points.

Runs or Straights—When a player lays down a card that forms, in combination with those immediately before it, a sequence or straight of three or more cards, he or she pegs 1 point for each card in the sequence (7, 8, 9, for example, is worth 3 points, while 7, 8, 9, 10 is worth 4 points). The order of the cards and the suits is irrelevant in these series. In other words, a sequence such a 10, 7, 8, 9 is a legitimate run worth 4 points.

During the play all the points are pegged as soon as they are earned. Also, the various combinations are cumulative. For example, let's say Player A lays down a six, then Player B lays down a seven, and next Player A lays down an eight. Player A gets to score 2 points for making 15 (the seven and eight), plus an additional 3 points for the run of 6, 7, 8.

Following the play of the hands, the second scoring phase in Cribbage begins. In this phase players count up the combinations that are left in their own hands in combination with the starter card on top of the deck. Each player, with the starter, has five cards. The non-dealer gets to count his or her cards first, a rule that has important implications late in the game when the scoring begins to approach the winning number of 121. In addition to the combinations described above, there are additional combinations available in counting hands. These are:

Flush—If a player has four cards of the same suit, not counting the starter, he or she pegs 4 points. If the starter is also the same suit the player pegs 5 points.

His Nibs—When a player has a jack of the same suit of the starter card, in either a regular hand or in the crib, he or she gets 1 point.

Double Run—A hand with a three-card sequence in which a player has two of one of the cards in the sequence (for example, 6, 7, 8, 8) earns 8 points.

Double Run of Four—A hand with a four-card sequence in which a player has two of one of the cards in the sequence (for example, 6, 7, 8, 8, 9) earns 10 points.

Triple Run—A hand with a three-card sequence in which a player has three of one of the cards in the sequence (for example, 6, 7, 8, 8, 8) earns 15 points.

Double-Double Run—A hand with a three-card sequence in which a player has a pair of two of the cards in the sequence (for example, 6, 7, 7, 8, 8) earns 16 points.

Muggins—An optional rule in Cribbage in which the players agree in advance that if a player overlooks any possible points in a hand, his or her opponent may take those points for himself or herself upon pointing them out. A player simply says, ''Muggins,'' describes the combination the other player missed, and pegs off those points.

Counting cards is notoriously difficult in Cribbage precisely because each card may be used in different combinations. Let us take a look at a typical hand:

This would earn 2 points for the first pair (♦5 and ♣5), 2 points for the second pair (♦5 and ♥5), 2 points for the third pair (♣5 and ♥5), and an additional 6 points for the three of a kind (♦5, ♣5, and ♥5), 2 points for the first five and the ten (♦5 and ♦10), 2 points for the second five and the ten (♣5 and ♦10), 2 points for the third five and the ten (♥5 and ♦10), 2 points for the first five and the king (♦5 and ♦K), 2 points for the second five and the king (♣5 and ♦K), and 2 points for the third five and the king (♥5 and ♦K)—for a grand total of 24 points.

Counting cards in Cribbage is actually an art form with its own protocol. It is the way scoring is done, not a system for winning as in Blackjack. In Cribbage you count cards by announcing the combination you are claiming first and the cumulative total of the hand second. For example, a hand with 5, 5, 8, J, and K would be counted verbally this way: "Fifteen-two" (for the first five and the jack), "fifteen-four" (for the second five and the jack), "fifteen-six" (for the first five and the king), "fifteen-eight" (for the second five and the king), "and a pair makes ten" (for the pair of fives).

After each player has counted his or her hand, the dealer then counts the cards in the crib and gets to take those points as an extra bonus for being the dealer.

After the dealer takes his or her points from the crib, the deck is handed to the other player, reshuffled, and another hand begins.

Strategy for Absolute Beginners

Believe it or not, strategy in Cribbage is simple. A player must carefully consider which cards to discard and place in the crib, depending upon whether he or she is the dealer, and who gets to take the points from the crib. Toward the end of a game, when the points are in the upper nineties, players must begin thinking about preventing each other from making any points that might push the opponent over 120. At this time, the order of counting hands is critical. Remember, the nondealer counts his or her hand first, which has important implications late in the game. For example, a nondealer with a lousy hand will do everything he or she can to prevent the dealer from scoring during play (the first scoring phase) because he or she may be able to win by counting cards first. The dealer's only chance in a tight game is to score enough points during play to win the game because chances are the nondealer will win by counting his or her hand first.

Usually, the way you decide which cards to discard is to simply figure out which four cards yield the highest scoring combinations and discard the two others that don't. However, players frequently will select a less-than-perfect hand to avoid giving the dealer certain powerful, sure-scoring cards. These dangerous cards, quite obviously, are those that easily add up to 15, such as fives, sevens, and eights. Sometimes, they also include sixes and nines. Just as obviously, players usually avoid discarding cards that make up a partial sequence (5, 6), pairs, or a partial flush. You should try to discard cards that are widely separated (for example, a two and a nine).

During actual play a player's goal is to lay down cards that will not allow his or her opponent to score on the next card. This is difficult because you have to lay your cards down eventually (unless a player gets a Go), but the order is everything. For example, if they can players avoid laying down a five or making a pair. If you lead with an ace or a two, three or four, it is impossible for your opponent to score 15. He or she may be able to make a pair, but there is nothing you can do to prevent that.

Sometimes a player can anticipate a sequence and will play a card strategically even if it means allowing his or her opponent to score a few points. For example, let's say Player A lays down a seven, and Player B, thinking ahead, follows that up with an eight for two points. Player A next lays down another seven, which scores 2 points for another 15. But then Player B lays down a six and scores 3 points for a run of three (6, 7, 8). Player A scores a total of 2 points, but Player B scores 5.

It takes a while to get the knack of Cribbage, but once you do you'll almost certainly enjoy it. The circle of Cribbage players is small but loyal, and many a player has been enticed to spend an afternoon with a friend, a Cribbage board, and some cold lemonade.

BRIDGE

Bridge, or Contract Bridge, as it is often called, is one of the most complex of all card games and, like chess, can be almost entirely a game of skill. Any attempt to describe it in a book for beginners must be somewhat inadequate and perhaps even confusing. As most readers know, entire books are dedicated to Contract Bridge strategy and in many newspapers there is a Bridge column daily that details the intricacies of the game. However, the section on Bridge in this book will probably be the simplest, most concise explanation of the game you are likely to encounter.

Modern Bridge evolved from a game called Whist, which itself can be dated to the late seventeenth century and which is still played today. The rules for Contract Bridge as we know it were formalized in the 1920s by a group of American players led by Harold Vanderbilt, a noted industrialist and yachtsman. Today there are two basic forms of Contract Bridge—Rubber Bridge, which utilizes a deal and therefore has an element of chance, and Duplicate Bridge, in which all four players use the same hand, eliminating any element of chance whatsoever.

The complexity of Bridge lies in both the scoring and in the way players predict how their hands will turn out. The actual rules for play can be described rather simply.

In many ways, Bridge is similar to Pinochle, which is why the section on Bridge came after the one on Pinochle. Like Pinochle, Bridge is a game in which both tricks and a trump suit play major roles. As in Pinochle, players attempt to win tricks by playing the highest card in a leading suit or by playing a trump card. The number of tricks a player, or pair of players, wins determines the scoring.

However, what makes Bridge so complicated is that players must predict how many tricks they will win. These predictions, or bids, are what determine the score. Players win so many points for winning tricks over and above the original bid. As in Pinochle, there are also extra points, or premiums, for certain combinations of cards that each player, or side, holds.

The Basic Game

Bridge is played with a standard 52-card deck and the rank of the cards is the same as in Poker (ace high). However, in Contract Bridge the suits are also ranked, with spades highest, followed by hearts, diamonds, and clubs. Usually, the game is played with four people, one pair of partners against the other.

The dealer is determined by cutting or selecting the cards, with the highest card winning, and the deal, the bidding, and the actual play all rotate clockwise from the left of the dealer. The game begins when the dealer deals one card at a time to each player, beginning with the player to his left, until everyone has thirteen cards. Players arrange the cards in their hands by suits, for convenience' sake.

Then the crucial and unique aspect of Bridge, the bidding, begins. Beginning with the player to the dealer's left, each player now must make a call—that is, must either make a bid, pass the bid, or offer to double or redouble a previous bid. A bid is a prediction from a player about how many tricks he or she will win in excess of six as well as a suit that will, if the player wins the bid, become the trump suit. For example, if a player announces "two diamonds," that means that he is predicting that he will win two tricks more than six, or eight total, and that he would name diamonds as the trump suit. A player can also bid no-trump, which means he or she declines to name a suit as trump. A bid of no-trump outranks bids of other suits, so that "three no-trump" is a higher bid than "three diamonds." A player must bid at least one and no more than seven.

Once the first player bids, each player in turn must either beat (raise) that bid, pass, double, or redouble it. To double or redouble does not affect the size of the actual bid, only the number of points that the players earn from a bid. In other words, if a player doubles an opponent's bid of "three diamonds," he is not, therefore, making a bid of "six diamonds." Rather, he is announcing that if his opponent wins the bid, the value of the tricks and penalties will be doubled when the scores are tallied. (I realize this is confusing.) A doubled or redoubled bid of three diamonds can still be beaten by a bid of four diamonds, but if the bid of three diamonds wins, then the value of the points from that bid will be double or redoubled accordingly. As was said above, it is the scoring, not the play, that makes bridge so difficult.

Bidding continues until there have been three passes in succession. Whichever player had the final bid wins what is called the contract—this is why it is called Contract Bridge—and his or her bid determines the game. The player winning the contract is called the Declarer and his partner is called the Dummy. The two opposing players are called the Defenders. If the Declarer named a suit as part of his or her bid, that suit becomes the trump suit.

Play consists of laying down cards, one card from each player, to form a trick of four cards. Whichever player lays down the highest card in the lead suit, or lays down the highest trump card, wins the trick. As in Pinochle, the winner of the previous trick leads the next trick. Players *must* follow suit if they can—meaning that they must lay down a card of the same suit as the one preceding it—but may use any other card in their hand if they cannot. When a player wins a trick, he or she gathers up the four cards and places them facedown on the table. The Declarer gathers up the tricks for his team, and the first defender to win a trick gathers up the tricks for his or her team. These players should arrange the won tricks neatly in stacks of four, and in order of winning, so everyone can see how many tricks have been won by each side.

There is one unusual apsect to Bridge, however, that makes it a little strange: the Dummy does not play his own cards. Rather he spreads the cards faceup on the table, with the cards arranged into suits, and the Declarer plays his cards for him. The Dummy must keep silent—hence, the name—and may not participate in the actual play, although he is permitted to point out an error in the game (such as if the Declarer attempts to play the wrong suit).

When the thirteenth trick—which is the last one—has been played, scoring begins. There are two scores—a trick score and a premium score. Special Bridge scoring sheets are used that divide the scores into the trick score (written below a horizontal line) and the premium score (written above the line). The first side to score 100 points in tricks, or "below the line," wins a game. When a side has won two games, it wins premium points for the rubber (discussed below). Then the two sides compare their overall cumulative points (both premium points and trick points) to determine who won the rubber. Players can then switch partners and start a new round.

When scoring tricks, each side counts up the number of tricks it has won. If the Declarer won the number of tricks he or she predicted in the original bid, then the value in points of those tricks is added to the score. For example, if a Declarer bid two spades, that means that he predicted that he would win two tricks over the required six, or eight total. If the Declarer makes this contract, then he scores 30 points for each of the two tricks over six—or 60 points. Any tricks won by the Declarer over and above his declared contract are called overtricks and earn premium points. When a Declarer wins fewer tricks than he predicted in the contract then his opponents score what are called undertrick premiums for each trick below the required number.

In addition to these points scored for the contract tricks, there are a number of premium points that may be scored—slams and rubbers. A slam is the extra points that a side wins if it bids a contract of six tricks and makes them. If the contract is for seven tricks, and a side makes them, then it wins a grand slam (which is the origin of the expression "grand slam"). A rubber means a side has won two games and gets an extra number of points for that (500 points if its opponents have won one game, 750 if they have not). A side is said to be vulnerable if it has won one game toward its rubber. A side is vulnerable because it can be subject to increased undertrick penalties, although it can also win extra points, if vulnerable, if it wins a slam or grand slam. For example, a vulnerable side wins 750 points for a slam, but only 500 points if it is not vulnerable. Finally, there are premium points for honors (A, K, Q, J, and 10 in a trump suit)—sides winning 100 points for holding four of the five honor cards, 150 points for all five.

As mentioned above, there is not sufficient room here to go into all of the complexities of scoring Contract Bridge. Here is a brief table of the scoring, however, to give you some idea of what it is like:

Scoring Tricks

	Points if trump suit is:			
Each Trick over Six	♣	♦	♥	♠
Regular Bid	20	20	30	30
Doubled	40	40	60	60
Redoubled	80	80	120	120

No-Trump Hands

	First Trick Over 6	Each Additional trick
Regular	40	30
Doubled	80	60
Redoubled	160	120

Bidding Strategy

The real strategy in Bridge lies not in the actual play itself but in the bidding—that is, in the subtle hints that players give to one another by the way in which they bid. Over the years there have developed certain conventions that allow players to signal to each other which cards they have in their hands. Players also calculate how they will bid according to which cards they have in their hands. A number of complex evaluation systems have been created that allow players to calculate precisely the value of the cards they are holding and what, therefore, they should bid and counterbid. The system most common today is called the Goren system, named after Charles Goren, in which an ace is worth 4 points, a king 3 points, a queen 2 points, and a jack 1 point. The other cards are worth no points. With 40 points in all available in all hands, a side usually must hold 26 points to win a game. Players add up the points in their hands and then signal to their partners, by their bidding, what they have. These signals or conventions must be learned by every player, which is why it takes so long to learn how to play Bridge. For example, one convention, called the Stayman Convention, is a way of bidding that asks a player's partner to bid a four-card major suit (spades or hearts) after the opener has bid one no-trump. Another convention, the Blackwood Convention, which is a bid of four no-trump, is used simply to ask a player's partner how many aces he has in his hand. The partner's response—five clubs means no aces or four aces, five diamonds means one ace, etc.—tells how many aces he has.

As a result, Bridge is frequently a game in which players go around and around making bids and counterbids, the only purpose of which is for partners to gradually tell each other what cards they are holding. The actual play is, in a sense, anticlimactic, although numerous legitimate signals are used. For example, if a player leads a trick and a partner follows that up with a six or higher, that is often a signal from the partner to the opener to continue playing that suit. A card lower than a six is a signal not to continue with that suit.

There is no way to explain all of these conventions and signals here, however, and all we can do is to recommend that interested players purchase one of the hundreds of books on Contract Bridge that go into more detail.

It takes a certain kind of person to play Bridge—someone with the mind of a chess master combined with the cool nerves of a Poker player. It is no accident that there are championship Bridge tournaments and that the best players achieve a status that's not exactly on a par with world chess masters, but which certainly comes close. Because of the partnership nature of Bridge, many husbands and wives take up the game and become amazingly good at telegraphing their hands to each other. Anyone wishing to learn the game should read a few books on Bridge and then inquire at local community colleges for adult education classes on the game. One may also call the entertainment editor at the local newspaper and ask about Bridge clubs.

Just as with chess, Bridge can be played for a lifetime without ever getting boring. And, as in chess, there is such a wide variety of skill levels, every player can find opponents on the same general plane.

How to Bet on Horse Racing if You've Never Been to the Track

Any gambler who knows anything about sports has a favorite parlor trick to pull on all the armchair quarterbacks and dedicated baseball fans in the United States or Canada. The gambler asks the sports fan if he or she knows which is the biggest spectator sport in North America. Almost invariably, the sports fan will insist it is professional football or baseball or, if a Canadian, hockey. The gambler just smiles. The answer is none of those. It's horse racing.

Each year more than 100 million people flock to thoroughbred horse racing at 56 tracks in the United States for a total of 5,695 days of racing. The largest of the racing tracks, such as the one at Santa Anita in Arcadia, California, will attract as many as 30,000 people *each day*. In comparison, a football team might have 50,000 fans at a home game every third weekend. Tracks see a lot of money as well: the average amount of money bet at a track such as Santa Anita is $200 per person per day.

Although the betting arrangements are primarily the same for all horse racing, there are three basic forms of racing today that involve gambling. The most well known is thoroughbred racing, in which a rider, or jockey, rides a thoroughbred horse around the track. A thoroughbred horse, the fastest and most elite of horses, differs from a standardbred horse in its overall structure, being generally taller with a shorter body and leaner legs. A second type of racing, much like thoroughbred racing, is a quarter horse race. Quarter horses are a distinct breed that have been bred especially for the short, one-quarter-mile races (actually between 200 to 600 yards) from which they get their name. In a quarter horse race, a jockey rides on the horse's back, but the race is so short it is run on a straightaway and at full speed. Often the results, measured in hundredths of a second, can only be determined by photographic examination. A third, increasingly popular form of racing is harness racing, in which standardbred horses are attached to a special two-wheeled cart, called a sulky, in which a driver sits riding behind the horse. Unlike thoroughbred or quarter horse racing, harness racing requires that the horses maintain a specific gait—either pacing or trotting. In this chapter we will discuss thoroughbred racing because it is the most common form of horse racing, and the betting principles of thoroughbred racing apply to harness and quarter horse racing as well.

The great advantage of horse racing over other forms

of gambling is that it is perfectly legal in almost all of the U.S. and in most countries, even in those that ban most other forms of gambling. There are historical reasons for why this is so. Human beings have been racing horses and betting on the outcome for at least five thousand years. Anyone who has seen the film *Ben-Hur* can imagine the ancient Romans betting on chariot races—which are merely the ancient equivalent of modern-day harness races. North American Indians also were dedicated horse-racing fans long before the colonists built tracks in North America in the 1660s.

In the U.S. and in Europe, gambling on horse racing has been made much easier through the illegal bookie and the legal institution of off-track betting (OTB) establishments. Because work and family obligations often made it difficult or impossible for ordinary people to go to the track, these two inventions served the betting needs of horse players. By the late 1940s, some gambling historians estimate that there were well over 250,000 illegal bookies operating in the United States alone with another half million employees—runners, accountants, and collectors—working to collect some $18 billion in horse-racing bets. The bookies were able to work through the establishment of what were called wire services, telegraph systems run by gangsters such as Benjamin "Bugsy" Siegel, that provided information about all of the races in the U.S. Bookies would get together to service an entire neighborhood and share the cost of a wire service subscription, which could be between $300 and $500 per week. With the gangland assassination of Bugsy Siegel in 1947, there was a nationwide crackdown on gambling that led to the famed Kefauver Commission in 1951–53. While

Kefauver did not succeed in elminating bookies in America, technology and a few federal laws eventually did in the wire services.

The establishment of completely legal off-track betting (OTB) shops took away some, but not all, of the betting action from ordinary bookies. These are just what they sound like—places where horse players can make and collect their bets on races in various parts of the country. Most OTBs feature video monitors and electronic posting machines that display the official results.

Dedicated horse players like to claim that betting on horses, unlike most other forms of gambling, is purely a matter of skill. With knowledge and discipline, they say, the talented few can overcome the odds and win consistently. This is possible because horse players are not betting against the house but, rather, betting against one another.

It is true that the track itself, the "house," is completely indifferent as to which horse wins or loses. In a way similar to Poker games in Las Vegas, the house merely collects a fixed take of 17 percent from the betting pool no matter who wins, which it shares with the state.

And it is true that the dedicated horse player is betting against the vast majority of casual fans, who spend a day at the track more for recreation and fun than to win money. The informed player, who takes the time to study the individual horses and races, can have a slight betting advantage over the vast majority of unprepared recreational racing spectators.

The bad news is that whatever small advantage the experienced horse player has—that is, someone who studies the *Racing Form* every day—is more than made up for by the structural disadvantages built into legalized horse betting. It is extremely difficult to win consistently at the races. This is because, even if the horse player has a superhuman amount of patience, self-discipline, and knowledge, he or she is still facing an almost unbelievably high tax burden. Most state governments collect between 17 and 25 percent of each and every dollar won at the track, depending on the type of bet. Thus, a horse player has to make at least 20 percent on every dollar wagered just to break even. What's more, there is an additional 2 percent lost on every dollar won that is called breakage, or the rounding off of winnings to the lowest dime, which the track collects. If you win $4.58 at the track, the cashier will only give you $4.50. The track keeps the difference. And if you place your bets at the legal OTB establishments, instead of with your favorite bookie, you have to pay even more for the privilege—an *additional* 5 percent.

It's quite possible, therefore, for horse players to have to give up a staggering 32 percent of their winnings in some states on some bets.

When track betting is compared to, say, the 1.5 percent house advantage in Bacarrat—with no taxes collected at all unless the winnings are really large—you can understand why so many seasoned gamblers prefer to lose their money in the casinos instead of at the racetrack.

A note about dog racing. Dog racing is very similar to thoroughbred horse racing because both use the parimutuel betting system discussed in the next section. Although each dog track is different, many also have the same types of bets found at horse tracks—Win, Place, and Show as well as the Exactas, Quinellas, Pick

Three, Pick Six, and so on (we'll discuss those in a moment). The primary differences between dog racing and horse racing, of course, are that dog racing makes use of the mechanical rabbit to lead the dogs around the track and the dogs do not have any riders; dog racing is easier to organize; it is usually held at night under the lights; it is much quicker; and there are often more races. Also, dog racing is not found in some states that permit thoroughbred horse racing.

The Pari-Mutuel Betting System

The backbone of contemporary horse racing is the "pari-mutuel betting system." Some experts on gambling, such as the late John Scarne, believe that the word *pari-mutuel* came from Paris Mutuel, because the pari-mutuel system was invented in Paris in the 1850s. Actually, though, pari-mutuel comes from the French words *pari,* for bet or equalize, and *mutuel,* for mutual. It is a betting system in which those backing the winners in a race divide, in proportion to their wagers, the total amount bet minus a fixed percentage that goes to the track operators.

The origins of the pari-mutuel system actually date back to the auction pools used for betting on horses in the United States. Eventually, though, a man named Pierre Oller invented a system that calculated the true payoff odds on a horse based on the amount of money actually bet on it. Before that, hapless bookies and other promoters had to figure out their own odds, and the possibility of corruption was great. Obviously, bettors placing a five-dollar bet on an old nag expected to receive better odds on that horse, which was a long shot to win, than he or she would when betting on a champion thoroughbred. The pari-mutuel system, as Oller conceived it, eliminated all of the ad hoc odds and gave a mathematical precision to betting.

The pari-mutuel is a fairly straightforward system, but it takes most absolute beginners a while to get used to it. The bets on each race are divided into three pools, "Win, Place, and Show." Place means second place and show means third place. The bets are divided into two-dollar segments or units, with the track rounding off, as we have seen, to the lowest dime. If you technically win $6.88, the track will pay only $6.80, keeping the eight cents for itself.

The number and distribution of two-dollar bets determine how the total amount of each pool is divided up. If a horse has $4 total bet on it by two players, and it wins, then the two players would divide up the entire pot bet on all of the horses in that pool, less the track's cut. For example, let's say that a horse has a total of $16 bet on it and it wins. Stephanie bet $2 but her sister Susan bet $14. What happens is that Stephanie receives one eighth of the total amount bet on all the horses because she had bet on eighth of the total, and Susan gets seven-eighths less the track's commission.

It sounds a lot more complicated than it is. Let's look at it another way. Let's say there is $100 in the Win pool. As we've seen, the track gets its 17 percent, or $17, right off the top, so in reality there is only $83 left. A horse named Spitting Image has a total of $40 bet on it to win by two players placing a twenty-dollar bet each. The rest of the money in the Win pool, $43, comes from bets to win placed by numerous people on the five other horses in the race. Now if Spitting Image wins then the two players split the entire pot of $43 contributed by the losing players plus their original $40. In other words, they receive $41.50 each on a twenty-dollar bet. Even if the two winners had only bet $2 each on Spitting Image, they would still divide the $43 equally. In this scenario they would receive 20 times return on their money instead of merely doubling it.

What you have to remember is that the pool of money is divided among the winners according to how much money they bet on the correct horse. Put simply, the winners divide all of the money contributed by the losers, less the track's take, plus they get their original bets back. That is how people can win big at the track on long shots.

If you and four other people place small bets on a long shot, and thousands of other people bet on other, more favored horses, and your horse wins, then you and the four other smart people divide all the money in the pool that came from the thousands of other people who bet on other horses.

It is the possibility of making big money on small bets that makes horse racing so addictive. Shrewd, dedicated horse players can occasionally outfox the masses and win big. This is because, as we noted earlier, you're not betting against the house but against all of your fellow bettors.

Each of the betting pools is separate, divided into the total amount of money bet on each horse. The mathematics involved is complicated because it is not merely the total amount of money bet on each horse that matters but also how many people made the bets. Obviously, if there is a total of $50,000 bet on a horse that wins, it makes a difference if one person placed it or 50 people. If a single person placed it, and the horse wins, then that one person gets the entire pool. If 50 people each placed $1,000 on the horse, then those 50 will divide up equally the total pool.

The way you figure out how much money has been bet on a given horse is by reading what is called a "tote board." The tote board shows the total amounts bet on each horse in each of the betting pools—Win, Place, and Show. Most of the time, the favorite horse to win, the one with the most money riding on it, will also have the greatest amount of money bet on it in the Place and Show pools. This is usually true, but not always.

A tote board displays a tremendous amount of information, including the race number, the condition of the track (e.g., "fast"), and the amount of money bet in each of the Win, Place, and Show pools. It also displays the total, and the so-called morning line odds on each horse, as well as the actual odds based on the wagers placed so far.

Each day, the track experts publish in a variety of publications what is called the "morning line." This consists of predictions of track experts about how each of the various horses will perform in each race. The morning line can, and frequently does, vary dramatically from the official odds on the tote board, which reflect the actual betting up to the minute. The real odds on each horse result from a rapid calculation, made by sophisticated computers, of the total amount of money bet in the pool. The tote board shows the real up-to-the-minute bets that are laid down. These are the official odds. The morning line, in contrast, is the experts' guesses.

A tote board's odds will look like this:

1.	8	7.	8–5
2.	35	8.	9–5
3.	9–2	9.	10
4.	10	10.	12
5.	15	11.	30
6.	5–2	12.	25

Each horse has a number, and by looking up the horse's number in the track program, you can tell what the official odds, or real bets, are on that horse.

In the above list the examples with just one number, such as 10, is shorthand for 10 to 1. The Number 1 horse has odds of eight to one—which means that if this horse wins, the winners will get back eight times their bet plus their original wager. Thus, the track will pay $40 back on an original five-dollar bet plus the $5. Horse Number 7, with odds of 8 to 5, will pay back $8 plus the original five-dollar bet for a total of $14. Obviously, the racing fans believe that horse Number 7 is considered more likely to win than horse Number 1.

Just as in most forms of gambling, however, the bets can be more complicated than simply betting on a single outcome. It is possible, for example, to place a bet on a horse "across the board," which means that you are betting on it to win, place, or show (come in first, second, or third). Obviously, if the horse wins, you get more money than if it merely places. For example, let us say Horse A goes off at odds of 4.45 to 1 and wins. On a two-dollar bet, a fan would win $10.90 for win, $4.30 for place, and another $2.80 for show—or a total of $18. If the horse only places, the fan would win

$4.30 plus $2.80, or $7.10. If the horse only shows, the fan would win just $2.80. The reason why the place and show pools pay off so much less is because the place pool must be divided between two horses. The winner pool is not divided.

The Morning Line

The morning line, as we have discussed, is the unofficial guide found in every track program of how the experts guess the various horses will perform. It predicts what the real odds will end up being on the tote board. The morning line does not rate how the horses will actually perform, however; it simply predicts how the racing fans will place their bets. That is an important point to remember. There is a major difference between predicting which horse will actually win and which horse the fans think, rightly or wrongly, will win.

Many horse players put too much faith in the morning line. It only reflects what one person, or a group of persons, believes the betting will be like.

This is what a typical morning line looks like:

Fourth Race	Morning Line
1. Tiny Dancer	6–1
2. Welcome Back	7–2
3. Dreamer	4–1
4. Wild One	9–5
5. Sugar and Spice	2–1

Obviously, this means that the track's resident experts believe that most of the money in the Fourth Race will be on Wild One, which, if the horse wins, will pay $9 on a five-dollar bet. The numbers in both the morning line and on the tote board are rounded off, which means that the payoffs can be greater than you might expect. For example, odds of 7–1 could actually be 7.2 to 1, so the track would pay $14.40 on a two-dollar bet, not just $14.00.

Of course, the people who prepare the morning line work for the track. This means that they have a built-in incentive to have the odds appear favorable, so people will bet more. It also means that, when you add up the odds, they amount to 120 percent or more. This reflects the extra 20 percent take of the track and the breakage.

How to Place a Bet

Betting on horse races is not a particularly complicated thing to do in and of itself, but choosing which horse to bet on, and how the horse will perform, is actually quite complicated. The horse player is confronted with a bewildering number of choices on how to place a bet. In the past a horse player's choices were much more limited. He or she was only allowed to bet on a horse to win, place, or show—with the occasional Daily Double. Today, however, the tracks have followed a trend similar to the state lotteries and have created a host of new, exotic bets with names such as Exactas, Triples, Pick Sixes, and so on. We'll discuss each of these briefly, but for the time being most absolute beginners should focus on the basics of betting, what is known as "straight betting."

The reason why a player wins so much more money on a win is because he or she only wins money if the horse wins. In contrast, if a player bets on a horse to show, he or she has three chances to collect. In such a case, the bet is that the horse will at least *show*—that is, be among the first three horses to cross the finish line. If the horse wins or places, the player also collects. Many people, not understanding this elementary principle of horse racing, *actually throw away winning tickets* because they believe, wrongly, that their horse didn't win when it placed instead of showed. There is a type of racetrack scavenger who spends his or her time looking on the ground for discarded winning tickets.

So, the question becomes: how do you know which way you should bet on a horse? The answer depends upon the amount of money already wagered in each of the pools and, more importantly, your own guess as to how the horse will perform. Often, it makes more sense to bet on a horse to place rather than to win. The statistical analysts and other experts have proven that favorites win only 35 percent of all races but place 53 percent of the time. Horses with odds of 9 to 2 or less are often considered prospects for place betting, but you should only make this bet if you, too, believe the horse has a good chance of winning. As we said, if the horse wins or places second, you collect. On the other hand, horses with high odds, more than 5 to 1, should usually be bet on to win. This is because the payoffs are so high and the prices so small. Once again, though, you should only bet on a horse if, in your judgment or in the judgment of some expert you trust, the horse has a good chance to win.

As in Craps, most absolute beginners have a hard time figuring out how much money they will actually win with a given set of odds. The best way, of course, is simply to look at the monitors at the track, which announce what the payoff is on a given horse in a given race. You can also figure out the payoffs by applying some simple arithmetic.

First, you have to know how to read posted odds. The first number always refers to how much money is won if the second number were, in fact, bet. For example, a horse with 2 to 5 odds means that if you bet $5, and the horse won, you would win $2 plus your original $5 back, or a total of $7. To figure out how much you would win on a two-dollar bet, you have to do some elementary proportional arithmetic. You're comparing 2:5 versus X:2, so you multiply the first number in the first proportion by the second number in the second proportion and then divide the result by the second number in the first proportion. In other words, you multiply 2 times 2 and divide by 5. The result is $0.80, which would be your profit on a two-dollar bet. On such a bet with 2 to 5 odds, you'd collect a total of $2.80.

Here is what a typical payoff chart would look like on a series of two-dollar bets with various odds:

1–5	$2.40	8–5	$5.20
2–5	$2.80	9–5	$5.60
1–2	$3.00	2–1	$6.00
3–5	$3.20	5–2	$7.00
4–5	$3.60	3–1	$8.00
1–1	$4.00	7–2	$9.00
6–5	$4.40	4–1	$10.00
7–5	$4.80	9–2	$11.00
3–2	$5.00	5–1	$12.00

Now, as we mentioned, there are bets other than simple straight bets for Win, Place, or Show. "The Daily Double" (DD), for example, is a bet in which you attempt to pick the winners of the first and second race of the day. Another bet is called the "Exacta," in which you bet on the precise outcome of a particular race. You bet that you can pick which two horses will finish first and second respectively. A "Quinella" bet is made when you wager that two horses will come in first and second, but you don't have to pick which one will actually win. As long as your two horses win or place, you win your bet. A "Triple" bet involves betting on the exact horses to win, place, and show. With a "Pick Six" bet, you bet on the winners of six races. Because of the difficulty of picking either the top three horses in a given race, or the winners of six races in a row, these two types of bets have tremendously high odds and tremendously high payoffs. The odds on a Pick Six bet can range between 100 to 1 to 500 to 1. That means on a two-dollar bet, you could win $202 for the 100 to 1 odds and $1,002 for the 500 to 1 odds.

How to Read the *Racing Form*

The ultimate source of most information about horse racing is the *Daily Racing Form,* a tabloid newspaper that sells for $3.00 per copy and well over two thousand dollars for a year's subscription. The paper is available in regional editions published all over the country and is found in liquor stores or at the racetrack. Individuals can order subscriptions by calling the newspaper's offices in Hightstown, New Jersey (Tel. 609-448-9100).

The paper is chock-full of articles by racing columnists and news stories about the various races run the previous day. However, most people buy the *Racing Form* for the detailed information it provides about the past racing performance of each horse. Each of the regional editions features information about all the horses racing on all the tracks in that region. The Los Angeles edition, for example, carries information about all the horses and races at Santa Anita, Los Alamitos, Del Mar, Golden Gate Fields, and so on.

How to Read the *Daily Racing Form* Past Performance Results

Following the news stories and the columns, there is a lengthy summary on The Handicapper's Page of all of the races that will be run that day at each local track, along with the morning line odds for each race (see Fig. 7-1). The amount of information is staggering: The horse's name, country of origin, owner, jockey, color, sex and age, month of foaling, the sire's name, the dam's sire, the breed, state of foaling, the trainer with his record at the meet, the medication allowed and weight to be carried, the horse's lifetime record as well as his race results for the current and prior year, the total claiming prize, all of the data from recent races, and so on. Above each horse's individual data are the specifications of the race. For example, one race might read: 350 yards, Quarter Horse Claiming, Purse $4,700, 3-year-olds. Weight, 122 pounds. Another race will be entirely different: 6 Furlongs. Arabian Maiden Claiming. Purse $2,700. 3-year-olds and upwards. Weights: 3-year-olds, 117 pounds. Older, 120 pounds.

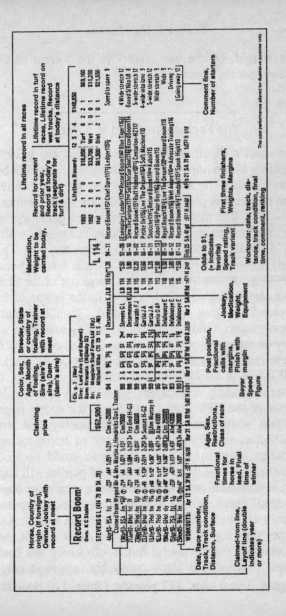

The weight, by the way, refers to the weight of the jockey, not the horse.

The Factors Involved in a Race

The most difficult aspect of gambling at the track is deciding which horse to bet on. What's an absolute beginner to do? The first thing to do, as we stated above, is to realize that playing the ponies is a losing proposition. It is, like most forms of organized gambling, an exciting way to spend the afternoon but one in which the odds are tremendously stacked against you. That said, however, the second thing an absolute beginner should do, if unwilling to pick a horse out of the blue, is to consult the so-called experts. In the jargon of the racetrack, picking horses is called "handicapping." Horse players handicap horses according to a wide variety of factors. Some look at the current condition of the horses, others at their recent speeds on the tracks, still others at which class the horses are racing in. In some large daily newspapers, such as the *Los Angeles Times* or the New York *Daily News,* the sports pages contain some handicapping information. Also, the *Daily Racing Form,* the newspaper of horse racing, contains more information than you could possibly want or digest on what all the experts predict will happen in each race. And, to make matters even more complicated, there are innumerable freelance experts, known as touts, who sell illegal tip sheets with lists of horses they say will win, place, or show. All of this information can be useful but is obviously not foolproof. There are so many intangible factors in horse racing—from the type and length of a race and the condition of a horse on a certain day to the condition of the track—that few experts are right even most of the time.

Most absolute beginners are unaware that in handicapped races the track's official handicappers actually require the horses to carry extra weight of a few pounds—in addition, of course, to the weight of the jockey—for each of their most recent wins. This extra weight is supposed to equalize the racing field so that each horse has a good chance of winning. Weight is also sometimes taken off a horse for a variety of reasons—including the use of a novice jockey, a lower asking price in a claiming race, and so on.

The first factor in picking a horse, therefore, is knowing which type of race the horses are running in. The most competitive and the most difficult race to bet on is called a "stakes race." In this race, usually run on the weekends, the horses are considered to be about equal in size, strength, and age. The second most competitive race is called a "handicapped race." The third most competitive race is an "allowance race." The fourth is called a "claiming race" and refers to the fact that prospective owners bid on, or "claim," the horses before the race. The least competitive race is called a "maiden claiming race"—this is for two-year-old thoroughbreds which have never won a race. Obviously, it's harder to pick a horse when none in the field has ever won. A maiden claiming race means that prospective owners "claim" a maiden horse by putting a bid to buy the horse before the race. Another category is "maiden special weights races," which divides the races according to the horses' weights. These various race classifications determine the size of the purses, the money the owners collect if their horse wins, which varies substantially.

Besides the different race classifications, races are also divided according to the ages of the horses—two-year-olds, three-year-olds, four-year-olds, or five-year-olds and up. Finally, in addition to the race classifications and the ages of the horses, there is the length of the race to consider. The lengths are: half mile, six furlongs, one mile, one mile and a quarter, one mile and a half, and two miles. It sometimes happens that a race has further conditions. For example, the race might be for three-year-olds which have never won two races.

Picking Horses

Horse players must take into account all of this information described above—the type of race, the condition of the track, the length of the race—when making their picks. It is very, very difficult, which is why, of course, most people lose at the track. This does not, however, prevent horse players from learning all they can about the various horses and continuing to bet.

If you have the time, therefore, and a little extra money to risk, you can take a stab at making your own picks. This is how various horse-racing experts advise beginners to pick horses. First, you should get yourself some old issues of the *Daily Racing Form*. Next, you have to classify all of the various horses by writing down the final odds of every favorite in every race over the past year. You divide these horses into four basic categories:

1. Odds-on favorites (less than even money)
2. Even money to 7–5 favorites
3. 2–1 to 5–2
4. All favorites above 5–2

Your next step is to further divide the above categories into the types of races—claiming, maiden, allowance, handicap, and stakes. Finally, you should try to calculate which percentage of favorites won in each type of race, by dividing them according to the four categories. When you finally go to the track, therefore, your job will be to discover which horses are the morning line favorites for the first three positions in each race and then you compare these race day favorites with your own historical information. What you're trying to do is to locate the favorites that won most of the time in each type of race and which are also the favorites in the morning line. You should try to pay particular attention to the odds for each type of race. In other words, figure out which group of favorites in the four categories won most of the time. Odds-on? Even money to 7–5? Find a pattern, if you can, and then try to find a morning line favorite that seems to fit that pattern.

Once you've used this system to identify some possible winners, you then must look up some more information about these horses in the *Racing Form*. For example, do your picks do well on slow tracks? Do they do well in claiming races but fade in allowance races? There is more than enough information on each horse available at the track. Track programs will tell you everything you could possibly want to know about a horse, including how many times it has run that year, its total earnings, and so on.

With all of this past and current information, you will then try to make an informed guess as to how your picks might perform. Unfortunately, you'll end up losing anyway—because there will always be other intangible factors involved, such as a particular horse's sore muscle or indigestion, which will influence the race's outcome—but at least you'll have had some fun.

Off-Track Betting (OTB)

By the early 1980s, many states legalized the establishment of what are called Off-Track Betting (OTB) locations that allow horse players to make bets long-distance for races all across the country. These establishments are also known in the trade as racing books. OTB parlors have programs that list all of the races in America as well as all of the horses. Beside each horse in the program is something called a post number, ranging from one up into the thousands. These post numbers vary according to the region of the country, but the idea is that there is just one post number for each horse for each race. For example, a horse running in the fifth race at Santa Anita might have a post number of 810. When you place a bet on that horse, you go up to the cashier window and say that you'd like to bet $10 to place on number 810. Just by the post number, the system is able to know which race the horse is in and what the current odds are.

The Racetrack and Systems

Sooner or later dedicated horse players, like all other gamblers, inevitably start to think about developing a system. Many use the classic Martindale or so-called progressive system, in which the player bets double his previous bet if he loses. As we saw in the introduction, the idea with this system is that, as the favorite horse wins between 35 and 37 percent of the time, the player will eventually win—and, because the amounts he wagers keep getting higher and higher, he will win big. A popular variation on a systems approach to betting favorites is to bet second choices to win—but, as second choices win only 18 percent of the time, the possibility of hitting a losing streak is even greater than when betting on favorites to win. A more promising method is to bet on horses to show because, historically, favorites show a little more than 50 percent of the time. The problem with this, however, is that the odds are so low on the favorites that a player doesn't make much money—he might make 20 cents on a two-dollar bet. With those odds, you have to bet $2,000 to make $200—and there is nearly a 50 percent chance that you'll lose the $2,000 and have to put up another $2,000, and then another, in order to win. As in any system, this system works great if you win consistently. But, if you hit a losing streak, you can rack up major losses very quickly.

Remember, in the long run all systems fail because the amounts you must bet quickly become so large that the average player cannot or will not sustain the increasingly high bets. A penny doubled in a progressive system becomes $1 million in just 30 turns. Not many people can keep risking upwards of $500, $800, or $1,000 to make, if they're lucky, $50.

Smart Money on Horses

So, what is the absolute beginner to make of all this? Is it possible to win at the track? The short answer is: Of course! Because players bet against one another and not against the house, shrewd, dedicated horse players, who study all of the historical data on the horses and jockeys, can occasionally pick winners. They can sometimes even beat the regular odds.

But the real question we face is whether you, an absolute beginner, who undoubtedly lack the time and interest to do this kind of exhaustive research, can win. That answer is: No, not consistently. Betting on horses for most fans is roughly the equivalent of betting on a slot machine. If you win, it's pure luck.

As a result, you should view horse racing as a form of recreation. The best advice is simply to keep your bets small, study the *Racing Form,* and make your picks as best you can. Stay away from systems of any kind and rely on your own judgment or on the judgment of a handicapper you like. Horse racing can be enormously fun, and there is a small element of scientific calculation about it. This is what makes it so exciting and challenging. But absolute beginners should view the horse track as they would a college football game, learn what you can, place bets on your favorites, and remember that, at least on your level, it is purely a game of chance. Look at it as a fun way to spend the day, not as an investment.

A Final Word

A final word about gambling in general and gambling for absolute beginners in particular. There is no doubt that gambling as an institution still has a bad reputation. Despite its rising popularity in the last quarter of the twentieth century, many well-meaning people still see gambling as a vice to be discouraged, with little or no redeeming social value. While there is no doubt that gambling, like alcohol, can be addictive for some people and can even ruin entire lives, for the vast majority of casual gamblers it is simply a form of recreation. Unlike television or even films, in which people sit passively in front of a screen and do nothing but stare, gambling at its best is a highly social activity. Card players, especially, are a naturally gregarious, usually friendly lot, the kind of people who would rather pass an evening chitchatting about life over a Cribbage board than sit at home watching the latest TV sitcom. The Friday night Poker game, in my opinion, is one of most enjoyable and cost-effective ways available to spend an evening with friends.

For gambling to be enjoyable, however, you have to

know how to keep it in perspective. As we stated at the outset of this book, gambling is recreation, not a way to make money. Except for the rare professional gambler, most people will, over the long term, lose money while gambling. It's a mathematical certainty. Anyone who wants to enjoy himself while learning how to gamble, therefore, has to view it as a leisure activity for which he or she must pay at least some, but hopefully not too much, money. When gambling starts to be more painful than pleasurable, it is obviously time to stop. As stated in the introduction, the smart gambler knows when to quit both when winning, and, just as importantly, when losing.

The key to success at any form of gambling, then, is to realize from the start that the odds are quite literally against you. But by following the tips outlined in this book, you can minimize these odds by avoiding dumb plays, knowing the correct odds for each game, staying away from systems, and betting with your head, not your instincts. You can take advantage of the science of probability theory by not drawing to an inside straight in Poker, avoiding field bets in Craps, never standing pat on a soft 17 and only playing Roulette when you have money to throw away.

Most important of all, you should have fun. Let's face it: people gamble because it's fun. It's thrilling to risk a little money in the hope that you can win enough money to, say, have a nice dinner for two. So when you venture out and begin gambling, remember that the purpose of the exercise is to have fun.

Relax, enjoy yourself . . . and good luck.

Appendix

DIRECTORY OF CASINOS, CARD HOUSES, AND RACETRACKS IN NORTH AMERICA AND THE CARIBBEAN

ABBREVIATIONS: Entertainment—Lounge Music (LM), Floor Show (FS), Dinner Show (DS), Adults Only (AO), Family Entertainment (FE), Children (CH). **Gaming**—Blackjack (B), Poker (P), Slot Machines (SM), Craps (C), Roulette (R), Keno (K), Bacarrat (Bac), Sports Book (SB), Race Book (RB), Video Gaming (VG), Video Poker (VP), Bingo (BI).

ALABAMA

Legal Staus: *Gambling restricted to Charitable Games, Horse/Dog Racing, and Class II gaming, which consists of Bingo, but no other casino-style games are included in this state's Indian Reservation Gaming Operations.*

Birmingham Race Course, 1000 John Rogers Dr., Birmingham, AL 35210. Tel. (205) 328-7223. Dog, harness, and thoroughbred racing.

Green Tracks, I-59 & 20, Exit 45 Union Rd., Eutaw, AL 35462; Tel. (205) 372-9318. Dog racing.

Mobile Greyhound Park, 7101 Old Pascagoula, Theodore, AL 36582. Tel. (205) 653-5000. Dog racing.

Victory Land, I-85, Exit 22, Shorter, AL 36075. Tel. (205) 727-0540. Dog racing.

ALASKA

Legal Status: *Gambling restricted to Charitable Games only.*

ARIZONA

Legal Status: *Gambling restricted to Charitable Games, Horse/Dog Racing, the Lottery, and Indian Reservation Gaming Operations.*

HORSE/DOG RACETRACKS

Prescott Downs, 1828 Rodeo Dr., Prescott, AZ 86301; Tel. (602) 257-9233. Horse racing in the summer. Thoroughbred racing.

Rillito Race Track, 4502 N. 1st. Ave., Tucson, AZ 85728; Tel. (602) 293-5011. Horse racing. Thoroughbred and quarter horse racing.

Turf Paradise, 1501 Bell Rd., Phoenix, AZ 85023; Tel. (602) 942-1101. Thoroughbred racing.

Apache Greyhound Park, 2551 W. Apache Trail, Apache Junction, AZ 85220; Tel. (602) 982-2371. Dog racing.

Phoenix Greyhound Park, 3801 E. Washington St., Phoenix, AZ 85036; Tel. (602) 273-7181. Dog racing.

Tuscon Greyhound Park, 2601 S. Third Ave., Tucson, AZ 85713; Tel. (602) 884-7576. Dog racing.

Yuma Greyhound Park, 4000 S. 4th Ave., Yuma, AZ 85366; Tel. (602) 726-4655. Dog racing.

INDIAN RESERVATION GAMBLING

Harrah's Ak-Chin Casino, 7304 W. Chicago, Chandler, AZ 85226; Tel. (602) 802-5000. Gaming: B, P, K, SM.

Cocopah Bingo, 15364 S. Ave. B, Somerton, AZ 85350; Tel. (602) 726-8066, Gaming: BI.

Fort McDowell, Route 87, Fountain Hills, AZ 85269; Tel. (602) 837-1424. Gaming: BI, SM, VG, B.

Gila River Gaming Operation, 1201 S. 56th St., Chandler, AZ 85226; Tel. (800) 946-4452. Gaming: VP, SM.

The Arizona Club & Yaqui Bingo, 7406 S. Camino de Oeste, Tucson, AZ 85746. Tel. (602) 883-1700. Gaming: B, P, VP, K, SM.

Apache Gold Casino, Hwy. 5, 5 mi. east of Globe, San Carlos, AZ 85550. Tel. (602) 425-7693. Gaming: B, P, VP, K, SM.

Desert Diamond Casino, 7350 S. Old Nogales, Tucson, AZ 85734. Tel. (602) 294-7777. Gaming: VP, K, SM.

Mazatzal Casino, Tonto Reservation #30, Payson, AZ 85541. Tel. (602) 474-6044. Gaming: SM.

Bucky's Casino, 1500 Hwy. 69, Prescott, AZ 86301. Tel. (602) 776-1666. Gaming: VP, SM.

Yavapai Gaming Center, Hwy. 69, Prescott, AZ 86301. Tel. (602) 445-8790. Gaming: SM.

ARKANSAS

Legal Status: *Gambling restricted to Horse/Dog Racing.*

HORSE/DOG RACETRACKS

Oaklawn Park, Arkansas Hwy. 7 South, Hot Springs, AR 71902; Tel. (501) 623-4411. Thoroughbred racing.

Southland Greyhound Park, 1550 N. Ingram Blvd., West Memphis, AR 72301; Tel. (501) 735-3670. Dog racing.

CALIFORNIA

Legal Status: *Gambling restricted to Cardrooms, Charitable Games, Horse Racing, Lottery, and Indian Reservation Gaming Operations.*

HORSE/DOG RACETRACKS

Bay Meadows Racecourse, 3600 S. Delaware St., San Mateo, CA 94402. Tel. (415) 574-7223. Thoroughbred racing.

California Exposition, 1600 Exposition Blvd., Sacramento, CA 95815. Tel. (916) 263-3000.

Del Mar, P.O. Box 700, Del Mar, CA 92014; Tel. (619) 755-1141. Thoroughbred racing.

Fairplex Park, 1101 W. McKinley, Pomona, CA 91766. Tel. (909) 623-3111. Thoroughbred racing.

Ferndale, 1255th St., Ferndale, CA 95536; Tel. (707) 786-9511. Thoroughbred racing.

Fresno, 1121 Chance Ave., Fresno, CA 93702; Tel. (209) 453-3226. Thoroughbred racing.

Hollywood Park Racetrack, 10885 S. Prairie Ave., Inglewood, CA 90301; Tel. (310) 419-1500. Thoroughbred racing.

Golden Gate Fields, 1100 East Shore Hwy., Albany, CA 94706; Tel. (510) 559-7300. Thoroughbred racing.

Los Alamitos Racecourse, 4961 E. Katella Ave., Los Alamitos, CA 90720. Tel (714) 995-1234.

Santa Anita Racecourse, 285 W. Huntington Dr., Arcadia, CA 91007; Tel. (818) 574-1161. Thoroughbred racing.

CARDROOMS

Jerry's Place & Card Palace, 2607 Oceanside Blvd., Oceanside, CA 92054; Tel. (619) 439-6988. Gaming: Hold 'Em, High-Low Split, Omaha, Pan, Pai Gow.

Oceanside Card Casino, 3232 Mission Ave., Oceanside, CA 92054, Tel. (619) 722-2828. Gaming: Poker, Hold 'Em, Hold 'Em Hi-Lo, 7-Card Stud, 7 Card Hi-Lo Split.

Commerce Casino, 6131 E. Telegraph, City of Commerce, CA 90040; Tel. (213) 721-2100. Gaming: Asian Poker, Asian Stud, Omaha, Lowball, Pan, Pai Gow Poker.

Bicycle Club, 7301 Eastern Ave., Bell Gardens, CA 90201; Tel. (310) 806-4646. Gaming: Texas Hold 'Em, High-Low Draw, Omaha, California Aces, Asian Stud, Asian Poker, Pai Gow, 7-Card Stud, Pan, Lowball.

Hollywood Park Casino, 1088 South Prairie, Inglewood, CA 90301; Tel. (310) 330-2800. Gaming: Texas Hold 'Em, High-Low Draw, Omaha, California Aces, Asian Stud, Asian Poker, Pai Gow, 7-Card Stud, Pan, Lowball.

Normandie Casino, 1045 W. Rosecrans Ave., Gardena, CA 90247; Tel. (310) 352-3400. Gaming: Hold 'Em, 7-Card Stud, Draw, Pan, Asian Poker.

El Dorado Club, 15411 S. Vermont Ave., Gardena, CA 90247; Tel. (310) 323-2800. Gaming: Texas Hold 'Em, Lowball, High-Low Split, Pai Gow, Pan, Pan 9.

Huntington Park Casino, 6611 S. Alameda St., Los Angeles, CA 90001; Tel. (213) 585-3050. Gaming: Hold 'Em, Omaha, Pineapple, Stud, Pai Gow Poker, Pan.

Empire Casino, 111 S. Main St., Yreka, CA 96097; Tel. (916) 842-1173. Cardroom.

The Casino Club, 1885 Hilltop Dr., Redding, CA 96002; Tel. (916) 221-5015. Gaming: Hold 'Em, Omaha Hi-Lo, Lowball, 7-Card Stud, Aces 22.

Lucky Derby, 7433 C. Greenback Lane, Citrus Heights, CA 95610; Tel. (916) 726-8946. Cardroom.

Lake Bowl Card Room, 511 E. Bidwell St., Folsom, CA 95630; Tel. (916) 983-6000. Gaming: Hold 'Em, Omaha, Pineapple.

Blacksheep Casino, 3330 Cameron Park Dr., Cameron Park, CA 95682; Tel. (916) 676-4251. Cardroom.

Rancho's Club, 2740 Mills Park Dr., Rancho Cordova, CA 95670; Tel. (916) 361-9186. Cardroom.

The Paragon, 726 2nd. St., Davis, CA 95616; Tel. (916) 758-7550.

Winner's Circle, 3020 Santa Rosa Ave., Santa Rosa, CA 95407; Tel. (707) 579-9424. Gaming: Hold 'Em, Omaha, Pineapple, Dealer's Choice, 7-Card Stud, Pan.

Cisco's Cardroom, 4904 Auburn Blvd., Sacramento, CA 95841; Tel. (916) 334-5141. Cardroom.

River City Casino, 5420 Auburn Blvd., Sacramento, CA 95841; Tel. (916) 332-7000.

South Bowl Card Room, 5005 Stockton Blvd., Sacramento, CA 95820; Tel. (916) 428-0418. Cardroom.

Delta Club Card Room, 6518 Pacific Ave., Stockton, CA 95207; Tel. (209) 951-1601. Cardroom.

The Cameo Club, 5757 Pacific Ave., Stockton, CA 95207; Tel. (209) 474-1777. Cardroom.

Artichoke Joe's, 659 Huntington Ave., San Bruno, CA 94066; Tel. (415) 589-8812. Texas Hold 'Em, Pai Gow, Pai Gow Poker, Pan, Super Pan 9.

Sonoma Joe's, 5151 Montero Way, Petaluma, CA 94954; Tel. (707) 795-6121. Gaming: Hold 'Em, Dealer's Choice, Stud, Asian Games.

Kelly's Cardroom, 408 O St., Antioch, CA 94509; Tel. (510) 757-5190. Cardroom.

Pete's 881 Sports Bar, 721 Lincoln Ave., San Rafael, CA 94901; Tel. (415) 453-5888. Cardroom.

California Grand, 5867 Pacheco Blvd., Pacheco, CA 94553; Tel. (415) 685-8397. Gaming: Hold 'Em, Lowball, Pai Gow.

Pacific News Card Club, 204-B 2nd Ave., San Mateo, CA 94401; Tel. (415) 348-9383. Cardroom.

The Garden City, 360 S. Saratoga Ave., San Jose, CA 95129; Tel. (408) 244-3333. Gaming: Double-Handed Poker, Hold 'Em, Panguinge, California Aces, Lowball.

Pleasure Point Casino, 3910 Portola Dr., Santa Cruz, CA 95062; Tel. (408) 479-7789.

Garcia's Club & Restaurant, 7275 Monterey St., Gilroy, CA 95020; Tel. (408) 848-5916. Cardroom.

Rusty's Cardroom, 112 North Main, Bishop, CA 93514; Tel. (619) 873-9066. Cardroom.

The Cottage, 106 W. 7th St., Hanford, CA 93230; Tel. (209) 583-1077. Gaming: Lowball, Omaha.

Sequoia Club Cardroom, 118 N. Irwin, Hanford, CA 93230; Tel. (209) 582-9945. Gaming: Hold 'Em, Omaha, High-Low Split.

B.J.'s Card Parlor, 8155 El Camino, Atascadero, CA 93422; Tel. (805) 466-2273. Cardroom.

Fremont Cardroom, 133 South Thompson, Nipomo, CA 93444; Tel. (805) 929-3308. Cardroom.

Sal's Town, 118 20th St. West, Rosamond, CA 93560; Tel. (805) 256-6724. Gaming: Texas Hold 'Em, Lowball, Crazy Pineapple, 7-Card Stud, Sal's Town 22.

Hi-Desert Casino, Hwy. 395 at Airbase Rd., Adelanto, CA 92301; Tel. (619) 246-8624. Gaming: Texas Hold 'Em, Lowball, Stud, Omaha, Pai Gow Poker, Super Pan 9.

INDIAN RESERVATION GAMBLING

Jackson Indian Bingo & Casino, 12222 New York Ranch Rd., Jackson, CA 95642; Tel. (209) 223-1677. Gaming: P, VG, BI.

Barona Casino & Bingo, 1000 Wildcat Canyon Rd., Lakeside, CA 92040; Tel. (619) 443-2300. P, VG, BI.

Win-River Casino & Bingo, 2100 Redding Rancheria Rd., Redding, CA 96001; Tel. (916) 243-3377. Gaming: P, VG.

Robinson Rancheria Bingo & Casino, 1545 East Hwy. 20, Nice, CA 95464; Tel. (707) 275-9000. Gaming: P, BI, VG.

Cache Creek Indian Bingo & Casino, 14455 Hwy. 16, Brooks, CA 95606; Tel. (916) 796-3118. Gaming: B, P, VG, BI.

Sycuan Indian Bingo & Poker Casino, 5469 Dehesa Rd., El Cajon, CA 92019; Tel. (619) 445-6002.

Cher-Ae Heights Casino & Bingo, 1 Cher-Ae Heights Ln., Trinidad, CA 95570; Tel. (707) 677-0211. Gaming: BI, P, VG, B.

COLORADO

Legal Status: *Gambling is restricted to Cardrooms, Casinos, Charitable Games, Horse/Dog Racing, the Lottery, and Indian Reservation Gaming Operations.*

HORSE/DOG RACETRACKS

Arapahoe Park, 26000 East Quincy, Aurora, CO 80016; Tel. (303) 690-2400. Thoroughbred racing.

Cloverleaf Kennel Club, 2527 W. Frontage Rd., Loveland, CO 80539; Tel. (303) 667-6211. Dog racing.

Mile High Greyhound Park, 6200 Dahlia St., Commerce City, CO 80022; Tel. (303) 288-1591. Dog racing.

Pueblo Greyhound Park, 3215 Lake Ave., Pueblo, CO 81005; Tel. (719) 566-0370. Dog racing.

Rocky Mountain Greyhound Park, 3701 N. Nevada, Colorado Springs, CO 80933; Tel. (719) 632-1391. Live dog racing during April–Sept. only.

CASINOS

Central City

Harrah's Casino, 131 Main St., Central City, CO 80422; Gaming: B, P, VP, SM.

Lady Luck Casino, 120 Main St., Central City, CO 80422; Tel. (303) 582-1603. Gaming: B, P, VP, SM.

Baby Doe's Silver Dollar, 102A Lawrence, Central City, CO 80422; Tel. (303) 582-5510. Gaming: B, VP, SM.

Central Palace, 132 Lawrence, Central City, CO 80422; Tel. (303) 582-0637. Gaming: B, VP, SM.

Doc Holliday, 101 Main St., Central City, CO 80422; Tel. (303) 582-1619. Gaming: B, VP, SM.

Famous Bonanza, 107 Main St., Central City, CO 80422; Tel. (303) 582-5914. Gaming: B, P, VP, SM.

Firehouse, 171 Lawrence, Central City, CO 80422; Tel. (303) 582-0405. Gaming: VP, SM.

Golden Rose, 102 Main St., Central City, CO 80422; Tel. (303) 582-1413. Gaming: B, VP, SM.

Papone's Palace, 118 Main St., Central City, CO 80422; Tel. (303) 582-5820. Gaming: B, VP, SM.

Pete's Place, 107 Main St., Central City, CO 80422; Tel. (303) 582-5914. Gaming: B, P, VP, SM.

Pony Express, 110 Gregory, Central City, CO 80422; Tel. (303) 582-0802. Gaming: SM.

Teller House, 120 Eureka, Central City, CO 80422; Tel. (303) 582-3200. Gaming: VP, SM.

Black Hawk

Blazing Saddles, 139 Main St., Black Hawk, CO 80422; Tel. (303) 582-0707. Gaming: B, VP, SM.

Harrah's Casino, 131 Main St., Black Hawk, CO 80422; Tel. (303) 582-3794. Gaming: B, P, VP, SM.

Gilpin Hotel, 111 Main St., Black Hawk, CO 80422; Tel. (303) 582-1133. Gaming: B, P, VP, SM.

Bullwhacker's Casino, 1819 Denver W. Dr., Bldg. 26, Suite 100, Black Hawk, CO 80422; Tel. (303) 271-2500. Gaming: B, P, VP, SM.

Bronco Billy's, 125 Gregory, Black Hawk, CO 80422; Tel. (303) 582-3311. Gaming: B, VP, SM.

Colorado Central Station, 340 Main St., Black Hawk, CO 80422; Tel. (303) 582-3000. Gaming: B, P, VP, SM.

Crook's Palace, 200 Gregory, Black Hawk, CO 80422; Tel. (303) 582-5094. Gaming: VP, SM.

Eureka! 211 Gregory, Black Hawk, CO 80422; Tel. (303) 582-1040. Gaming: B, VP, SM.

Gold Mine, 130 Clear Creek Hwy. 119, Black Hawk, CO 80422; Tel. (303) 582-0711. Gaming: B, VP, SM.

Golden Gates, 261 Main St., Black Hawk, CO 80422; Tel. (303) 582-1650. Gaming: B, P, VP, SM.

Gregory Street, 380 Gregory, Black Hawk, CO 80422; Tel. (303) 582-1006. Gaming: B, VP, SM.

Jazz Alley, 321 Main St., Black Hawk, CO 80422; Tel. (303) 582-1125. Gaming: B, VP, SM.

Lucky Star, 221 Gregory, Black Hawk, CO 80422; Tel. (303) 582-1122. Gaming: B, VP, SM.

Otto's, 260 Gregory, Black Hawk, CO 80422; Tel. (303) 582-0150. Gaming: B, VP, SM.

Pick-A-Dilly, 121 Main St., Black Hawk, CO 80422; Tel. (303) 582-1844. Gaming: SM.

Red Dolly, 530 Gregory, Black Hawk, CO 80422; Tel. (303) 582-1100. Gaming: B, VP, SM.

Rich Man, 101 Richmond, Black Hawk, CO 80422; Tel. (303) 582-0400. Gaming: B, VP, SM.

The Station Casino, 141 Gregory, Black Hawk, CO 80422; Tel. (303) 582-5582. Gaming: B, VP, SM.

Cripple Creek

The Aspen Mine & Casino, 166 East Bennett Ave., Cripple Creek, CO 80813; Tel. (719) 689-0770. Gaming: B, VP, SM.

Brass Ass, 264 East Bennett Ave., Cripple Creek, CO 80813; Tel. (719) 689-2104. Gaming: B, VP, SM.

Bronco Billy's, 233 East Bennett Ave., Cripple Creek, CO 80813; Tel. (719) 689-2142. Gaming: B, VP, SM.

Black Diamond, 425 East Bennett Ave., Cripple Creek, CO 80813; Tel. (719) 689-2898. Gaming: B, VP, SM.

Colorado Grande, 300 East Bennett Ave., Cripple Creek, CO 80813; Tel. (719) 689-3517. Gaming: B, VP, SM.

Gold Rush Hotel & Casino, 209 East Bennett Ave., Cripple Creek, CO 80813; Tel. (719) 689-2646, Reservations (800) 235-8239. Hotel, 14 rooms, $49–79. Restaurants include The Golden Grill. Gaming: B, VP, SM.

Gold Digger's Casino, 217 East Bennett Ave., Cripple Creek, CO 80813; Tel. (719) 689-3911. Gaming: B, VP, SM.

Creeker's, 274 East Bennett Ave., Cripple Creek, CO 80813; Tel. (719) 689-3239. Gaming: B, VP, SM.

Imperial Hotel & Casino, 279 East Bennett Ave., Cripple Creek, CO 80813; Tel. (719) 689-7777, Reservations (800) 235-2922. Hotel, 29 rooms, $40–$145. Restaurants include The Imperial Dining Room. Gaming: B, P, VP, SM.

The Independence Hotel & Casino, 157 East Bennett Ave., Cripple Creek, CO 80813; Tel. (719) 689-2744. Hotel, 8 rooms, $45–$75. Restaurants include Sam's House of Prime Rib. Gaming: SM.

Johnny Nolan's Saloon, 301 East Bennett Ave., Cripple Creek, CO 80813; Tel. (719) 689-2080. Gaming: B, P, VP, SM.

Jubilee Casino, 351 East Myers Ave., Cripple Creek, CO 80813; Tel. (719) 689-2519. Gaming: B, VP, SM.

Loose Caboose Casino, 400 East Bennett Ave., Cripple Creek, CO 80813; Tel. (719) 689-2935. Gaming: B, VP, SM.

Long Branch Casino, 200 East Bennett Ave., Cripple Creek, CO 80813; Tel. (719) 689-3242. Gaming: B, VP, SM.

Lucky Lola's, 400 East Bennett Ave., Cripple Creek, CO 80813; Tel. (719) 689-2994. Gaming: B, VP, SM.

Midnight Rose Hotel & Casino, 256 East Bennett Ave., Cripple Creek, CO 80813; Tel. (719) 689-2865, Reservations (800) 635-5825. Hotel, 19 rooms, $69–$89. Entertainment: LM. Gaming: B, P, VP, SM, Horse/Dog racing.

Maverick's, 411 East Bennett Ave., Cripple Creek, CO 80813; Tel. (719) 689-2737. Gaming: B, VP, SM.

Old Chicago Casino, 419 East Bennett Ave., Cripple Creek, CO 80813; Tel. (719) 689-2992. Gaming: B, VP, SM.

The Palace Hotel & Casino, 172 East Bennett Ave., Cripple Creek, CO 80813; Tel. (719) 689-2992. Hotel, 15 rooms, $35–$70. Restaurants include The Gilded Cage. Gaming: B, SM.

Phoenix House Casino, 232 East Bennett Ave., Cripple Creek, CO 80813; Tel. (719) 689-2030. Gaming: B, P, VP, SM.

Silver Palace Casino, 404 East Bennett Ave., Cripple Creek, CO 80813; Tel. (719) 689-3980. Gaming: B, VP, SM.

Virgin Mule Casino, 269 East Bennett Ave., Cripple Creek, CO 80813; Tel. (719) 689-2734. Gaming: B, VP, SM.

Wild Bill's Pub, 220 East Bennett Ave., Cripple Creek, CO 80813; Tel. (719) 689-2707. Gaming: B, VP, SM.

Wild West Brewer, 443 East Bennett Ave., Cripple Creek, CO 80813; Tel. (719) 689-3736. Gaming: B, VP, SM.

Womack's Casino, 210 East Bennett Ave., Cripple Creek, CO 80813; Tel. (719) 689-0333. Gaming: B, VP, SM.

INDIAN RESERVATION GAMBLING

Sky Ute Lodge & Casino, Hwy. 172, Ignacio, CO 81137; Tel. (303) 563-4531, Reservations (800) 876-7017. Hotel, 37 rooms, $29–$65, pool. Gaming: B, P, VG, SM.

Ute Mountain Casino, Weeminuche Dr. at Yellow Hat, Towaoc, CO 81334; Tel. (303) 565-8800. Gaming: SM, P, B.

CONNECTICUT

Legal Status: *Gambling restricted to Charitable Games, Horse/Dog Racing, the Lottery, and Indian Reservation Gaming Operations.*

HORSE/DOG RACETRACK

Plainfield Greyhound Park, 1337 Lathrop Rd., Plainfield, CT 06374; Tel. (800) RACES-ON. Dog racing.

INDIAN RESERVATION GAMBLING

Foxwoods High Stakes Bingo & Casino, Route 2, Ledyard, CT 06339. Tel. (203) 885-3000, Reservations (800) Play Big. Resort Hotel, 283 rooms, $135–$175, pool, gym, massage. Restaurants include The Al Dente, The Han Garden. Entertainment: LM, CH. Gaming: B, P, VP, C, R, BI, K, SM, SB, RB, Bac. Two Trees Hotel, 280 rooms, $100–$125, is also part of the Foxwoods Casino & Resort.

DELAWARE

Legal Status: *Gambling restricted to Charitable Games, Horse Racing, and the Lottery.*

HORSE/DOG RACETRACKS

Delaware Park, Rt. 7, Wilmington, DE 19804; Tel. (302) 994-2521. Thoroughbred racing.

Dover Downs, 1131 N. Dupont Hwy., Dover, DE 19901 Tel. (302) 674-4600. Harness racing.

Harrington Race Way, Rt. 13, Harrington, DE 19952; Tel. (302) 398-3269. Harness Racing.

FLORIDA

Legal Status: *Gambling restricted to Charitable Games, Horse/Dog Racing, and Class II gaming which consists of Bingo, but no other casino-style games are included in this state's Indian Reservation Gaming Operations.*

HORSE/DOG RACETRACKS

Calder Racecourse, Inc., 21001 Northwest 27th Ave., Miami, FL 33055; Tel. (305) 625-1311. Thoroughbred racing.

Gulfstream Park Racing Assoc., Inc., 901 S. Federal Hwy., Hallandale, FL 33008; (305) 931-7223. Thoroughbred racing.

Hialeah Park, 2200 East 4th Ave., Hialeah, FL 33011; Tel. (305) 885-8000. Thoroughbred racing.

Payson Park, 9700 Kanner Hwy., Indiantown, FL 34956; Tel. (407) 597-3555. Thoroughbred racing.

Pompano Park, 1800 Southwest 3rd St., Pompano Beach, FL 33089; Tel. (305) 970-0882. Harness racing.

Tampa Bay Downs, 11225 Racetrack Rd., Tampa, FL 34677; Tel. (813) 855-4401. Thoroughbred racing.

Tropical Park, 21001 Northwest 27th Ave., Miami, FL 33056; Tel. (305) 625-1311.

INDIAN RESERVATION GAMBLING

Seminole Gaming Palace, 7439 E. Hillsborough Ave.,

Tampa, FL 33610; Tel. (813) 621-1302. Gaming: VG, P, BI.

GEORGIA

Legal Status: *Gambling restricted to Charitable Games and the Lottery.*

HAWAII

Legal Status: *No Gambling Permitted.*

IDAHO

Legal Status: *Gambling restricted to Horse/Dog Racing, the Lottery, and Class II gaming which consists of Bingo, but no other casino-style games are included in this state's Indian Reservation Gaming Operations.*

HORSE/DOG RACETRACK
Les Bois Park, 5610 Glenwood, Boise, ID 83714; Tel. (208) 376-3991. Thoroughbred racing.

Pocatello Downs, 10588 Fairgrounds Rd., Pocatello, ID 83204; Tel. (208) 238-1721.

Coeur D'Alene Greyhound Park, 5100 Riverbend Ave., ID 83854; Tel. (208) 773-0545. Horse/Dog Racing.

ILLINOIS

Legal Status: *Gambling restricted to Charitable Games, Riverboats, Horse/Dog Racing, and the Lottery.*

RIVERBOATS

The Alton Belle Riverboat Casino, 219 Piasa St., Alton, IL 62002; Tel. (618) 474-7500, Reservations (800) 336-7568. Restaurants include Belle's Buffet, Victor's. Entertainment: LM. Gaming: B, Caribbean Stud Poker, VG, C, R, SM.

Casino Rock Island, 18th St., Mississippi Riverfront, Rock Island, IL 61201; Tel. (800) 477-7747. Gaming: B, Caribbean Stud Poker, VG, C, R, K, SM.

Empress River Casino, 2300 Empress Dr., Joliet, IL 60431; Tel. (708) 345-6789. Gaming: B, Caribbean Stud Poker, VG, C, R, K, SM, Bac.

Harrah's Casino Cruises, 150 N Joliet St., Joliet, IL 60431; Tel. (800) 3-HARRAH. Restaurants include Andreotti's. Gaming: B, Caribbean Stud Poker, VG, C, R, SM, Mini-Bac.

Hollywood Casino, 1 New York St. Bridge, Aurora, IL 60506; Tel. (800) 888-7777. Restaurants include Cafe Harlow and Fairbanks. Entertainment: LM. Gaming: B, Caribbean Stud Poker, C, R, VG, SM, Mini-Bac.

Par-a-dice Pavillion, 21 Blackjack Blvd., E. Peoria, IL 61611; Tel. (800) DEAL-ME IN. Restaurants include The Grill and The Buffet. Gaming: B, P, VG, K, C, R, SM, Bac.

Silver Eagle Casino Cruise, 19731 U.S. Route 20 West, East Dubuque, IL 61025; Tel. (800) SILVER-1. Restaurants include Wings. Entertainment: LM. Gaming: B, VG, C, R, SM.

HORSE/DOG RACETRACKS

Arlington International Racecourse, Inc., Intersection of Euclid & Wilke, Arlington Heights, IL 60006; Tel. (708) 255-4300. Thoroughbred racing.

Balmoral Park, 26435 Dixie Hwy., Crete, IL 60417; Tel. (708) 672-7544. Harness racing.

Du Quoin State Fair, U.S. Route 51 South, Du Quoin, IL 62832; Tel. (618) 542-3000. Harness racing.

Fairmont Park, Route 40, Collinsville, IL 62234; Tel. (618) 345-4300. Thoroughbred and harness racing.

Hawthorne Racecourse, 3501 S. Laramie Ave., Cicero, IL 60650; Tel. (708) 780-3700. Thoroughbred and harness racing.

Sportsman's Park, 3302 S. Laramie Ave., Cicero, IL 60650; Tel. (708) 976-8300. Thoroughbred and harness racing.

Springfield, 801 East Sangamon Ave., Springfield, IL 62794; Tel. (217) 782-4231. Harness racing.

INDIANA

Legal Status: *Gambling restricted to Charitable Games, Horse Racing, and the Lottery. Indiana Supreme Court ruled a state law authorizing riverboat gaming is constitutional, reversing a decision originally made by a lower court in May 1994.*

HORSE/DOG RACETRACKS
Hoosier Park, 4500 Dan Patch Circle, Anderson, IN 46013; Tel. (317) 642-7223. Thoroughbred racing.

IOWA

Legal Status: *Gambling restricted to Cardrooms, Charitable Games, Riverboats, Horse/Dog Racing, the Lottery, and Indian Reservation Gaming Operations.*

RIVERBOATS

Belle of Sioux City, 1800 Larson Park Rd., Sioux City, IA 51103; Tel. (800) 424-0080. Restaurants include The Speakeasy. Gaming: B, P, VG, C, R, K, SM.

Catfish Bend, Cruise Season (May–Oct.) Fort Madison Landing, Riverview Park US 61 & 6th St., Fort Madison, IA 52627; Dockside Season (Nov.–April) Big Muddy's Landing, N. Front St., Burlington, IA. Tel. (800) 372-2WIN. Gaming: B, P, VG, C, R, SM.

Diamond Jo, 400 E. 3rd. St., Dubuque, IA 52001; Tel. (800) 582-5956. Gaming: B, VG, C, R, SM.

Mississippi Belle II, 311 River View Dr., Clinton, IA 52732; Tel. (800) 457-9975. Gaming: B, P, VG, C, R, SM, Bac.

The President, 130 W. River Dr., Davenport, IA 52801; Tel. (800) 262-8711. Gaming: B, P, VG, C, R, SM.

HORSE/DOG RACETRACKS

Prairie Meadows, 1 Prairie Meadows Dr., Altoona, IA 50009; Tel. (800) 325-9015. Horse racing (thoroughbred and quarter).

Bluff's Run, 2710 23rd Ave., Council Bluffs, IA 51502; Tel. (800) 462-9378. Dog racing.

Dubuque Greyhound Park, 1855 Greyhound Dr., Dubuque, IA 52004; Tel. (800) 373-3647. Dog racing.

Waterloo Greyhound Park, 3250 Greyhound Dr., Waterloo, IA 50701; Tel. (800) 922-3006. Dog racing.

INDIAN RESERVATION GAMBLING

Casino Omaha, 1 Blackbird Bend Blvd., Onawa, IA 51040; Tel. (800) 858-8238. Gaming: B, VP, P, C, R, SM, BW.

Winna Vegas Casino, 1500–330th St., Sloan, IA 51055; Tel. (712) 428-9466. Gaming: B, VP, P, C, R, K, BI, SM.

Mesquaki Bingo & Casino, Rt. 2, Tama, IA 52339; Tel. (515) 484-2108. Gaming: B, P, VG, C, R, BI, K, SM, RB.

KANSAS

Legal Status: *Gambling restricted to Charitable Games, Horse/Dog Racing, the Lottery, and Class II Gaming which consists of Bingo, but no other casino-style games are included in this state's Indian Reservation Gaming Operations.*

HORSE/DOG RACETRACKS
Woodlands Racetrack, 99th & Leavenworth Rd., Kansas City, KS 66109; Tel. (800) 695-RACE. Thoroughbred racing and dog racing.

Wichita Greyhound Park, 1500 E. 77 St. N., Valley Center, KS 67147; Tel. (800) 535-0482. Dog racing.

KENTUCKY

Legal Status: *Gambling restricted to Horse Racing and the Lottery.*

HORSE/DOG RACETRACKS
Blue Grass Downs, 150 Downs Dr., Paducah, KY 42001; Tel. (800) 755-1244.

Churchill Downs, 700 Central Ave., Louisville, KY 40208; Tel. (502) 636-4400. Thoroughbred racing.

Ellis Park, U.S. Hwy. 41, Henderson, KY 42402; Tel. (800) 333-8110. Thoroughbred racing.

Keeneland, 4201 Versailles Rd., Lexington, KY 40592; Tel. (800) 456-3412. Thoroughbred racing.

Red Mile, 1200 Red Mile Rd., Lexington, KY 40504; Tel. (606) 255-0752.

Turf Way Park, 7500 Turf Way Rd., Florence, KY 41042; Tel. (800) 733-0200. Thoroughbred racing.

LOUISIANA

Legal Status: *Gambling restricted to Cardrooms, Casinos, Charitable Games, Riverboats, Horse/Dog Racing, the Lottery, and Indian Reservation Gaming Operations.*

RIVERBOATS

Harrah's Shreve Star, 315 Clyde Fant Parkway, Shreveport, LA 71163; (318) 424-7777. Restaurants include Andreotti's, Wild Rose Grill. Gaming: B, P, C, R, SM, Mini-Bac.

Isle of Capri Casino, 711 Isle of Capri Blvd., Boossier City, LA 71111; Tel. (318) 678-7777. Restaurants include Calypso's and Coral Reef. Gaming: B, P, VP, C, R, K, SM, Mini-Bac.

Boomtown Belle New Orleans, 4132 Peters Rd., Harvey, LA 70058; Tel. (504) 366-7711. Reservations (800) 366-7711. Gaming: B, P, VP, C, R, SM.

Showboat Star Casino, 1 Star Casino Blvd., New Orleans, LA 70126; Tel. (504) 243-0400, Reservations (800) 504-STAR. Restaurants include Star Casino Grill. Gaming: B, VG, C, R, SM.

Horseshoe Entertainment, 711 Horseshoe Blvd., Boosier, LA 71171; Tel. (504) 742-0711. Restaurants include Branding Iron. Gaming: B, R, C, SM, VG.

Treasure Chest, 5050 Williams Blvd., Kenner, LA 70064; Tel. (504) 443-8000, Reservations (800) 298-0711. Gaming: B, C, R, SM.

Flamingo Casino & Resort of New Orleans, Poydras St., New Orleans, LA 71040; Tel. (504) 587-1600, Reservations (800) 587-LUCK. Hotel, 1600 rooms, $150–$300, pool, gym, massage. Restaurants include Kabby's, Horizons. Entertainment: Jazz Band. Gaming: B, P, VP, C, R, SM, Bac.

Belle of Baton Rouge, 103 France St., Baton Rouge, LA 70802; Tel. (504) 378-6000. Restaurants include The Pantry. Gaming: B, VP, C, R, SM, Bac.

Players Casino Lake Charles, 507 N. Lake Shore Dr., Lake Charles, LA Tel. (318) 437-1580. Reservations (800) ASK-MERV. Gaming: B, P, VP, K, C, R, SM, Mini-Bac.

Note: **Casino Rouge** and **Catfish Queen** in Baton Rouge and the **Horseshoe Entertainment** in Bossier are in the process of construction, but at press time there was no opening date available.

HORSE/DOG RACETRACKS

Delta Downs Racetrack, Hwy. 3063, Vinton, LA 70668; Tel. (318) 589-7441. Thoroughbred racing.

Evangeline Downs, U.S. Hwy. 167 N., Lafayette, LA Tel. (318) 896-7223. Thoroughbred racing.

Fair Grounds, 1751 Gentilly Blvd., New Orleans, LA 70119; Tel. (504) 944-5515. Thoroughbred racing.

Louisiana Downs, 8000 E. Texas St., Bossier City, LA 71171; Tel. (318) 742-5555. Thoroughbred racing.

INDIAN RESERVATION GAMBLING

Cypress Bayou Casino/Chitimacha Bayouland Bingo, 832 Martin Luther King Rd., Charenton, LA 70523; Tel. (800) 284-4386. Gaming: B, C, R, SM.

Coushatta Gaming Operation, 11920 Hwy. 165, Kinder, LA 70640; Tel. (318) 738-7320. Gaming: B, C, R, SM, VG, Mini-Bac.

Grand Casino Avoylles, 711 E. Tunica, Marksville, LA 71351; Tel. (318) 253-1946. Gaming: B, P, C, R, VG, Bac, SM.

MAINE

Legal Status: *Gambling restricted to Charitable Games, Horse Racing, the Lottery, and Class II Gaming which consists of Bingo, but no other casino-style games are included in this state's Indian Reservation Gaming Operations.*

HORSE/DOG RACETRACKS
Scarborough Downs, Rt. 1, Scarborough, ME 04074; Tel. (207) 883-4331. Harness racing.

Bangor Raceway, P.O. Box 614, Bangor, ME 04402; Tel. (207) 947-6744. Harness racing.

MARYLAND

Legal Status: *Gambling restricted to Charitable Games, Horse/Dog Racing, and the Lottery.*

HORSE/DOG RACETRACKS
Delmarva Downs, Routes 50 & 589, Berlin, MD, 21811; Tel. (410) 641-0600. Harness racing.

Laurel Racecourse, Racetrack Rd. & Route 198; Laurel, MD 20725; Tel. (301) 725-0400. Thoroughbred racing.

Pimlico Racecourse, Hayward Ave., Baltimore, MD 21215; Tel. (410) 542-9400. Thoroughbred racing.

Rosecroft Raceway, 6336 Rosecroft Dr., Fort Washington, MD 20744; Tel. (301) 567-4000. Harness racing.

Timonium, 2200 York Rd., Timonium, MD 21093; Tel. (410) 252-0220. Thoroughbred racing.

MASSACHUSETTS

Legal Status: *Gambling restricted to Charitable Games, Horse/Dog Racing, and the Lottery.*

HORSE/DOG RACE TRACKS

Foxboro Park, Route 1, Foxboro, MA 02035; Tel. (508) 543-3800. Harness racing.

Suffolk Downs, 111 Waldemar Ave., East Boston, MA 02128; Tel. (617) 567-3900. Thoroughbred racing.

MICHIGAN

Legal Status: *Gambling restricted to Charitable Games, Horse Racing, the Lottery, and Indian Reservation Gaming Operations.*

HORSE/DOG RACETRACKS

Hazel Park Harness Raceway, 1650 E. Ten Mile Rd., Hazel Park, MI 48030; Tel. (810) 398-1000. Harness racing.

Jackson Raceway, 200 W. Ganson St., Jackson, MI 49204; Tel. (517) 788-4500. Harness racing.

Ladbroke Detroit Racecourse, 28001 Schoolcraft Rd., Livonia, MI Tel. (313) 525-7300. Thoroughbred racing.

Mt. Pleasant Meadows Horse Racing, 500 N. Mission, Mt. Pleasant, MI 48858; Tel. (517) 773-0012.

Muskegon Racecourse, 4800 Harvey St., Fruitport, MI 49415; Tel. (616) 798-7123. Harness racing.

Saginaw Harness Raceway, 2701 E. Genesee St., Saginaw, MI 48601; Tel. (517) 755-3451.

Sports Creek Raceway, 4290 Morrish Rd., Swartz Creek, MI 48473; Tel. (313) 635-3333. Harness racing.

INDIAN RESERVATION GAMBLING

Vegas Kewadin Casino, 2186 Shunk Rd., Sault Ste. Marie, MI 49783; Tel. (906) 635-5274. Gaming: B, P, K, R, C, BI.

Ojibwa Casino Resort Motel/Big Bucks Bingo Hall, Route 1, M-38, Baraga, MI 49908; Tel (906) 353-6333, Reservations (800) 323-8045. Hotel, 40 rooms, $50-$55, pool. Restaurants include The Bear's Den. Entertainment: LM and Bowling Lanes. Gaming: B, VP, C, R, SM.

Kings Club Tribal Casino, Rte. 1, Brimley, MI 49715; Tel. (906) 248-3227. Gaming: B, VP, C, K, SM. (Caribbean Stud Poker.)

Lac Vieux Desert Casino, Choate Rd., Watersmeet, MI 49969; Tel. (906) 358-4227. Gaming: B, VP, P, C, K, BI, SM.

Soaring Eagle Casino, 2395 S. Leaton Rd., Mt. Pleasant, MI 48858; Tel. (800) 992-2306. Gaming: B, P, VG, BI, SM.

Saginaw Chips Card Room & Casino, 7498 E. Broadway, Mt. Pleasant, MI 48858; Tel. (517) 772-5700. Gaming: B, P, SM, BI.

Chip-In Casino, U.S. 2 & 41, Harris, MI 49845; Tel. (906) 466-2941; Reservations (800) 682-6040. Hotel, 29 rooms, $58-$68. Gaming: B, P, VG, C, K, SM.

Kewaden Shores Casino, 3039 Mackinac Trail, St. Ignace, MI 49783; Tel. (906) 643-7071. Gaming: B, VG, C, R, K, SM, BW.

Leelanau Sands Casino, 2521 N. West-Bay Shore Dr., Suttons Bay, MI 49682; Tel. (616) 271-4104. Gaming: B, P, R, C, VG, K, SM, BW.

MINNESOTA

Legal Status: *Gambling restricted to Charitable Games, Horse Racing, the Lottery, and Indian Reservation Gaming Operations.*

HORSE/DOG RACETRACKS
Canterbury Downs, 1100 Canterbury Rd., Shakopee, MN 55379; Tel. (612) 445-7223. Horse racing.

INDIAN RESERVATION GAMBLING
Lake of the Woods Casino, 1001 1/2 Lake St. Warroad, MN 56763; Tel. (218) 386-3381. Gaming: B, VP, BI, SM.

River Road Casino, RR 3, Thief River Falls, MN 56701; Tel. (218) 681-4062. Gaming: B, VP, BI, SM.

Red Lake Casino & Bingo, Red Lake, MN 56671; Tel. (218) 679-2500. Gaming: B, VP, BI, SM.

Palace Bingo & Casino, Rt. 3, Cass Lake, MN 56633; Tel. (218) 335-6787, (800) 228-6676. Gaming: B. VG, SM.

Northern Lights Casino, HCR 73, Walker, MN 56484; Tel. (218) 547-2744, (800) 252-PLAY. Gaming: B, VG, SM.

Grand Casino Mille Lacs, 777 Grand Ave., HCR 67, Onamia, MN 56359; Tel. (800) 626-5825. Gaming: B, VG, BI, SM.

Jackpot Junction Casino, Rt. 1, Morton, MN 56270; Tel. (507) 644-2645. Gaming: B, VG, BI, SM.

Mystic Lake Casino & Dakota Country Casino, 2400 Mystic Lake Blvd., Prior Lake, MN 55372; Tel. (612) 445-9000. Gaming: B, BI, SM.

Treasure Island Bingo & Casino, Red Wing, MN 55066; Tel. (612) 385-2535, (800) 222-7077. Gaming: B, BI, SM.

Grand Casino Hinckley, 777 Lady Luck Dr., Hinckley, MN; Tel. (612) 384-7777, (800) Grand-21. Restaurant, buffet, and snack bar. Gaming: B, VG, SM.

Black Bear Casino, 601 Hwy. 210, Carlton, MN 55718; Tel. (218) 878-2412. Gaming: B, BI, SM.

Fond-Du-Luth Gaming Casino, 129 East Superior St., Duluth, MN 55802; Tel. (218) 722-0280, (800) 873-0280. Gaming: BI, SM.

Fortune Bay Casino, 1430 Bois Forte Rd., Tower, MN 55790; Tel. (218) 753-6400, (800) 992-2647. Gaming: B, VG, BI, SM.

Grand Portage Lodge & Casino, Grand Portage, MN 55605; Tel. (218) 475-2441; (800) 543-1384. Gaming: B, BI, SM.

Shooting Star Casino, Mahnomen, MN 56557; Tel. (218) 935-2701. Gaming: B, VG, SM.

MISSISSIPPI

Legal Status: *Gambling restricted to Charitable Games, Riverboats, Horse/Dog Racing, and Indian Reservation Gaming Operations.*

RIVERBOATS

Bay St. Louis

Casino Magic, 711 Casino Magic Dr., Bay St. Louis, MS 39521; Tel. (800) 562-4425. Hotel, 201 rooms, $55–$95, pool, spa. Restaurants include The Torgy's, The Veranda Buffet. Entertainment: LM. Gaming: B, P, VG, K, C, R, SM, Bac.

Bayou Caddy's Jubilee Casino, 5005 S. Beach Blvd., Lakeshore Ave., Bay St. Louis, MS 39576; Tel. (800) 552-0707. Gaming: B, P, VG, C, R, SM, Bac.

Biloxi

Biloxi Belle Casino & Resort, 857 Beach Blvd., Biloxi, MS

39576; Tel. (800) 245-6947. Hotel, 153 rooms, $69–$89, pool. Restaurants include The Biloxi Steamer, The Biloxi Landing. Entertainment: LM. Gaming: B, C, R, VG, SM, Bac.

Boomtown Casino, 460 Cailevet St., Biloxi, MS 39530; Tel. (601) 435-7000, Reservations (800) 627-0777. Restaurants include The Long Horn. Gaming: B, P, VP, C, R, K, SM.

Casino Magic, 167 E. Beach Blvd., Biloxi, MS 39533; Tel. (601) 435-2559, Reservations (800) 562-4425. Gaming: B, P, VG, C, R, SM.

Gold Shore Casino, 867 Howard Ave., Biloxi, MS 39530, Tel. (601) 435-3111, Reservations (800) 946-4653. Restaurants include The Steakhouse. Gaming: B, VP, C, R, SM, Bac.

Grand Casino Biloxi, 265 Beach Blvd., Biloxi, MS 39530; Tel. (601) 436-2946, Reservations (800) 946-2946. Gaming: B, P, VP, C, R, K, SM, Bac.

Isle of Capri, 151 Beach Blvd., Biloxi, MS 39530; Tel. (601) 435-5400, Reservations (800) 843-4753. Gaming: B, P, C, R, SM, Mini-Bac.

Lady Luck Biloxi, 1848 Beach Blvd., Biloxi, MS 39531; Tel. (601) 388-1364, Reservations (800) 539-5825. Restaurants include The Fisherman's Wharf. Gaming: B, VP, C, R, SM.

Palace Casino, 158 Howard Ave., Biloxi, MS 39530; Tel. (601) 432-8888, Reservations (800) PALACE-9. Restaurants include The Crown Room. Gaming: B, VP, Caribbean Stud Poker, R, C, SM, Bac.

President Casino, 2110 Beach Blvd., Biloxi, MS 39530; Tel. (601) 385-3500, Reservations (800) 843-7737. Gaming: B, VP, P, C, R, SM.

Treasure Bay Casino & Resort, 1980 Beach Blvd., Biloxi, MS 39531; Tel. (601) 385-6000, Reservations (800) 388-3955. Hotel, 254 rooms, $45–$65, pools. Restaurants include The Terrace Bay. Entertainment: LM. Gaming: B, VP, C, R, SM, Bac.

Other Locations

Copa Casino, East Pier 52, Gulfport, MS 39501; Tel. (601) 863-3330, Reservations (800) 946-2672. Restaurants include Raintree Lounge. Gaming: B, P, R, C, SM. Bac.

Grand Casino, 943-B 33rd Ave., Gulfport, MS 39501; Tel. (601) 870-7777, Reservations (800) 946-7777. Gaming: P, SM.

Lady Luck Natchez Under the Hill, 21 Silver St., Natchez, MS 39120; Tel. (601) 445-0605, Reservations (800) 722-5825. Restaurants include Victorian Room, Boiler Deck. Gaming: B, P, C, R, SM.

Silver Star Resort & Casino, Hwy. 16, 9 mi. west of Philadelphia, MS; Tel. (601) 550-1234, Reservations (800) 922-9988. Hotel, 100 rooms, $59–$69, pool. Restaurants include Phillip M's, The Terrace Cafe. Gaming: B, P, VP, C, R, K, SM, Bac.

Ameristar Casino Vicksburg, 4146 S. Washington St., Vicksburg, MS 39180; Tel. (601) 638-1000, Reservations (800) 700-7770. Hotel, 54 rooms, $39–$50, pool. Entertainment: CH. Gaming: B, P, VG, C, R, SM.

Isle of Capri, Vicksburg, 3990 Washington St., Vicksburg, MS 39180; Tel. (601) 636-5700, Reservations (800) 946-4753. Restaurants include Calypso's, Trade Winds. Gaming: B, P, VG, C, R, K, SM, Bac.

Harrah's Casino & Hotel, 1310 Mulberry St., Vicksburg, MS 39180; Tel. (601) 636-3423, Reservations (800) 843-2343. Hotel, 117 rooms, $59–$129. Restaurants include Winning Streak Sports Bar. Entertainment: LM. Gaming: B, VG, C, R, SM.

Rainbow Casino, 1380 Warrenton Rd., Vicksburg, MS 39180; Tel. (601) 636-7575, Reservations (800) 503-3777.

In the process of building a hotel, restaurants, and theme park. Gaming: B, VG, C, R, SM.

Cotton Club, 333 Washington Ave., Greenville, MS 38701; Tel. (601) 335-1111, Reservations (800) 946-6673. Gaming: B, P, C, R, SM.

Las Vegas Casino, Waterfront at Central St., Greenville, MS 38701; Tel. (601) 335-5800, Reservations (800) 834-2721. Gaming: B, VP, C, R, Caribbean Stud Poker.

Lady Luck Mississippi, 777 Lady Luck Parkway, Lula, MS 38644; Tel. (601) 363-4600, Reservations (800) 789-5825. Restaurants include The River View Room. Gaming: B, VP, Caribbean Stud Poker, R, C, SM.

Bally's Saloon & Gambling Hall, Moon Landing, Lot 5, Tunica, MS 38676; Tel. (800) 382-2559. Gaming: B, C, R, Caribbean Stud Poker.

Circus Circus, 11 Casino Center Dr., Robinsonville, MS 38664; Tel. (601) 357-1111, Reservations (800) 9CIRCUS. Restaurants include The Amazing Linguini Brothers. Gaming: B, P, C, R, SM.

Fitzgerald's Casino Tunica, Off Commerce Rd., Rt. 304, Tunica, MS 38676; Tel. (800) 766-LUCK.

Harrah's Tunica Casino, Commerce Landing, Robinsonville Rd. West, Tunica, MS 38664; Tel. (601) 363-7000, Reservations (800) 427-7247. Restaurants include Magnolia's Gardens. Gaming: B, C, R, Caribbean Stud Poker.

Hollywood Casino, Rt. 1 Commerce Landing, Robinsonville, MS 38664; Tel. (601) 357-7700, Reservations (800) 871-0711. Hotel, 154 rooms, $59–$99. Restaurants inlcude Fairbanks Steakhouse. Gaming: B, P, VG, C, R, SM.

Sam's Town Hotel & Gambling Hall, Commerce Landing Rd., Tunica, MS 38676; Tel. (601) 363-0711, Reservations (800) 456-0711. Hotel, 500 rooms, $59–$79. Restaurants include Billy Bob's Steakhouse, Calamity Jane. Gaming: B, P, K, C, R, SM.

Sheraton Casino, 1 Casino Center Dr., Robinsonville, MS 38664; Tel. (601) 363-4900, Reservations (800) 391-3777. Gaming: B, P, C, R, SM.

Splash Casino, 35 mi. south of Memphis, Tennessee off Hwy. 61, Tunica, MS 38676; Tel. (601) 278-3515, Reservations (800) 949-3423. Gaming: B, VP, C, R, SM.

Treasure Bay Casino, Off Commerce Rd., Rt. 304, Tunica, MS 38676; Tel. (601) 363-6600, Reservations (800) 727-7684. Gaming: B, P, VP, C, R, SM, Bac.

MISSOURI

Legal Status: *Gambling restricted to Charitable Games, Riverboats, and the Lottery. Horse/Dog racing is allowed, although there are no horse/dog racetracks in the state at this time.*

RIVERBOATS

Harrah's, One Riverboat Dr., North Kansas City, MO 64116; Tel. (816) 472-7777. Restaurants include One-Eyed Jack and Winning Streak Bar & Grill. Gaming: B, P, VG, C, R, SM.

President Riverboat Casino, 600 Leonora K. Sullivan, St. Louis, MO 63102; Tel. (314) 622-3000. Restaurants include The St. Louis Room. Gaming: B, P, VG, C.

St. Charles Riverfront Station, 1260 S. Main, St. Charles, MO 63302; Tel. (314) 940-4300. Gaming: B, P, VG, C, R, SM.

St. Joe's Frontier Casino, Riverfront Park, St. Joseph, MO 64501; Tel. (816) 233-8218. Gaming: B, VP, C, R, SM.

The Argosy Riverside Casino, 4443 Northwest Gateway, Riverside, MO 64150; Tel. (816) 746-3100. Restaurants include Winner's Row. Gaming: B, P, VP, C, R, SM.

MONTANA

Legal Status: *Gambling restricted to Cardrooms, Charitable Games, Horse/Dog Racing, the Lottery, and Indian Reservation Gaming Operations.*

CARDROOMS

Billings

Custer's Card Club, 101 28th N., Billings, MT 59101; Tel. (406) 259-5148. Gaming: Hold 'Em, Dealer's Choice.

Desperados, 145 Regal, Billings, MT 59101; Tel. (406) 248-2969. Gaming: Dealer's Choice.

Eagle's Nest, 1516 4th Ave. North, Billings, MT 59101; Tel. (406) 259-1104. Gaming: Hold 'Em.

Horseshoe Club, 1412 4th Ave. North, Billings, MT 59101; Tel. (406) 248-9870.

Lucky Grand Casino, 1411 13th St. W., Billings, MT 59102; Tel. (406) 245-4976.

Ole's Little Nevada, 1413 13 St. W., Billings, MT 59102; Tel. (406) 256-5366. Gaming: P, K.

Player's Club, 131 Main St., Billings, MT 59105; Tel. (406) 245-6494. Gaming: Dealer's Choice, Omaha High-Low 8.

Riverboat, 444 24th St. West, South, Billings, MT 59102; Tel: (406) 652-4766. Gaming: Dealer's Choice.

Shooters Card Club, 1600 Ave. D, Billings, MT 59102; Tel: (406) 652-4766. Gaming: Dealer's Choice.

Turn of the Century, 1744 Grand Ave., Billings, MT 59102; Tel. (406) 248-1131. Gaming: Cardroom.

Other Locations

Cat's Paw Cardroom, 700 7th St., Bozeman, MT 59715; Tel. (406) 586-3542. Gaming: Cardroom.

Grand Tree Poker Room, 1325 N. 7th St., Bozeman, MT 59715; Tel. (406) 587-5261. Gaming: Cardroom.

Scoop Bar, 412 W. Main, Bozeman, MT 59715; Tel. (406) 587-9968. Gaming: Cardroom.

R & R Cardroom, 3811 10th Ave. S., Great Falls, MT 59405; Tel. (406) 727-5876. Gaming: Cardroom.

5 W's Bingo & Poker Room, 619 Main, Helena, MT 59601; Tel. (406) 442-4304. Gaming: Cardroom and Bingo.

Pancho Magoo's, 1301 S. Main, Kalispell, MT 59901; Tel. (406) 755-4778. Gaming: Cardroom.

Locomotive Inn Casino, 216 1st Ave., South, Laurel, MT 59044; Tel. (406) 628-7969. Gaming: Cardroom.

Ida's Cardroom, 123 W. Broadway, Missoula, MT 59801; Tel. (406) 543-9044. Gaming: Cardroom.

Milwaukee Station, 250 Station Dr., Missoula, MT 59801; Tel. (406) 721-7777. Gaming: Cardroom.

Silvership Lounge & Dining Room, 680 S. Higgins Ave., Missoula, MT 59801; Tel. (406) 728-9664. Gaming: Cardroom.

Gilded Garter, Broadway Ave., Red Lodge, MT 59068; Tel. (406) 446-3351. Gaming: Cardroom.

Casey's Casino, 101 Central Ave., Whitefish, MT 59937; Tel. (406) 862-8150. Gaming: Cardroom.

HORSE/DOG RACETRACKS

Great Falls, 400 3rd. St., NW., Great Falls, MT 59403; Tel. (406) 727-8900. Thoroughbred racing.

MetraPark, 308 6th Ave. North, Billings, MT 59103; Tel. (406) 256-2400. Thoroughbred racing.

INDIAN RESERVATION GAMBLING

Silverwolf Casino, Hwy. 13 West, Wolf Point, MT 59201; Tel. (406) 653-3476. Gaming: VG, BI.

4 C's Cafe & Casino, Box Elder, MT 59521; Tel. (406) 395-4863.

Little Big Horn Casino, Interstate 90, Exit 510, Crow Agency, MT 59022; Tel. (406) 638-4444. Gaming: B, VG, P.

NEBRASKA

Legal Status: *Gambling restricted to Charitable Games, Horse/Dog Racing, the Lottery, and Class II Gaming (Bingo) on reservations. No casino-style games are included in this state's Indian Reservation Gaming Operations.*

HORSE/DOG RACETRACKS
Aksarben Park, 6800 Mercy Rd., Omaha, NE 68106; Tel. (402) 444-4000. Thoroughbred racing.
Atokad Park, Hwy. 77, South Sioux City, NE 68776; Tel. (402) 494-3611. Thoroughbred racing.
Columbus Agricultural Park, 12th Ave. & 15th St., Columbus, NE 68601; Tel. (402) 564-0133. Thoroughbred racing.
Fonner Park, 700 E. Stolley Park Rd., Grand Island, NE 68801; Tel. (308) 382-4515. Thoroughbred racing.
Nebraska State Fair Park, 1800 State Fair Park, Lincoln, NE 68508; Tel. (402) 474-5371. Thoroughbred racing.

NEVADA

Legal Status: *Gambling legal throughout the state, including Cardrooms, Casinos, Charitable Games, Indian Reservation Gaming Operations, and sports betting.*

CASINOS

Las Vegas

Las Vegas Hilton, 3000 Paradise Rd., Las Vegas, NV 89109; Tel. (702) 732-5111, Reservations (800) 732-5584. Hotel, 3,300 rooms, $79–$249, pool, spa, gym, massage. Restaurants include The Hilton Steak House, The Montrachet, and The Socorro Springs. Entertainment: LM, FS. Gaming: B, P, VP, C, R, K, SM, SB, RB, Bac.

Sahara Hotel & Casino, 2535 Las Vegas Blvd. South, Las Vegas, NV 89109; Tel. (702) 737-2111, Reservations (800) 634-6666. Hotel, 2,100 rooms, $35–$115, pools. Restaurants include The House of Lords, The Mexican Village. Entertainment: LM, FS. Gaming: B, P, VP, C, R, K, SM, RB, SB, Bac.

Sands Hotel Casino, 3355 Las Vegas Blvd. South, Las Vegas, NV 89109; Tel. (702) 733-5000, Reservations (800) 634-6901. Hotel, 730 rooms, $35–$205, pool, spa, gym, massage. Restaurants include The Garden Terrace, The Shangri La. Entertainment: LM, FS. Gaming: B, P, VP, C, R, BI, K, SM, SB, RB, Bac.

Stardust Resort & Casino, 3000 Las Vegas Blvd. South, Las Vegas, NV 89109; Tel. (702) 732-6111, Reservations (800) 824-6033. Hotel, 2,500 rooms, $30–$100, pool, spa, gym, massage. Restaurants include Tony Roma's, Tres Lobos, William B's. Entertainment: LM, FS. Gaming: B, P, VP, C, R, K, SM, SB, RB, Bac.

Showboat Hotel & Casino Bowling Center, 2800 E. Fremont, Las Vegas, NV 89109; Tel. (702) 385-9123, Reservations (800) 826-2800. Hotel, 480 rooms, $65–$180, pool. Restaurants include The Captain's Buffet, The Plantation Room. Entertainment: LM. Gaming: B, P, VP, C, R, BI, K, SM, SB, RB.

Luxor Hotel Casino, 3900 Las Vegas Blvd. South, Las

Vegas, NV 89109; Tel. (702) 262-4000, Reservations (800) 288-1000. Hotel 2,500 rooms, $49–$169, pool, Full service spa, gym, massage. Restaurants include The Sacred Sea Room, Nile Deli, The Pyramid Cafe. Entertainment: LM, FS, DS. Gaming: B, P, VP, C, R, K, SM, SB, RB, Bac.

Excalibur Hotel Casino, 3850 Las Vegas Blvd. South, Las Vegas, NV 89109; Tel. (702) 597-7777, Reservations (800) 937-7777. Hotel, 4,032 rooms, pool. Restaurants include The Camelot, Sir Galahad's. Entertainment: LM, DS. Gaming: B, P, VP, C, R, K, SM, SB, RB, Bac.

Caesars Palace, 3570 Las Vegas Blvd. South, Las Vegas, NV 89109; Tel. (702) 731-7110, Reservations (800) 634-6001. Hotel, 1,500 rooms, $115–$190, pools, spa, gym, massage. Restaurants include The Palace Court, Bacchanal. Entertainment: LM, FS. Gaming: B, VP, C, R, K, SM, SB, RB, Bac.

Treasure Island, 3300 Las Vegas Blvd. South, Las Vegas, NV 89109; Tel. (702) 894-7111, Reservations (800) 944-7444. Hotel, 5,000 rooms, $49–$249, pools, spa, gym, massage. Restaurants include The Buccaneers' Bay, The Plank. Entertainment: LM. Gaming: B, P, VP, C, R, BI, K, SM, SB, RB, Bac.

MGM Grand, 3799 Las Vegas Blvd. South, Las Vegas, NV 89109; Tel. (702) 891-1111, Reservations (800) 929-1111. Hotel, 5,005 rooms, pool, spa, gym, massage, tennis courts. Restaurants include Wolfgang Puck's Cafe, Leonardo's, The Cracked Crab, Ocean Grille, Sir Reginald's Steakhouse. Entertainment: LM, Grand Theatre, Comedy Store, Complete Theme Park. Gaming: B, P, VP, C, R, K, SM, SB, RB, Bac.

Tropicana Resort & Casino, 3801 Las Vegas Blvd. South, Las Vegas, NV 89109; Tel. (702) 739-2222, Reservations (800) 634-4000. Hotel, 2,000 rooms, $59–$125, pool, spa, gym, massage. Restaurants include El Gaucho, DiMartino,

Mizuno. Entertainment: FS, DS. Gaming: B, P, VP, C, R, K, SM, SB, Bac.

Rio Suite Hotel & Casino, 3700 W. Flamingo, Las Vegas, NV 89109; Tel. (702) 252-7777, Reservations (800) 752-9746. Hotel, 1,410 rooms, pools, spa, gym, massage. Restaurants include All American Bar & Grill, Antonio's, Fiore's. Entertainment: DS. Gaming: B, P, VP, C, R, K, SM, SB, RB, Bac.

Lady Lucky Casino Hotel, 206 N. Third St., Las Vegas, NV 89109; Tel. (702) 477-3000, Reservations (800) LADY-LUC. Hotel, 791 rooms, $40–$60, pool. Restaurants include The Winner's Cafe, Burgundy Room, Emperor's Room. Entertainment: LM, DS, AO. Gaming: B, P, VP, C, R, K, SM, Bac.

Riviera Hotel Casino, 2901 Las Vegas Blvd. South, Las Vegas, NV 89109; Tel. (702) 734-5110, Reservations (800) 634-6753. Hotel, 2,000 rooms, $59–$95, pool, spa, gym, massage. Restaurants include Christopher's, Rigatori. Entertainment: LM, FS. Gaming: B, P, VP, C, R, K, SM, SB, RB, Bac.

Flamingo Hilton, 3555 Las Vegas Blvd. South, Las Vegas, NV 89109; Tel. (702) 733-3111, Reservations (800) 732-2111. Hotel, 3,034 rooms, $69–$145, pools, spa, gym, massage. Restaurants include The Altavilla, Peking Market, Beef Baron. Entertainment: LM, DS. Gaming: B, P, VP, C, R, K, SM, SB, RB. Wedding Chapel.

Hacienda, 3950 Las Vegas Blvd. South, Las Vegas, NV 89109; Tel. (702) 739-8911, Reservations (800) 634-6713. Hotel, 1,400 rooms, $28–$98, pool. Restaurants include The New York Pasta Shop, The Cactus Room, The Charcoal Room. Entertainment: LM, FS. Gaming: B, P, VP, C, R, K, SM, SB, RB.

Harrah's Las Vegas, 3475 Las Vegas Blvd. South, Las Vegas, NV 89109; Tel. (702) 369-5000, Reservations (800)

634-6765. Hotel, 1,735 rooms, $50–$250, pool, spa, gym, massage. Restaurants include The Veranda Cafe, Derby Deli, All That Jazz, Joe's Bayou. Entertainment: LM, Magic Show. Gaming: B, P, VP, C, R, BI, K, SM, SB, RB.

Bally's Casino Resort, 3645 Las Vegas Blvd. South, Las Vegas, NV 89109; Tel. (702) 739-4111, Reservations (800) 634-3434. Hotel, 2,832 rooms, $89–$169, pool, spa, gym, massage, shops. Restaurants include Seasons, The Steakhouse. Entertainment: LM, FS. Gaming: B, VP, C, R, K, SM, SB, RB, Bac. Wedding Chapel.

Aladdin Hotel & Casino, 3667 Las Vegas Blvd. South, Las Vegas, NV 89109; Tel. (702) 736-0111, Reservations (800) 634-3424. Hotel, 1,100 rooms, $45–$105, pools, tennis courts. Restaurants include The Wellington Steak House, Fishermen's Port. Entertainment: Theatre. Gaming: B, P, VP, C, R, BI, K, SM, SB, RB, Bac.

Sheraton Desert Inn, 3145 Las Vegas Blvd. South, Las Vegas, NV 89109; Tel. (702) 733-4444, Reservations (800) 634-6906. Hotel, 823 rooms, $120–$165, pools, spa, gym, massage, 18-hole golf course, tennis courts. Restaurants include La Promenade, Monte Carlo, The Portofino. Entertainment: LM. Gaming: B, P, VP, C, R, K, SM, SB, RB, Bac.

Fitzgerald's Hotel Casino, 300 Fremont St., Las Vegas, NV 89109; Tel. (702) 388-2400, Reservations (800) 274-5825. Hotel, 654 rooms, $24–$160. Restaurants include Cassidy Steakhouse, Molly's Buffet. Entertainment: LM. Gaming: B, P, VP, C, R, K, SM, SB, Bac.

The Mirage, 3400 Las Vegas Blvd. South, Las Vegas, NV 89109; Tel. (702) 791-7111, Reservations (800) 456-4564. Hotel, 3,000 rooms, $89–$299, pool spa, gym, massage. Restaurants include Moon Gate, The Bistro, California Pizza Kitchen, Mikado. Entertainment: Theatre. Gaming: B, P, VP, C, R, K, SM, SB, RB, Bac.

Circus Circus Las Vegas, 2880 Las Vegas Blvd. South, Las Vegas, NV 89109; Tel. (702) 734-0410, Reservations (800) 634-3450. Hotel, 2,800 rooms, $21–$100, pools. Restaurants include Pink Pony, Sky Rise, The Steakhouse. Entertainment: LM, Circus acts, Enclosed amusement park, shops. Gaming: B, P, VP, C, R, K, SM, SB.

Stardust, 3000 Las Vegas Blvd. South, Las Vegas, NV 89109; Tel. (702) 732-6111, Reservations (800) 824-6033. Hotel, 2,500 rooms, $32–$100, pools, spa, massage. Restaurants include Two Can Harry's, Tony Roma's, Tres Lobos. Entertainment: LM, FS. Gaming: B, P, VP, C, R, K, SM, SB, RB, Bac.

Four Queens Hotel Casino, 202 Fremont St., Las Vegas, NV 89109; Tel. (702) 385-4011, Reservations (800) 634-6045. Hotel, 700 rooms, $47–$57. Restaurants include Pastina's, Italian Bistro, Magnolia Veranda. Entertainment: LM. Gaming: B, VP, C, R, K, SM, SB.

Reno

Peppermill Hotel & Casino, 2707 S. Virginia St., Reno, NV 89502; Tel. (702) 826-2121, Reservations (800) 282-2444. Hotel, 640 rooms, $29–$99, pool, spa, gym, massage. Restaurants include Le Moulin, Island Buffet. Entertainment: LM, FS. Gaming: B, P, VP, C, R, BI, K, SM, SB, RB, Bac.

Harrah's Reno, 219 N. Center St., Reno, NV 89501; Tel. (702) 786-3232, Reservations (800) HARRAHS. Hotel, 625 rooms, $85–$105, pool, spa, gym, massage. Restaurants include The Garden Room, Cafe Andreotti, The Steakhouse. Entertainment: LM, FS, DS, AO. Gaming: B, P, VP, C, R, K, SM, SB, RB, Bac.

Flamingo Hilton, 255 N. Sierra St., Reno, NV 89501; Tel. (702) 322-1111, Reservations (800) 648-4882. Hotel, 600 rooms, $59–$219, gym. Restaurants include The Top of the Hilton, Flamingo Room, The Emperor's Garden. Entertainment: LM, FS. Gaming: B, P, VP, C, R, K, SM, SB, RB, Bac.

Sparks

John Ascuaga's Nugget, 1100 Nugget Ave., Sparks, NV 89431; Tel. (702) 356-4198, Reservations (800) 648-1177. Hotel, 750 rooms, $65–$104, pools, spa, gym, massage. Restaurants include The Steakhouse Grill, John's Oyster Bar, Gabe's Pub & Deli. Entertainment: LM, CH. Gaming: B, P, VP, C, R, BI, K, SM, SB, RB.

Lake Tahoe

Caesars Tahoe, 55 Highway 50, Stateline Nevada, NV 89449; Tel. (702) 588-3515, Reservations (800) 648-3353. Hotel, 432 rooms, $65–$135, pool, spa, gym, massage. Restaurants include The Broiler Room, Emperor's Court Room, Pisces, Primavera. Entertainment: FS, CH. Gaming: B, VP, C, R, K, SM, SB, RB, Bac. Wedding Chapel.

Harvey's Resort Hotel Casino, Highway 50, Stateline Nevada, NV 89449; Tel. (702) 588-2411, Reservations (800) HARVEYS. Hotel, 741 rooms, $95–$155, pool, spa, gym, massage. Restaurants include Llewellyn's, The Sage Room, El Vacquero, The Carriage House. Entertainment: LM. Gaming: B, P, VP, C, R, K, SM, SB, RB, Bac. Wedding Chapel.

Harrah's Lake Tahoe, Highway 50, Stateline Nevada, NV 89449; Tel. (702) 588-6611, Reservations (800) HARRAHS. Hotel, 534 rooms, $119–$179, pool, spa, gym, massage. Restaurants include The Summit, Friday's Station Steak & Seafood Grill, Cafe Andreotti Adventures in Pasta & Pizza. Entertainment: FE, Theatre. Gaming: B, P, VP, C, R, K, SM, SB, RB, Bac.

Laughlin

Edgewater, 2020 S. Casino Dr., Laughlin, NV 89029; Tel. (702) 298-2453, Reservations (800) 756-3343. Hotel, 1,450 rooms, $18–$28, pool, spa. Restaurants include The Garden Room, Hickory Pit. Gaming: B, P, VP, C, R, K, SM, SB, RB.

Colorado Belle, 2100 S. Casino Dr., Laughlin, NV 89029; Tel. (702) 298-4000, Reservations (800) 458-9500. Hotel, 1,230 rooms, $18–$45, pools. Restaurants include Mark Twain's, The Orleans Room. Entertainment: LM. Gaming: B, P, VP, C, R, K, SM, SB, RB.

Pioneer Hotel & Gambling Hall, 2200 S. Casino Dr., Laughlin, NV 89029; Tel. (702) 298-2442, Reservations (800) 634-3469. Hotel, 414 rooms, $17–$80, spa. Restaurants include The Boarding House, Granny's Gourmet. Gaming: B, VP, C, R, K, SM.

Riverside, 1650 Casino Dr., Laughlin, NV 89029; Tel. (702) 298-2535, Reservations (800) 227-3849. Hotel, 613 rooms, $16–$79, pool. Restaurants include Prime Rib, The Gourmet. Entertainment: LM, FS. Gaming: B, P, VP, C, R, BI, K, SM, SB, RB.

NEW HAMPSHIRE

Legal Status: *Gambling restricted to Charitable Games, Horse/Dog Racing, and the Lottery.*

HORSE/DOG RACETRACKS

Rockingham Park, Route 28 & I93, Salem, NH 03079; Tel. (603) 898-2311. Thoroughbred racing.

Hinsdale Greyhound Racing, Route 119, Hinsdale, NH 03451; Tel. (603) 336-5382. Dog racing.

Seabrook Greyhound Park, Route 107, New Zealand Rd., Seabrook, NH 03874; Tel. (603) 474-3065.

Lake's Region Greyhound Park, Route 106, Belmont, NH 03220; Tel. (603) 267-7778.

NEW JERSEY

Legal Status: *Gambling restricted to Casinos, Charitable Games, Horse/Dog Racing, and the Lottery.*

HORSE/DOG RACETRACKS

Freehold Raceway, Routes 9 & 3, Freehold, NJ 07728, Tel. (908) 462-3800. Harness racing.

Garden State Park, Route 70 & Haddonfield Rd., Cherry Hill, NJ 08034; Tel. (609) 488-3778. Thoroughbred and harness racing.

Monmouth Park, Oceanport Blvd., Oceanport, NJ 07757; Tel. (908) 222-5100. Thoroughbred racing.

The Meadowlands, 50 State Hwy. 120, East Rutherford, NJ 07073; Tel. (201) 935-8500. Thoroughbred racing.

CASINOS

Atlantic City

Showboat Casino & Hotel, Delaware Ave., Atlantic City, NJ 08401; Tel. (609) 343-4100, Reservations (800) 970-9666. Hotel, 496 rooms, $122–$172, pool, spa, gym, massage. Restaurants include Mississippi Steak & Seafood & Company, Casa di Napoli. Entertainment: LM, FS, Bowling Alley. Gaming: B, P, VP, C, R, BI, K, SM, SB, RB, Bac.

Sands Hotel & Casino, Indiana Ave. & Brighton Park, Atlantic City, NJ 08401; Tel. (609) 441-4000, Reservations (800) 257-8580. Hotel, 534 rooms, $109–$229, pool, spa, gym, massage. Restaurants include Brighton Steakhouse, China Moon. Entertainment: LM, FS, CH. Gaming: B, P, VP, C, R, K, SM, RB, Bac.

Harrah's Casino Hotel Atlantic City, 1725 Brigantine Blvd., Atlantic City, NJ 08401; Tel. (609) 441-5000, Reservations (800) HARRAHS. Hotel, 1,000 rooms, $65–$150, pool, spa, gym, massage. Restaurants include Shear Water Bar & Grill, The Deli, Andreotti's Italian Restaurant. Entertainment: LM, Theatre. Gaming: B, P, VP, C, R, K, SM, Bac. Miniature golf in season.

Tropworld, Brighton & Boardwalk, Atlantic City, NJ 08401; Tel. (609) 340-4000, Reservations (800) 257-7227. Hotel, 1,020 rooms, $85–$200, pool, spa, gym, massage. Restaurants include Regent Court Pier 7, Il Verdi. Entertainment: LM, CH, Enclosed amusement park. Gaming: B, P, VP, C, R, BI, K, SM, Bac.

Trump's Castle, Huron & Brigantine Blvd., Atlantic City, NJ 08401; Tel. (609) 441-2000, Reservations (800) 777-1177. Hotel, 725 rooms, $89–$130, pool, spa, gym, massage, tennis courts, jogging track. Restaurants include Castle Steakhouse, Harbor View, Portofino, Broadway Deli. Entertainment: LM, FS, CH. Gaming: B, P, VP, C, R, K, SM, SB, RB, BW, Bac. Miniature Golf Course.

Caesars Atlantic City, 2100 Pacific Ave., Atlantic City, NJ 08401; Tel. (609) 348-4411, Reservations (800) CAESARS. Hotel, 620 rooms, $115–$275, pool, spa, gym. Restaurants include The Primavera, Oriental Palace, Hyakumi, Planet Hollywood. Entertainment: LM, Magic Show. Gaming: B, P, VP, C, R, K, SM, SB, RB, Bac.

Bally's Park Place Casino & Hotel & Tower, Park Place & Broadwalk, Atlantic City, NJ 08401; Tel. (609) 340-2000, Reservations (800) 225-5977. Hotel, 1,255 rooms, $115–$195, pool, spa, gym, massage, basketball and racquetball courts. Restaurants include Mr. Ming's, Prime Palace, Arturo's. Entertainment: LM, FS. Gaming: B, P, VP, C, R, K, SM, SB, RB, Bac.

Claridge Hotel & Casino, Indiana Ave & Boardwalk, Atlantic City, NJ 08401; Tel. (609) 340-3434, Reservations (800) 257-8585. Hotel, 500 rooms, $100–$145, pool, spa, gym, massage. Restaurants include The Twenties, Martino's, The Garden Room. Entertainment: CH. Gaming: B, P, VP, C, R, BI, K, SM, SB, RB, Bac.

Bally's Grand Casino Resort Hotel, Boston & Pacific Ave., Atlantic City, NJ 08401; Tel. (609) 340-7100, Reservations (800) 257-8677. Hotel, 518 rooms, pool, spa, gym, massage. Restaurants include The Oaks, Caruso's, Peregrine's. Entertainment: Theatre. Gaming: B, VP, C, R, BI, SM, Bac.

Merv Griffin's Resorts, 1133 Boardwalk, Atlantic City, NJ 08401; Tel. (609) 344-6000, Reservations (800) 438-7424. Hotel, 698 rooms, $50–$120, pool, spa, gym, massage. Restaurants include Le Palais, Camelot Steak & Seafood, Capriccio, Club Griffin. Entertainment: LM, FS, CH, DS. Gaming: B, P, VP, C, R, K, SM, SB, RB, Bac.

Trump Plaza, Mississippi & Boardwalk, Atlantic City, NJ 08401; Tel. (609) 441-6000, Reservations (800) 677-7378. Hotel, 556 rooms, pool, spa, gym, massage. Restaurants include Max's Steak House, Ivana's, Fortune's, Roberto's. Entertainment: LM, FS, CH. Gaming: B, VP, C, R, BI, K, SM, Bac.

Trump Taj Mahal, 1000 Boardwalk & Virginia Ave., Atlantic City, NJ 08410; Tel. (609) 449-1000, Reservations (800) 825-8786. Hotel, 609 rooms, $115–$125, pool, spa, gym, massage. Restaurants include Marco Polo, Sinbad's, Dynasty, Scheherazade International. Entertainment: LM, FS, CH, FE, Sporting events, Theatre, Amusement park. Gaming: B, P, VP, C, R, K, SM, RB, Bac.

NEW MEXICO

Legal Status: *Gambling restricted to Charitable Games, Horse/Dog Racing, and Class II gaming (Bingo). No casino-style games are included in this state's Indian Reservation Gaming Operations.*

HORSE/DOG RACETRACKS

Albuquerque, 201 California Northeast, Albuquerque, NM 87108; Tel. (505) 266-5555. Thoroughbred racing.

Ruidoso Downs, Hwy. 70 East, Ruidoso Downs, NM 88346; Tel. (505) 378-4431. Thoroughbred racing.

Santa Fe Downs, 27475 I 25, W. Frontage Rd., Santa Fe, NM 87505; Tel. (505) 471-3311. Thoroughbred racing.

Sunland Park Racetrack, 101 Futurity Dr., Sunland Park, NM 88063; Tel. (505) 589-1131. Thoroughbred racing.

NEW YORK

Legal Status: *Gambling restricted to Charitable Games, Horse/Dog Racing, the Lottery, and Indian Reservation Gaming Operations.*

HORSE/DOG RACETRACKS

Aqueduct, Rockaway Blvd. & 108th St., Queens, NY 11417; Tel. (718) 641-4700. Thoroughbred racing.

Belmont Park, Hemstead Turnpike, Elmont, NY 11003; Tel. (516) 488-6000. Thoroughbred racing.

Finger Lakes, Route 96, Farmington, NY 14564; Tel. (716) 924-3232. Thoroughbred racing.

Historic Track-Goshen, Park Place, Goshen, NY 10924; Tel. (914) 294-5333. Harness racing.

Saratoga Harness, Nelson Ave., Saratoga Springs, NY 12866; Tel. (518) 584-2110. Harness racing.

The Syracuse Mile, Route 690, Hamburg, NY 14075; Tel. (315) 487-7711 Harness racing.

Vernon Downs Racetrack, Route 5, Vernon, NY 13476; Tel. (315) 829-2201. Harness racing.

Yonkers Raceway, 810 Central Ave., Yonkers, NY 10704; Tel. (914) 968-4200. Harness racing.

NORTH CAROLINA

Legal Status: *Gambling restricted to Charitable Games Only.*

NORTH DAKOTA

Legal Status: *Gambling restricted to Cardroom, Charitable Games, Horse/Dog Racing, and Indian Reservation Gaming Operations. North Dakota permits mini-casinos that carry blackjack and pull tabs.*

MINI-CASINOS

Dakota Lounge, 104 South 12 St., Bismarck, ND 58504; Tel. (701) 223-3514.

Blue Wolf Casino, I-94 & University, Fargo, ND 58102; Tel. (701) 232-2019.

Cactus Jack's Gold Rush Casino, 3402 Interstate Blvd., Fargo, ND 58108; Tel. (701) 280-0400.

Doublewood Inn Casino Lounge, 3333 13th Ave., South Fargo, ND 58108; Tel. (701) 235-3333.

Charlie Brown's Casino, 414 Gateway Dr., Grand Forks, ND 58203; Tel. (701) 772-7620.

Southgate Casino, 2525 Washington St. South, Grand Forks, ND 58201; Tel. (701) 775-6174.

Silver Spur, 501 Pleasant Ave., Surry, ND 58785, Tel. (701) 838-3616.

Big 'O' Casino, 512 Dakota Ave., Wahpeton, ND 58705; Tel. (701) 642-2407.

M & J Brand Saloon, 817 Main Ave., West Fargo, ND 58078; Tel. (701) 281-1639.

INDIAN RESERVATION GAMBLING

Dakotah Sioux Casino, Hwy 20 S, Toyko ND 58379; Tel. (701) 294-2109. Gaming: B, P, C, SM, VG, K.

Prairie Knights Casino, Hwy. 1806, Fort Yates, ND 58538; Tel. (701) 854-7777. Gaming: B, P, SM.

Four Bear Casino & Lodge, 5 mi. west of New Town on Hwy. 23, New Town, ND 58763; Tel. (701) 627-4343; Hotel, 40 rooms, $55–60. Restaurants include Lucky Cafe. Gaming: B, P, C, R, SM, BI, VG.

Tribal Gaming Operations, Hwy. 5, Belcourt, ND 58316; Tel. (701) 477-6451. Gaming: B, P, VG, SM, BI, R, C.

Turtle Mountain Casino, Belcourt, ND 58316; Tel. (701) 477-3171. Gaming: B, C, VG, P, SM.

OHIO

Legal Status: *Gambling restricted to Charitable Games, Horse/Dog Racing, and the Lottery.*

HORSE/DOG RACETRACKS

Beulah Park, 3664 Grant Ave., Grove City, OH 43123; Tel. (614) 871-9600. Thoroughbred racing.

Delaware Ohio Fair, 236 Pennsylvania Ave., Delaware, OH 43015; Tel. (614) 363-6000. Harness racing.

Northfield Park, 10705 Northfield Rd., Northfield, OH 44067; Tel. (216) 467-4101.

River Downs, 6301 Kellogg Ave., Cincinnati, OH 45230; Tel. (513) 232-8000. Thoroughbred racing.

Raceway Park, 5700 Telegraph Rd., Toledo, OH 43612; Tel. (419) 476-7751. Harness racing.

Scioto Downs, 6000 South High St., Columbus, OH 43207; Tel. (614) 491-2515. Harness racing.

Thistledown, 21501 Emery Rd., North Randall, OH 44128; Tel. (216) 662-8600. Thoroughbred racing.

OKLAHOMA

Legal Status: *Gambling restricted to Charitable Games, Horse/Dog Racing, and Class II gaming (Bingo). No casino-style games are included in this state's Indian Reservation Gaming Operations.*

HORSE/DOG RACETRACKS

Blue Ribbons Downs, Hwy. 64 E., Sallisaw, OK 74955; Tel. (918) 775-7771. Thoroughbred racing.

Remington Park, One Remington Pl., Oklahoma City, OK 73111; Tel. (405) 424-1000. Thoroughbred racing.

OREGON

Legal Status: *Gambling restricted to Cardrooms, Charitable Games, Horse/Dog Racing, the Lottery, and Indian Reservation Gaming Operations.*

HORSE/DOG RACETRACKS

Portland Meadows, 1001 NE Schmeer Rd., Portland, OR 97217; Tel. (503) 285-9144. Thoroughbred Racing.

INDIAN RESERVATION GAMBLING
Umatillas Casino & Bingo, 72777 Hwy. 331, Pendleton,
OR 97801; Tel. (503) 276-3165. Slot machines and casino-
style games.

PENNSYLVANIA

Legal Status: *Gambling restricted to Charitable Games,
Horse/Dog Racing, and the Lottery.*

HORSE/DOG RACETRACKS
Ladebroke at the Meadows, Race Track Road, Meadow
Lands, PA 15347; Tel. (412) 225-9300. Harness racing.
Penn National Racecourse, Rd. 1, Grantville, PA 17028;
Tel. (717) 469-2211. Thoroughbred racing.
Philadelphia Park, 3001 St. Road, Bensalem, PA 19020;
Tel. (215) 639-9000. Thoroughbred racing.
Pocono Downs, Route 315, Wilkes-Barre, PA 18702; Tel.
(717) 825-6681. Harness racing.

RHODE ISLAND

Legal Status: *Gambling restricted to Charitable Games,
Horse/Dog Racing, and the Lottery.*

SOUTH CAROLINA

Legal Status: *Gambling restricted to Charitable Games
only.*

SOUTH DAKOTA

Legal Status: *Gambling restricted to Cardrooms, Casinos, Charitable Games, Horse/Dog Racing, the Lottery, and Indian Reservation Gaming Operations.*

INDIAN RESERVATION GAMBLING

Fort Randall Casino & Hotel, P.O. Box 756, W. Hwy. 46, Wagner, SD 57380; Tel. (605) 487-7871, Reservations (800) 362-6333. Hotel, 57 rooms, $40–$49. Entertainment: LM. Gaming: B, P, BI, SM.

Dakota Sioux Casino, Sioux Valley Rd., Watertown, SD 57201, Tel. (605) 882-2051. Gaming: B, P, SM.

Golden Buffalo Casino & Resort, 123 Crazy Horse, Lower Brule, SD 57548; Tel. (605) 473-5577, Reservations (800) 341-8000. Hotel, 38 rooms, $45–$50, pool. Gaming: B, P, VG, BI, SM.

Rosebud Casino, Hwy 83, Mission, SD 57555; Tel. (800) 786-ROSE. Gaming: B, P, SM.

Royal River Casino, 326 Veterans St., Flandraeu, SD 57028; Tel. (800) 234-2WIN. Gaming: B, P, BI, SM.

TENNESSEE

Legal Status: *Gambling restricted to Horse/Dog Racing Only.*

TEXAS

Legal Status: *Gambling restricted to Charitable Games, Horse/Dog Racing, the Lottery, and Indian Reservation Gaming Operations.*

HORSE/DOG RACETRACKS

Bandera Downs, Hwy. 16, Bandera, TX 78003; Tel. (210) 796-7781. Thoroughbred racing.

Retama Park Association, San Antonio, TX 78292; Tel. (512) 677-8380. Thoroughbred racing.

Sam Houston Race Park, One Sam Houston Pl., Houston, TX 77252; Tel. (713) 807-8700. Thoroughbred racing.

Trinity Meadows Raceway, Inc., West Hwy. 80, Fort Worth, TX 76121; Tel. (817) 441-6284. Thoroughbred racing.

INDIAN RESERVATION GAMBLING

Speaking Rock Casino & Entertainment Center, 122 S. Old Pueblo Rd., El Paso, TX 79917; Tel. (915) 860-7777. Gaming: B, P, BI.

UTAH

Legal Status: *No gambling is permitted.*

VERMONT

Legal Status: *Gambling restricted to Charitable Games, Horse/Dog Racing, and the Lottery.*

VIRGINIA

Legal Status: *Gambling restricted to Charitable Games, Horse/Dog Racing, and the Lottery.*

WASHINGTON

Legal Status: *Gambling restricted to Cardrooms, Charitable Games, Horse/Dog Racing, the Lottery, and Indian Reservation Gaming Operations.*

CARDROOMS

5t's Restaurant & Cardroom, 845 Valley Mall Park, East Wenatchee, WA Tel. (509) 886-0199. Gaming: Dealer's Choice

Grove Tavern & Cardroom, 6504 Evergreenway, Everett, WA 98203; Tel. (206) 347-0677. Gaming: Blackjack, Texas Hold 'Em, High-Low Draw.

Jack O' Diamonds Card Room, 1216 Broadway, Everett, WA 98201; Tel. (206) 259-1500. Gaming: Blackjack, Texas Hold 'Em, Poker.

Sports Center Cafe, 1709 Hewitt Ave., Everett, WA 98301; Tel. (206) 252-6200. Gaming: Cardroom.

Petosa's Restaurant, 13640 Hwy. 99, S. Everett, WA 98201; Tel. (206) 742-5844.

P.J. Pockets Cardroom, 1320 South 324th, Federal Way, WA 98003; (206) 839-9922. Gaming: Cardroom.

Cedars Tavern, 2023 Main St., Ferndale, WA 98248; Tel. (206) 384-9953. Gaming: Cardroom.

Cal Clark's Red Rooster, Walker Way & Hwy. 101, Haquiam, WA 98550; Tel. (206) 987-2255. Gaming: Cardroom.

Desperado Saloon, 411 S. Pacific Ave., Kelso, WA 98626; Tel. (509) 586-9780. Gaming: Cardroom.

Totem Bowl Cardroom, 13033 NE 70th Place, Kirkland, WA 98033; Tel. (206) 827-9272. Gaming: Cardroom.

Last Frontier, 125 East 5th St., La Center, WA 98390; Tel. (206) 263-1255. Gaming: Blackjack, Texas Hold 'Em.

Timmen's Landing Restaurant, 318 Old Pacific Hwy., La Center, WA 98629; Tel. (206) 263-2426. Gaming: Blackjack, Texas Hold 'Em, Pan.

The Carriage, 1334 12th Ave., Longview, WA 98632; Tel. (206) 425-3134. Gaming: Cardroom.

The Club, 1251 Commerce Ave., Longview, WA 98632; Tel. (206) 577-9787. Gaming: Cardroom.

Shagg Tavern, 205 S. Pioneer Way, Moses Lake, WA 98337; Tel. (509) 765-7502. Gaming: Cardroom.

Town Pump Tavern, 1903 S. 3rd., Mount Vernon, WA 98273; Tel. (206) 336-5858. Gaming: Cardroom.

De Frazio's, 16261 Redmond Way, North Bend, WA 98052; Tel. (206) 883-6463. Gaming: Cardroom.

Oak Bowl, 1153 Midway Blvd., Oak Harbor, WA 98277; Tel. (206) 491-7515. Gaming: Cardroom.

Loomis Tavern, 2815 Hwy. 101 W., Port Angeles, WA 98362; Tel. (206) 457-0254. Gaming: Cardroom.

Hotel Cafe, 7844 Leary Way, Redmond, WA 98052; Tel. (206) 885-4454. Gaming: Blackjack, Texas Hold 'Em Poker.

Diamond Lil's, 321 Rainier Ave. So., Renton, WA 98055; Tel. (206) 255-9037. Gaming: Blackjack, Texas Hold 'Em Poker.

Cliff's Cardroom, 910 North 145th, Seattle, WA 98133; Tel. (206) 367-0343. Gaming: Blackjack, Dealer's Choice, Texas Hold 'Em, High-Low Draw Poker.

Drift-On-Inn, 16708 Aurora Ave. North, Seattle, WA 98133; Tel. (206) 546-8040. Gaming: Blackjack, High-Low Split, Texas Hold 'Em, Stud Poker.

Hideway Restaurant, 9636 16th SW, Seattle, WA 98106; Tel. (206) 764-6363. Gaming: Cardroom.

Hideway Tavern, 14525 Aurora N., Seattle, WA 98133; Tel. (206) 362-9494. Gaming: Cardroom.

Kings & Queens, 20060 Balinger Rd. NE, Seattle, WA 98155; Tel. (206) 363-6694. Gaming: Blackjack and Poker.

Midway Tavern, 13409 Pacific Hwy. S., Seattle, WA 98168; Tel. (206) 824-0642. Gaming: Cardroom.

Skyway Park Bowl, 11819 Renton Ave. S., Seattle, WA 98178; Tel. (206) 772-4125. Gaming: Blackjack, Dealer's Choice, Texas Hold 'Em Poker.

Rod's Inn, 1911 N. Maple, Spokane, WA 99205; Tel. (509) 325-0960. Gaming: Cardroom.

Sports Page, East 12828 Sprague Ave., Spokane, WA 99216; Tel. (509) 924-5141. Gaming: Cardroom.

Stockyards Inn, East 2837 Boone Ave., Spokane, WA 99202; Tel. (509) 534-1251. Gaming: Cardroom.

Vic's Cafe Cocktail Lounge, West 425 Main, Spokane, WA 99201; Tel. (509) 747-1812. Gaming: Cardroom.

Wilks & Wilks, 5005 N. Division, Spokane, WA 99205; Tel. (509) 482-2007. Gaming: Cardroom.

Safari Restaurant, 616 Edison Ave., Sunnyside, WA 98944; Tel. (509) 837-4212. Gaming: Blackjack, Texas Hold 'Em Poker, Pull tabs.

Aba Daba Cardroom, 12825 Pacific Hwy., SW, Tacoma, WA 98404; Tel. (206) 584-9612. Gaming: Cardroom.

Harry's Place, 3529 McKinley Ave. E., Tacoma, WA 98404; Tel. (206) 272-0555. Gaming: Cardroom.

Heena's Airport Tavern, 5406 S. Tacoma Way, Tacoma, WA 98409; Tel. (206) 474-4942. Gaming: Cardroom.

New Frontier, 4702 Center St., Tacoma, WA 98466; Tel. (206) 564-8555. Gaming: Cardroom.

Pete's Place, 5050 S. Tacoma Way, WA 98409; Tel. (206) 473-4028. Gaming: Cardroom.

The Pub Card Room, 1209 South 38th St., Tacoma, WA 98408; Tel. (206) 474-8781. Gaming: Blackjack, Texas Hold 'Em Poker, Pull tabs.

Red Roof Pub, 12314 Pacific Highway SW, Tacoma, WA 98499; Tel. (206) 588-9446. Gaming: Blackjack, Texas Hold 'Em, High-Low Draw, Omaha Poker, Pull tabs.

Golden Nugget Restaurant, 14025 Interurban Ave. South, Tukwila, WA 98188; Tel. (206) 246-8545. Gaming: Blackjack, Dealer's Choice, Pan, Pull tabs.

Riverside Inn, 14060 Interurban Ave. S., Tukwila, WA 98168; Tel. (206) 244-4542. Gaming: Cardroom.

Sports Center, 214 E. Yakima Ave., Yakima, WA 98901; Tel. (509) 453-3300. Gaming: Cardroom.

Mac's Tavern & Card Room, 210 E. Heron, Aberdeen, WA 98520; Tel. (206) 533-3932. Gaming: Blackjack, Texas Hold 'Em, Stud Poker.

Vito's T & C, 3805 Auburn Way, N., Auburn, WA 98002; Tel. (206) 833-0702. Gaming: Cardroom.

Danny's Tavern, 1313 State St., Bellingham, WA 98225; Tel. (206) 671-3100. Gaming: Blackjack, Texas Hold 'Em, High-Low Draw, Stud Poker.

Shenandoah Pub & Casino, 1313 Railroad Ave., Bellingham, WA 98225; Tel. (206) 676-9527. Gaming: Cardroom.

International Cafe & Hotel, 758 Peace Portal Dr., Blaine, WA 98230; Tel. (206) 332-6035. Gaming: Blackjack, High Draw, Texas Hold 'Em, Stud Poker.

Smith's Nut Shop, 906 6th St., Clarkston, WA 99403; Tel. (509) 758-8447. Gaming: Blackjack, Texas Hold 'Em, Stud Poker.

HORSE/DOG RACETRACKS

Playfair, N. Altamont & Main, Spokane, WA 99220; Tel. (509) 534-0505. Thoroughbred racing.

Yakima Meadows, 1301 S. 10th St., Yakima, WA 98907; Tel. (509) 575-7980. Thoroughbred racing.

INDIAN RESERVATION GAMBLING

Jamestown Band of Klallam Indians, 305 Old Blyn Hwy., Sequim, WA 98382; Tel. (206) 683-1109. Gaming: B, K, C, P.

Lummi Casino, 2559 Lummi View Dr., Bellingham, WA 98226; Tel. (206) 758-7559, (800) 776-1337. Gaming: Blackjack, Poker tables, Pai Gow.

Muckleshoot Tribal Council, 39015 172 Street SE, Auburn, WA 98002; Tel. (206) 939-5311.

Nooksack River Casino, 5048 Mount Baker Hwy., Deming, WA 98244; Tel. (206) 592-5472. Gaming: B, P, VG, C, R.

Swinomish Indian Bingo & Casino, 837 Casino Dr., Anacortes, WA 98221; Tel. (206) 293-4687. Gaming: B, P, C, R.

Tulalip Casino, 6410 33rd Ave. N.E., Marysville, WA 98271; Tel. (206) 651-1111. Gaming: B, P, C, R, Bac.

WASHINGTON, D.C.

Legal Status: *Gambling restricted to Charitable Games and the Lottery.*

WEST VIRGINIA

Legal Status: *Gambling restricted to Charitable Games, Horse/Dog Racing, and the Lottery.*

HORSE/DOG RACETRACKS

Charles Town Races, Flowing Springs Rd., Charles Town, WV 25414; Tel. (304) 725-7001. Thoroughbred racing.

Mountaineer Park, State Route 2, Chester, WV 26034; Tel. (304) 387-0700. Thoroughbred racing.

WISCONSIN

Legal Status: *Gambling restricted to Charitable Games, Horse/Dog Racing, the Lottery, and Indian Reservation Gaming Operations.*

HORSE/DOG RACETRACKS

Geneva Lakes Kennel Club, Hwys 50 & I-43, 1600 East Geneva St., Delavan, WI 53115; Tel. (800) 477-4552. Dog racing.

St. Croix Meadows Greyhound Racing Park, 2200 Carmichael Rd., Hudson, WI 54016; Tel. (715) 386-6800.

Dairyland Greyhound Park, 5522 104th Ave., Kenosha, WI 53144; Tel. (800) 233-3357.

Wisconsin Dells Greyhound Park, Winners Way, Wisconsin Dell, WI 53965; Tel. (608) 253-DOGS.

INDIAN RESERVATION GAMBLING

Bad River Bingo & Casino, Odanah, WI 54861; Tel. (712) 682-7111. Gaming:

Northern Lights Casino, Hwy. 32, Wabeno, WI 54566; Tel. (800) 487-9522. Gaming: B, SM.

Lac Courte Oreilles Casino, Hwy. B & I K, Hayward, WI 54843; Tel. (715) 634-5643. Gaming: B, VG, SM.

Lake of the Torches Casino, 562 Peace Pipe Rd., Lac du Flambeau, WI 54538; Tel. (715) 588-7070. Gaming: B, VG, SM.

Menominee Crystal Palace, Keshena, WI 54135; Tel. (715) 799-5114. Gaming: B, VG, SM.

Isle Vista Casino, Bayfield, WI 54814; Tel. (715) 779-3701. Gaming:

Grand Royal, Hwy. 55, Crandon, WI 54520; Tel. (715) 478-2604. Gaming: B, VG, SM.

Regency Resort, Hwy. 55, Crandon, WI 54520; Tel. (715) 478-2604. Gaming: B, VG, SM.

Hole in the Wall Casino, Hwy. 35 & 77, Danbury, WI 54830; Tel. (715) 656-3444. Gaming: B, VG, SM.

St. Croix Casino & Hotel, 777 Hwy. 8, Turtle Lake, WI 54889; Tel. (715) 986-2877, Reservations (800) 782-9987. Hotel, 158 rooms, $49–$59. Gaming: B, VG, SM.

Mohican North Star Casino & Bingo, W12180 A Country Rd. A, Bowler, WI 54416; Tel. (715) 793-4090. Gaming: B, VG, SM.

Hochunk Bingo & Casino, 902 Sock Ave., Baraboo, WI 53913; Tel. (800) 533-1956. Gaming: B, VG, SM.

Majestic Pines Bingo & Casino, Hwy. 54, Black River Falls, WI 54615; Tel. (715) 284-9098. Gaming: B, VG, SM.

Rainbow Bingo/Casino, 4950 Creamery Rd., Nekoosa, WI 54457; Tel. (715) 886-4551.

WYOMING

Legal Status: *Gambling restricted to Charitable Games, Horse/Dog Racing, and Class II gaming (Bingo). Casino-style games are not permitted in this state's Indian Reservation Gaming Operations.*

HORSE/DOG RACETRACKS

Wyoming Downs, 10180 Hwy. 89 North, Evanston, WY 82931; Tel. (509) 452-1124. Thoroughbred racing.

CANADA

Legal Status: *The laws regarding gambling in Canada vary from province to province just as in the U.S. they vary from state to state. Horse-racing tracks are legal throughout the country. Casinos are now legal in seven provinces, Alberta, British Columbia, Manitoba, Quebec, Saskatchewan, Yukon Territory, and Ontario.*

HORSE/DOG RACETRACKS

Assiniboia Downs, P.O. Box 10, Station A, 3975 Portage Ave., Winnipeg, MB R3K 2C7, Canada. Tel. (204) 885-3330. Thoroughbred racing.

Hastings Park, British Columbia Jockey Club, Vancouver, BV VSK 3NB, Canada. Tel. (604) 254-1631. Thoroughbred racing.

Marquis Downs, 2326 Herman Ave., P.O. Box 6010, Saskatoo, SK, S7K 4E4 Canada. Tel. (306) 242-6100. Thoroughbred racing.

Northlands Park, P.O. Box 1480, Edmonton, AB T5J 2N5, Canada. Tel. (403) 471-7379. Thoroughbred racing.

Stampede Park, Calgary Exhibition, Box 1060 "M," Calgary, AB T2P 2K8, Canada, Tel. (403) 261-0214. Thoroughbred racing.

Woodbine, P.O. Box 156, Rexdale, ON M9W 5L2, Canada. Tel. (416) 675-6110. Thoroughbred racing.

CASINOS

Casino de Charlevoix, Ave. Richelieu, Pointe-au-pic, Quebec GOT 1M0, Canada. (418) 665-5300, Reservations (800) 965-5355. Gaming: B, R, SM, Mini-Bac.

Casino de Montreal, 1 Ave du Casino, Montreal Quebec, H3C 4W7, Canada. Tel. (514) 392-2746, Reservations

(800) 665-2274. Restaurants include Nuances, La Bonne Carte. Gaming: B, R, VG, SM, K.

Cash Casino Place, 4040-B Blackfoot Trail SE, Calgary, Alberta T2G 4E6, Canada. Tel. (403) 287-1635. Gaming: B, R, Mini-Bac.

River Park Casino, 1919 Macleod Trail S., Calgary, Alberta T2G 4S1 Canada. Tel. (403) 272-3215. Gaming: B, R, Mini-Bac.

Casino ABS, 10549-102th St., Edmonton, Alberta T5H 4K6 Canada. Tel. (403) 424-9467. Gaming: B, R, SM, Mini-Bac.

Great Canadian Casino, 8440 Bridgeport Rd., Richmond, B.C. V6X 3C7. Tel. (604) 273-1895. Gaming: B, R, SM.

Casino World, 147-16200 McKay Ave., No. 147, Burnaby, BC V5H 4L7. Tel. (604) 439-0222. Gaming: B, R.

Prince George Casino, 444 George St., Prince George, B. C. V2L IR6. Tel. (604) 561-2421.

Royal Diamond Casino, 1195 Richards St. Vancouver, British Columbia. Tel. (604) 685-2340. Gaming: Canadian Craps, B, R.

Vancouver Casino, 611 Main St., Vancouver, British Columbia. Tel. (604) 253-4263. Gaming: B, R.

Crystal Casino, Hotel Fort Garry, 7th Floor, 222 Broadway, Winnipeg, Manitoba R3C OR3. Tel. (204) 957-2623. Gaming: B, R, P, VG, SM, Bac.

Note: **Casino Windsor** in Ontario, Canada, includes a showroom, three restaurants, entertainment area, a 300-room hotel, plus an enormous gaming area. The permanent casino is scheduled to open in early 1996.

CARIBBEAN ISLANDS

CASINOS

Aruba

Americana Aruba Beach Resort & Palace Casino, 83 L.G. Smith Blvd., Palm Beach, Oranjestad. Tel. 297-8-24500, Reservations (800) 447-7462. Hotel, 419 rooms, $75–$550, pool, spa, gym, massage, two tennis courts, water sports, shopping arcade. Restaurants include Le Petit Cafe. Gaming: B, C, R, P, SM, Bac, Caribbean Stud Poker.

Alhambra Casino & Divi Divi Beach Resort, 63 and 93 L.G. Smith Blvd., Puta Brabu Beach, Oranjestad, Aruba. Tel. 297-8-25434, Reservations (800) 367-3484. Hotel, 203 rooms, $225–$580, two pools, tennis courts, water sports, shopping. Restaurants include Pelican Terrace Cafe, The Red Parrot. Gaming: B, C, R, Mini-Bac, SM.

Aruba Royale Renaissance Resort & Casino, 75 L.G. Smith Blvd., Oranjestad, Aruba, Tel. 297-8-3700, Reservations (800) 228-9898. Hotel, 298 rooms, $155–$275, pool, spa, gym, massage, tennis and squash courts, water sports, children's playground, shopping. Restaurants include Palm Breeze Bar & Restaurant. Entertainment: LM, DS, Night club.

Hyatt Regency Aruba Resort & Copacabana Casino, L.G. Smith Blvd. #85, Palm Bay, Aruba, Tel. 297-8-31234, Reservations (800) 233-1234. Hotel, 360 rooms, pool, spa, gym, massage, tennis courts, water sports. Restaurants include Cafe Piccolo. Gaming: B, C, R, SM, Bac.

Sonesta Hotel Beach Club & Crystal Casino, 82 L.G. Smith Blvd., Oranjestad, Aruba. Tel. 297-8-36000, Reservations (800) SONESTA. Hotel, 300 rooms, pool, spa, gym, massage. Restaurants include L'Escale Gourmet Int'l & French Cuisine, Seabreeze Restaurant. Entertainment: LM, Nightclub. Gaming: B, R, C, SM, Bac. A Luxurious Resort & Casino.

Aruba Concorde Hotel & Casino, Tel. 297-8-24466. Hotel, 500 rooms, pool, tennis courts, water sports, shopping arcade. Restaurants include Kadushi Coffeeshop. Gaming: B, R, C, P, SM, Bac.

Aruba Palm Beach Hotel & Palm Casino, 79 L.G. Smith Blvd., Oranjestad. Tel. 297-8-23900, Reservations (800) 345-2782. Hotel 200 rooms, $155–$250, pool, tennis courts, water sports, shopping. Restaurants include Seawatch, Palm Garden Cafe. Gaming: B, R, SM, Caribbean Stud Poker.

Holiday Inn Aruba Beach Resort & Grand Holiday Casino, 23 L.G. Smith Blvd., Palm Beach, Oranjestad, Aruba. Tel. 297-8-636000, Reservations (800) 331-3831. Hotel, 600 rooms, $92–$200, pool, spa, gym, tennis court, water sports, shopping arcade.

Harbortown Suites & Seaport Casino, 9 L.G. Smith Blvd., Oranjestad, Aruba. Tel. 297-8-35600, Reservations (800) 223-9815. Hotel, 250 rooms, $165–$365, pool, spa, gym, massage, tennis courts, Seaport Market Place featuring a variety of restaurants and boutique shops. Restaurants include La Cafe Dining. Gaming: B, C, R, SM, Caribbean Stud Poker.

La Cabana All-Suite Beach Resort & Casino, 250 L.G. Smith Blvd., Oranjestad, Aruba. Tel. 297-8-39000, Reservations (800) 835-7193. Hotel, 441 suites, $165–$635, pool, spa, gym, tennis courts, racquetball, squash, water sports, children's playground, shopping arcade. Restaurants include Spats, Prawn Broker, La Cabana Trading Company, Captain's Table, Pool Grille. Gaming: B, C, R, SM, VP, Bac.

Puerto Rico

Candelero Hotel & Villas, Palmas Del Mar Resort, Route 906, Humacao, Puerto Rico 00661; Tel. (809) 852-6000, Reservations (800) 221-4874. Hotel, 325 rooms, 223 suites, $115–$420, five pools, spa, gym, massage, 20 tennis courts, 18-hole golf course, water sports, professional scuba diving. Entertainment: Disco. Gaming: B, C, R, SM.

Caribe Hilton, Fort San Jeronimo, Pta. De Tierra, San Juan, Puerto Rico 00903; Tel. (809) 721-0303, Reservations (800) 548-9951. Hotel, 667 rooms, 60 suites, $102–$285, private beach, two pools, spa, gym, massage, racquetball and squash courts, water sports, fishing. Restaurants include Caribe Terrace, La Rotisserie, El Cafe, El Batey. Entertainment: Club Caribe Nightclub, Juliana's Discotheque, LM. Gaming: B, C, R, SM, Bac.

Condado Plaza Hotel & Casino, 999 Ashford Ave., Condado, San Juan, Puerto Rico 00902; Tel. (809) 721-1000, Reservations (800) 468-8588. Hotel, 560 rooms, 63 Jr. Suites, $75–$600, four pools, spa, gym, massage, water sports center, two tennis courts, horseback riding, children's game room and playground. Restaurants include Lotus Flower, Las Palmas, La Posada, La Cantina, Capriccio's, Tony Roma's, L.K. Sweeney & Son, Ltd. Entertainment: LM, FS, Isadora's Disco. Gaming: B, C, R, VP, SM, Mini-Bac, Bac.

Dutch Inn and Tower, 55 Condado Ave., Condado, San Juan, Puerto Rico 00908; Tel. (809) 721-0810. Hotel, 146 rooms, 44 suites, $65–$105, pool. Gaming: B, C, R, Bac.

Radisson Ambassador Plaza Hotel & Casino, 1369 Ashford Ave., Condado, San Juan, Puerto Rico 00907; Tel. (809) 721-7300. Reservations (800) 654-2000. Hotel, 250 rooms, 84 suites, $148–$185, pool, spa, gym. Gaming: B, C, R, Bac.

Sands Hotel & Casino Beach Resort, 187 Isla Verde Rd.,

San Juan, Puerto Rico 00914; Tel. (809) 791-6141, Reservations (800) 443-2009. Hotel, 429 rooms, 51 suites, pool, spa, water sports, shops. Gaming: B, C, R, VP, SM, Bac.

El San Juan Hotel & Casino, Avenida Isla Verde, San Juan, Puerto Rico 00902; Tel. (809) 791-1000, Reservations (800) 468-2818. Hotel, 392 rooms, 28 suites, $265–$385, two pools, spa, gym, massage, three tennis courts, water sports, discotheque. Restaurants include Dar Tiffany's, La Veranda, Back Street Hong Kong, La Piccola Fontana. Gaming: B, R, C, SM, VP, Mini-Bac, Bac.

Hyatt Regency Cerromar Beach Hotel & Casino, Route 693, Dorado Beach, Puerto Rico 00646; Tel. (809) 796-1010, Reservations (800) 228-9000. Hotel, 508 rooms & suites, $115–$355, six pools, spa, gym, massage, fourteen tennis courts, 18-hole golf course, water sports, fishing, shops. Gaming: B, C, R, SM, Mini-Bac.

Hyatt Dorado Beach Resort & Casino, Route 693, Dorado Beach, Puerto Rico 00646; Tel. (809) 796-1600, Reservations (800) 228-9000. Hotel, 300 rooms, $125–$655, pool, spa, tennis courts, golf courses, water sports, hiking. Gaming: B, C, R, SM, Mini-Bac.

El Conquistador Resort, Country Club & Casino, Route 987, Las Croabas, Puerto Rico 00748; Tel. (809) 860-1000, Reservations (800) 468-8365. Hotel, 917 rooms & suites, $165–$900, six pools, water sports, tennis courts, golf. Gaming: B, C, R, SM, Mini-Bac.

Mayagüez Holiday Inn & Casino, Route 2, km 152.5, Mayagüez, Puerto Rico 00731; Tel. (809) 841-5381. Hotel, 146 rooms, $130–$180, pool, spa, gym, disco. Gaming: B, C, R, SM.

Hilton International Mayagüez Hotel & Casino, Marina Station, Mayagüez, Puerto Rico 00709; Tel. (809) 834-7575. Hotel, 145 rooms, 5 suites, $132–$170, pool, three tennis courts, water sports. Gaming: B, C, R, SM.

Ponce Hilton & Casino, Route 14, San Caballeros, Ponce, Puerto Rico 00732; Tel. (809) 259-7676, Reservations (800) 981-3232. Hotel, 156 rooms, $120–$160, pool, spa, tennis courts. Gaming: B, C, R, SM, Mini-Bac.

Bahamas

Bahamas Princess Resort & Casino, Ranfurly Circus, Freeport, Grand Bahama Island, Bahamas. Tel. (809) 352-7811, Reservations (800) 432-2994. Hotel, 965 rooms, 44 suites, $100–$175, two pools, spa, gym, massage, twelve tennis courts, water sports, deep-sea fishing. Restaurants include Crown Room, Morgan's Bluff, Rib Room, La Trattoria, Garden Cafe. Entertainment: LM, DS. Gaming: B, C, R, VP, SM, Mini-Bac.

Lucayan Beach Resort & Casino, Lucaya, Grand Bahamas Island, Bahamas. Tel. (809) 373-7777, Reservations (800) 772-1227, Hotel, 247 rooms, 8 suites, $105–$180, pool, spa, four tennis courts, water sports, horseback riding. Restaurants include Les Oursins, Hibiscus Brasserie, Hemingway's, Countyard Terrace. Entertainment: LM, DS. Gaming: B, C, R, VP, SM, Bac.

Crystal Palace Resort & Casino, West Bay St., Cable Beach, Nassau, Bahamas. Tel. (809) 327-6200, Reservations (800) 222-7466. Hotel, 867 rooms, pool, spa, gym, message, tennis courts, indoor squash and racquetball courts, water sports, golf, shopping. Entertainment: LM, DS, Discotheque. Gaming: B, C, R, VP, SM, Bac.

Paradise Island Resort & Casino, Nassau. Tel. (809) 363-3000, Reservations (800) 821-1139. Hotel, 1186 rooms, 67 suites, 80 Villa-Single Units, two pools, spa, gym, massage, tennis courts, water sports, shopping, children's playground. Restaurants include twelve restaurants from gourmet to ethnic to steak/seafood. Entertainment: LM, DS, Discotheque. Gaming: B, C, R, VP, SM, Bac.

Index

About the Author

Robert J. Hutchinson, the former managing editor of *Hawaii* magazine, has made a career out of writing about popular modern pastimes, from scuba diving to the obscure Japanese game of Go. He has written hundreds of magazine articles and is the author of *The Book of Vices: A Collection of Classic Immoral Tales*.

Hutchinson lives in southern California with his wife, Glenn Ellen, also a writer, and their three sons, Robert John, James Timothy, and William Kelly.